Gather the Children

Celebrate the Word with Ideas, Activities, Prayers & Projects

MARY CATHERINE BERGLUND

PASTORAL PRESS

PORTLAND · OREGON

Acknowledgements

Scriptural selections are taken from or based upon the New American Bible with Revised New Testament. © 1986 Confraternity of Christian Doctrine, Washington, D.C. Used with permission. All rights reserved.

"Matilda: Who Told Lies and Was Burned to Death" from *Cautionary Verses* by Hilaire Belloc. © 1941 Alfred Knopf, Inc. Used with permission. All rights reserved.

"A Eucharistic Prayer" adapted by the author from "A Prayer of Thanksgiving" as found in Lucien Deiss, *Springtime of the Liturgy*. © 1979 The Order of St. Benedict, Inc. Published by The Liturgical Press, Collegeville MN. Used with permission. All rights reserved.

"You Are My Own" by Dan Schutte. © 1970 North American Liturgy Resources/Oregon Catholic Press. All rights reserved.

ISBN 1-56929-012-1

© 1987, 1993 Pastoral Press
A Division of OCP Publications
5536 N.E. Hassalo
Portland, OR 97213
Phone: 800-LITURGY (548-8749)
Email: liturgy@ocp.org
Web site: www.pastoralpress.com
Web site: www.ocp.org

Nihil obstat: Br. Philip Dougherty, CFX, Censor librorum
Imprimatur: ✠ Walter F. Sullivan, Bishop of Richmond, April 8, 1987

Table Of Contents

The Tenth through the Thirty-Fourth Sundays of the Year

Introduction

When children are disappointed that they cannot attend Sunday liturgy, the church of the future looks bright! Just such eagerness on the part of little ones is the most rewarding aspect of a genuine, imaginatively celebrated liturgy of the word for children. *Gather the Children* offers adult leaders practical helps for celebrating liturgy of the word with children. It also offers them enrichment in our scriptures, both for their own spiritual benefit and for the benefit of the children whose lives they touch.

Gather the Children envisions a celebration of the eucharistic liturgy in which a large number of adults and a smaller number of children are present, such as the typical parish Sunday liturgy. The children arrive with their parents and join the assembly for the introductory rites. After the opening prayer the presider invites the children to attend their own special liturgy of the word in an area removed from the church proper. Then, while the adults hear the word of God proclaimed and reflect upon its meaning for their lives, the children of the assembly also listen to God's word and ponder its meaning, but in a way suited to their abilities and their interests. At the conclusion of the liturgy of the word, the children rejoin their parents for the entire assembly's celebration of the liturgy of the eucharist.

The advantages of a special liturgy of the word for children are striking. Children hear God's word with far greater meaning when its proclamation and explanation are designed especially for them. They experience the loving concern of a community which responds to their special needs. Their parents and, in fact, the entire adult assembly are free to participate in the liturgy of the word without the distraction of children. The presider can plan the homily more easily and deliver it more effectively when the group addressed consists of only adults. Adults who lead children in liturgy of the word find greater richness and new life in God's word even for themselves as they read and ponder the scriptures in preparation for sharing them with children. In short, everyone involved in the program benefits.

The *Directory for Masses with Children* recognizes the difficulties children face as they attempt to participate in liturgical celebrations, especially the eucharist, whose words and symbols speak effectively only to persons of considerable maturity. Children cannot understand much of daily adult experience; it easily wearies them; and, in fact, in the realm of the spiritual "we may fear spiritual harm if over the years children repeatedly experience in the Church things that are scarcely comprehensible to them" (#2). At the same time the *Directory* affirms recent psychological studies that establish "how profoundly children are formed by the religious experience of infancy and early childhood" (#2). In considering the typical parish Sunday situation in which a large number of adults and a smaller number of children are present for the celebration of the eucharistic liturgy, the Directory suggests that "great care" be taken so that "children do not feel neglected because of their inability to participate or to understand what happens and what is proclaimed in the celebration" (#17). The *Directory* suggests specifically that parishes consider the possibility of the celebration of a special liturgy of the word for children (#17). *Gather the Children* responds to the suggestions of the *Directory* by forming and enriching adults who will lead a weekly children's liturgy of the word.

Every adult who leads children in liturgy of the word should be familiar with the *Directory for Masses with Children*. The *Directory* was prepared by the Sacred Congregation for Divine Worship and approved and confirmed by Paul VI in 1973. It was published in English the next year by the United States Catholic Conference. With beautiful sensitivity this short document addresses the needs of children at worship and offers creative and practical suggestions for adapting liturgical celebrations to help the children of our Christian community "quickly and joyfully to encounter Christ together in the eucharistic celebration and to stand in the presence of the Father with him" (#55).

The structure of *Gather the Children* is simple.

The structure of *Gather the Children* is simple. Beginning with the First Sunday of Advent and proceeding Sunday by Sunday through the liturgical year, *Gather the Children* provides, in outline form, a procedure for proclaiming and explaining each Sunday's readings to children. The order of Sundays in *Gather the Children* differs from the order of Sundays in the Lectionary for Mass. The lectionary places the Advent, Christmas, Lenten and Easter seasons first, the Sundays of the Year (which the sacramentary, but not the lectionary, calls the "Sundays of Ordinary Time") next, and the solemnities of the Lord last. *Gather the Children* treats the Sundays in the order in which they occur in the course of the year. Thus the Advent and Christmas seasons come first, then the Sundays of the Year which occur before Lent, then the Lenten and Easter seasons, then the remaining Sundays of the Year. The feasts of Trinity Sunday and Corpus Christi have been inserted immediately after the feast of Pentecost, just as they occur as the church progresses through the liturgical year. The feasts of Christmas and Ascension have been included. The present volume covers the Sundays of year B. The Sundays of years C and A and the remaining holydays and special feasts that replace the usual celebration of Sunday will appear in additional volumes.

The reader of *Gather the Children* will discover quickly that each outline addresses the needs of children of widely different ages. The abilities and interests of younger children usually dominate the earlier parts of an outline, while the later parts look more specifically to the needs of older and more mature children. The leader of a group of older children should have no difficulty in adapting the simpler ideas for use with older children. The leader of a group of younger children will find it helpful, indeed necessary, to read the entire outline because the background information supplied for use with older children will enrich the leader as well as the children.

Individual outlines do not correspond exactly to the structure of the full liturgy of the word. That would defeat their purpose. The aim of children's liturgy of the word is twofold. On the one hand, it intends to simplify for children our celebration of God's word while insisting upon genuine liturgy in the best of taste. On the other hand, it intends to familiarize children with the full adult celebration of God's word in anticipation of the day when they will join the adult Christian assembly. *Gather the Children* reflects this twofold goal. Although each individual outline abbreviates the liturgy of the word and may change its order, the outlines touch upon all parts of the liturgy of the word as the weeks and the months progress.

Each outline offers many more suggestions than it is possible to utilize during the brief time span of a liturgy of the word. The leader, therefore, must never attempt to use an outline exactly as it appears. An outline should be viewed only as a catalyst for the leader's thoughts. The leader must not hesitate to personalize an outline by changing and adapting it, by discarding some of its suggestions, by adding new ideas. Only in this way will the final liturgy plans reflect the leader's unique Christian understanding and experience, as well as the needs of a particular group of children. It should be evident also that the more the leader reads and reflects upon the day's readings for his or her personal enrichment as an adult Christian, even before turning to the corresponding liturgy outline, the richer will be the liturgy.

Readings, prayer, music.

Some special comment upon the use of the readings is appropriate. The proclamation of the gospel is essential to every celebration of the liturgy of the word and should be its highlight. The ritual surrounding the proclamation of the gospel should reflect its importance. It is not necessary, however, for the leader to include all the prescribed readings each Sunday; in fact, to do so is usually confusing to children. The outlines comment upon some, but not all, of the readings, and the leader should choose to include or to omit a reading with the needs of a particular group of children in mind. The outlines usually suggest that the leader simplify a reading in order to make the word of God more comprehensible to children. A simplified reading should always respect the sense and the style of the biblical text and must, therefore, be prepared with the greatest care. Clearly, older children do not need as much simplification of the readings as younger children do. Occasionally an outline suggests that several children, or even the whole group of children, read a scriptural text in parts.

Good liturgy is always prayerful. *Gather the Children* recognizes that prayer, and especially children's prayer, need not always be formal and need not ever be stuffy. *Gather the Children* suggests prayer of many kinds. It invites children to pray in traditional ways. It encourages their spontaneous prayer. It suggests prayer in song and gesture and dance. It leaves time for individual reflection and for quiet personal prayer.

Good music is necessary for good liturgy, and good liturgical music abounds. But music that is effective for adult liturgy may be inappropriate for children's liturgy. At the back of the book the leader will find an appendix, "Music to Gather the Children," written by Fred Moleck, who is minister of music and liturgy in the author's parish. The essay offers incisive comment on the musical needs of children at worship, and then continues with an extensive list of musical possibilities arranged Sunday by Sunday.

Consistent with its intention of proclaiming and explaining God's word effectively to children, *Gather the Children* draws upon the principles of modern religious educational psychology. Children learn far more by seeing and doing than solely by listening. *Gather the Children* suggests music and singing, gesture and mime, storytelling, drama, group reading, visual aids, discussion, art activities and projects, and many other activities that appeal to children and at the same time form them. The children can carry out many of the suggestions during their brief time together. The leader should, however, view the more time-consuming activities as suggestions for home or school projects. The leader must always choose activity with the greatest of care. Because activity keeps children busy and happy, the leader constantly faces the temptation of misusing it. Overuse of activity or use of poorly chosen activity reduces children's liturgy to mere activity time. Children may learn and children may be happy with activity, but even good activity does not make genuine liturgy.

Liturgy is not class.

Although a good leader of liturgy and a good educator have common vital skills, it is essential that the leader of children's liturgy of the word recognize that liturgy and religious education are distinct. The leader must strive repeatedly to avoid confusing the two in the minds of the children or in the minds of their parents. In conversation with the children or with their parents, for example, the leader should avoid referring to liturgy as "class" or to an outline as a "lesson plan." The leader should remind the children frequently that the purpose of their gathering is to celebrate the presence of God in the word proclaimed. The adult assembly should be reminded occasionally of the nature of the program. Such a reminder might take the form of an explanation of the program coupled with an invitation to the children of the parish to take part in it.

A simple rite of dismissal is an effective and touching means of reminding the children and the entire assembly of the purpose of a separate children's celebration of God's word. The following rite, planned by Fred Moleck, works well. One of the adult leaders joins the entrance procession carrying a children's lectionary, places the book on the lectern near the adult lectionary, and returns to the assembly. After the opening prayer, the presider calls the children to gather before him. Handing the book to the leader, who has joined the children, and addressing the leader by his or her given name, the priest says: " . . ., receive the word of God. Proclaim it to our young people as we shall have it proclaimed to us." Then the presider, joined now by the assembly, addresses the children: "Children, may the Lord be with you there." The children respond: "May the Lord be with you here." The leader, holding the lectionary high, then leads the children away from the adult assembly to their separate gathering space.

The manner in which the children are assembled in their separate gathering space requires careful forethought. It is most effective to divide the children into groups according to their ages. If, for example, children from about the age of three or four to about the age of eleven or twelve wish to attend children's liturgy of the word, then at least three separate groups of children and three leaders would be appropriate. First graders and younger children might be grouped together, second and third graders together, and children in fourth and higher grades together. The number of willing adult leaders, the total number of children and the physical conditions of the gathering space, of course, affect the details of the program. It is ideal to include all youngsters who wish to participate, with the simple requirement that they be old enough to benefit, however simply, from a session of about twenty minutes which has been planned with their needs and interests in mind. Older children who wish to participate but who are self-conscious about their ages often make wonderful helpers.

The physical arrangement of the children's gathering space is vital to their good celebration of liturgy. The atmosphere need not be formal, but it must always remind the children of the purpose of their coming together. It is best not to celebrate children's liturgy in a classroom. If the parish has no other place for the celebration, the leader should remove the desks, or at least arrange them so that the children do not sit in rows and columns. The leader may gather the children around a simple cloth which the children themselves have made. Children are comfortable sitting on the floor in a circle around the gathering cloth. The leader may join the children on the floor, or use a chair. The lectionary should be prominently and attractively displayed. Candles enhance the spirit of a celebration, but obviously the leader must exercise the greatest of care with lighted candles. The liturgy outlines contain numerous other suggestions for enhancing the atmosphere of the children's gathering space, including suggestions for adapting it to specific liturgical feasts and seasons.

Timing.

Timing a children's liturgy of the word is always tricky. The length of the leader's time with the children depends on the length of the adult celebration of the liturgy of the word; in particular, it depends on the length of its homily. The leader must plan each presentation so that there will surely be enough time for its most important elements. It is unwise, for example, to leave until last the proclamation of the gospel. On the other hand, the leader also faces the possibility of exhausting all his or her plans before it is time for the children to return to their parents. It is thus useful for the leader to have ready an extra song or a story or a discussion which, while enriching the celebration, is not essential to it. In a word the leader's plans must be open-ended. Such planning may seem nearly impossible to the novice, but a little experience will soon render the leader capable of handling the difficulties with ease.

A word of practical advice about timing will be helpful. Usually the most appropriate moment for the children to rejoin the assembly is during the collection. If an adult "messenger," chosen in advance, leaves the assembly shortly before the collection, for example when the assembly begins the profession of faith, and quietly signals the leaders of the children, then the leaders will have a few moments to conclude their presentations and lead the children to the door of the church, where the group may wait quietly until the start of the collection. It is remarkable that the children almost always find their parents immediately.

Additional uses for Gather the Children.

Although the primary objective of *Gather the Children* is to aid leaders of a weekly children's liturgy of the word, it can be used in additional ways. Religion teachers can use it to prepare children for the coming Sunday liturgy or to deepen their celebration of the previous Sunday liturgy. Religion teachers can also find in it many ideas for sharing scripture with children in presentations not directly related to Sunday liturgies. Adults will find its background information about the scriptures helpful in preparing for their own Sunday celebrations, and, less specifically, simply in studying the bible. Adults who prepare parish Sunday liturgies will find that they can adapt many of its ideas to the interests and needs of their communities. The index of readings, included as an appendix, will be helpful in finding where particular scripture passages are discussed in the book. The index of readings will be helpful also in finding all the Sundays on which a particular book of the bible is discussed. The asterisks marking the readings at the beginning of each outline indicate how much attention the outline places on particular readings. Two asterisks indicate that the outline devotes considerable attention to a reading; one asterisk, less attention; the absence of an asterisk, little or no attention.

I have worked in children's liturgy of the word for over ten years. It is with deep gratitude and much affection that I remember the many children with whom I have celebrated God's word through these years, from the child who identified the greens on my Advent wreath as poison ivy to the children whose simple comments crystallize what theologians cannot say in volumes. This project could never have been completed without the support of John, my husband, who, among countless other helps, cooked many dinners while I struggled with my thoughts and my indispensable, though not entirely reliable, word processor. My own three children, one of whom was not even born when my ideas began to take shape, have consistently been my most honest critics. Without their enthusiasm and practical help I would have abandoned my work long ago. I thank my dear friend Sister Elaine McCarron who, by her beautiful attitude toward children and her many creative ideas, has taught me more than I can ever sufficiently acknowledge. I thank the many leaders of children's liturgy of the word at St. Bridget's and St. Mary's parishes in Richmond, Virginia, who have worked with me faithfully Sunday after Sunday, using the outlines and helping me to test and improve them. I thank Fred Moleck for his many musical suggestions and, more generally, for his persistent and encouraging support of this entire project. I acknowledge and thank Father Reginald Fuller for his wonderful knowledge of our scriptures and his penetrating insights which came to me primarily through his book *Preaching the New Lectionary*. I acknowledge and thank also the many other scholars whom I have come to know and love through their written words and, sometimes, their spoken words. I thank Lawrence Johnson of The Pastoral Press for the care with which he read the manuscript and for his successful handling of all the difficulties, large and small, which surfaced as the manuscript took its final form. Finally, while it is clear that much of the credit for what is good in this book belongs to my friends, I myself take full responsibility for its failings.

It is my hope that *Gather the Children* will help young Christians to celebrate God's word with joy. If God's word is nearer to even one child because of this work, then I shall be happy.

Advent 1986

Introduction to the Revised Edition

The occasion for the second edition of *Gather the Children* is the publication of the *Lectionary for Masses with Children*. The new edition of the three volumes of *Gather the Children* takes account of the contribution of the new children's lectionary to the ministry of celebrating parish Sunday liturgy of the word with children.

The new lectionary has been prepared by the Committee on the Liturgy of the National Conference of Catholic Bishops in response to the recommendation of the now two-decades-old *Directory for Masses with Children* (#43) and a formal request of the Federation of Diocesan Liturgical Commissions. Those gifted and generous women and men who serve the church by engaging in the ministry of planning and leading children's liturgy of the word will welcome the children's lectionary with enthusiasm both because of the impetus the lectionary gives to their ministry and because of its practical help.

The children's lectionary is based firmly upon the *Lectionary for Mass*, an essential property of any legitimate liturgical aid to the authentic participation of children in the church's liturgy of the word. The new lectionary adheres closely to the order of readings of the *Lectionary for Mass*, though it frequently judges one of the pre-gospel readings inappropriate for children and omits it without replacement. In a few instances the compilers of the lectionary have deemed both pre-gospel readings of the *Lectionary for Mass* inappropriate, in which case they have omitted both readings and provided a new reading. The responsorial psalms and refrains of the *Lectionary for Mass* have also been adapted for children. The most striking feature of the children's lectionary, however, is the simplicity of its language, a quality which the compilers have ensured by their almost exclusive use of American Bible Society translations of the scriptures.

While a thorough evaluation of the new lectionary is not possible until the lectionary has been widely used, a few comments on the lectionary relative to the objectives of *Gather the Children* are here in order. The author offers these comments in an effort to encourage healthy dialog which will lead eventually to a revised children's lectionary of greater excellence. As *Gather the Children* recognizes, the "typical child" is an illusion: if only by virtue of their varying ages, pre-adolescent children span an enormous range of capabilities and interests. No simplification of the scripture, therefore, can adequately meet the needs of all children simultaneously; thus, we will misuse the new lectionary if we expect its simplified readings to be maximally effective for all groups of children. Furthermore, the lectionary's frequent omission of readings of the *Lectionary for Mass* seems in principle unwise. The author believes that the compilers of the lectionary would have been more sensitive to the growing biblical literacy of children if they had included all the readings, except, possibly, those judged to be harmful to children, and then allowed planners and presiders of children's liturgy of the word to omit or to retain readings based upon the characteristics of specific groups of children. In some particular cases the omission of a reading impoverishes the liturgy of the word. For example, on the Fourth Sunday of Advent in Year B, the children's lectionary omits the Old Testament reading from II Sm 7, a passage not only essential to the theology of the Davidic covenant, but also of fundamental Messianic, hence fundamental Advent, importance. Even if children cannot grasp the rich implications of the passage, we should not deny them access to the story, a firm segment of our biblical tradition. Finally, the simplified readings seem occasionally to discount the formative power of liturgy. Why, for example, on the Feast of Corpus Christi in Year B should children not hear the word "covenant"? The lectionary substitutes "promises" in the Old Testament (an inadequate translation of the Hebrew) and "agreement" in the gospel. By not using the word "covenant," as the *Lectionary for Mass* does, and, if necessary, explaining the term in the homily, the proclaimer would pass up opportunity to lead children towards more "active, conscious and authentic participation" (*Directory for Masses with Children*, #12) not only in the liturgy of the word, but also in the liturgy of the eucharist during which, as part of the institution narrative, the presider always says the word "covenant." The last-mentioned deficiency of the lectionary reflects the fact that the children's lectionary does not use a simplification of the text prepared intentionally for liturgical use. Copyright laws, of course, prevent easy changing of the translated text.

The new edition of *Gather the Children* attempts to make the best possible use of the *Lectionary for Masses with Children*, while at the same time insisting that leaders of specific groups of children know best what is most appropriate for the children to whom they proclaim God's word. Wherever, for example, the new lectionary omits a reading and the original edition of *Gather the Children* has comments on the reading, the comments have been retained. Wherever the translation of the new lectionary fails to take into account the liturgical capabilities of children, the new edition of *Gather the Children* gives suggestions for countering the failure. On the other hand, in view of the usually satisfactory simplifications of the new lectionary, the constant injunction of the original edition of *Gather the Children* to proclaim the readings "simplified appropriately for children" has been omitted, although further simplification may at times be wise. In order to facilitate combining the best of both lectionaries, the reader will find listed at the beginning of each liturgy outline the readings of the *Lectionary for Masses with Children* on the left and, where there has been a change, the readings of the *Lectionary for Mass* on the right.

The author rejoices with the publication of revised edition of *Gather the Children*. In the years since the original edition of the books, children's liturgy of the word has flourished. Mixed with the chorus of praise for the program, however, are a few dissident voices who would eliminate the program and simply allow the adult liturgy to exercise its power over the entire assembly. The author believes that criticism of children's liturgy of the word arises either from an idealism that sees in the present Sunday liturgy and the present Sunday assembly the perfect liturgy and the perfect assembly of the kingdom, or from a judgment issued on children's liturgy of the word when it is not well done. The former criticism is inevitable and even beneficial: the Christian community will always have idealists, and, in fact, the Christian community needs idealists to impart vision to the whole people of God. The latter criticism is a call to those engaged in the ministry to strive continually to ensure that their liturgy with children is really the liturgy of the church, however simplified it may be. Neither criticism is reason for abandoning the program. The author hopes that the revised edition, as well as the original edition, of *Gather the Children* will help make the latter criticism unnecessary.

July 1993

Abbreviations

AB   Anchor Bible

DOB   Dictionary Of the Bible—J. McKenzie

IDB   The Interpreter's Dictionary of the Bible

JBC   The Jerome Biblical Commentary

LM   Lectionary for Mass

LMC   Lectionary for Masses with Children

PNL   Preaching the New Lectionary—R. Fuller

UOT   Understanding the Old Testament—B. Anderson

Gather the Children

Celebrate the Word with Ideas, Activities, Prayers & Projects

First Sunday of Advent

Lectionary for Masses with Children	Lectionary for Mass
--------- Ps 85:8,9,10 *I Cor 1:3–9 **Mk 13:33–37	**Is 63:16-17,19; 64:2-7 Ps 80:2-3,15-16,18-19 *I Cor 1:3-9 **Mk 13:33-37

Focus: We long for the coming of Jesus.

Gather the Children

1. The children's gathering space should speak to the children visually and audibly of the joy and the longing of the season of Advent, which begins today. Gather the children around a purple cloth. In the center of the gathering cloth have an Advent wreath. Display the lectionary prominently. Play quiet, reflective music as the children enter the room.

2. Welcome the children joyfully. Remind them why we gather for our special liturgy of the word: we are here to listen to God's word and to seek its meaning for our lives. Remind the children that the adults who have remained in the church proper are also listening right now to God's word. Our children's celebration, however, is planned specifically for children.

3. Help the children to understand the meaning of Advent:

• Ask the children what special decorations they noticed in the church today. Ask them special decorations are present here at our children's celebration.

•Tell the children that we begin today a time of preparation for a joyful feast. Ask them if they know what wonderful day is coming soon. They will know!

• Let the children share what they know of the meaning of Christmas. Be patient with their materialistic expectations, gently turning their attention to the deeper meaning of the great feast.

• Point out the Advent wreath. Let the children count the candles. Tell them that there are four candles because there are four Sundays of Advent, four Sundays until Christmas. For four weeks the church waits and prepares for the celebration of the coming of Jesus.

• Tell the children that we call this time of waiting and preparing for the coming of Jesus the season of Advent. The word "Advent" means "coming."

• Remind the children that Jesus will not be born again on Christmas day this year. He was born as a baby only once, nearly two thousand years ago. On every Christmas, however, we remember the birth of the Lord Jesus long ago and we ask him to come anew into our hearts to fill our lives ever more fully with his love.

4. Light the wreath and pray for the coming of Jesus:

• Teach the children a simple, prayerful Advent hymn and plan to sing it with them on each of the four Sundays of Advent.

• Tell the children that today, on this first Sunday of our four-week wait, we will light just one candle of our wreath.

• Light one purple candle, and sing the Advent hymn prayerfully.

Proclaim the Old Testament Reading

Note: The LMC omits today's magnificent Old Testament reading. The leader who wishes to proclaim it may find the following suggestions helpful.

1. Prepare the children to hear the reading:

• Tell the children of the hopes of the people of Israel of long ago: these people wanted God to come into their lives and take away their sorrows. Through the years God responded to their hopes and needs by promising to send a person to save them, but God did not reveal who that special person would be.

• Tell the children of the long wait for the savior: it was hundreds of years before the people of Israel saw the fulfillment of God's promise. Generations of people died without seeing the realization of their hopes. Sometimes God seemed very far away, as if he had forgotten the people. Sometimes the people lived as if they had forgotten about God, about God's love, about how God wanted them to act.

• Tell the children about the prophets: God sometimes sent special persons to remind the people of the promise of a savior and to remind them how they should live. We call such persons "prophets."

• While the people of Israel waited for the savior, they often prayed that God would keep the promise soon. In the book of the prophet Isaiah we can read some of these prayers. Our liturgy of the word on this First Sunday of Advent presents us with one of these prayers.

2. Ask the children to listen carefully to part of this prayer for the coming of the savior. Then proclaim the reading, simplified appropriately for younger children.

3. Relate the reading to our celebration of Advent:

• Tell the children that during Advent we remember the long wait of the people of God for the savior. During all their years of waiting, the people of Israel did not know who the savior would be.

• But we know who the savior was: it was Jesus. While we wait for the coming of Jesus at Christmas, we pray that God will help us prepare our hearts and our lives for the presence of Jesus.

• Ask the children to pray silently that Jesus will fill us with his presence and his love.

Proclaim the Gospel

1. Introduce the gospel by telling the children that in today's gospel Jesus urges his disciples, in the words of Mark, to be ready and waiting for his coming. With younger children, in order not to confuse them, the leader need not dwell on the distinction between the

coming of Jesus into our hearts at Christmas and his coming at the end of the world.

2. Ask the children to stand for the proclamation of the gospel. Acclaim the gospel joyfully in song and then proclaim it.

3. Review the gospel, making sure the children understand its meaning.

4. Apply the gospel to our lives:
• Point out that Jesus, who spoke our gospel to his disciples, meant his words also for us.
• Lead the group in discussing how we can take the words of Jesus seriously and prepare ourselves for his coming. Give practical suggestions, not merely "pious" thoughts, to make Advent real to the children. Drawing upon our two previous Sunday liturgies, include ideas for making good use of our talents and for finding Jesus in each other.
• Give the children a few moments of silent reflection to decide on something specific to do during Advent.

Make Our Own the Good News of the Coming of the Savior

1. Make a poster to symbolize our longing for the coming of the savior:
• Give each child a simple paper figure of a person standing with arms upraised.
• Have already painted on a piece of deep green poster board Isaiah's words (Is 63:19) "Oh, that you would come!" We use green for the poster because green is the color of hope. Have ready "the heavens," which the leader should cut beforehand from white paper. As the children watch, glue "the heavens" across the top of the poster. The leader need not explain overly, but simply let the symbols speak.
• Ask the children to hold up their figures and respond "yes" to the following questions:

> Do you want the savior to come soon into your heart? Do you want the savior to fill your heart with his presence and his love? Will you prepare your heart for the coming of the savior by trying to make other people happy?

• Collect the figures from the children and glue them onto the poster as a sign that we are waiting and preparing for the coming of the savior.
• Carry the poster into the church in the gift procession and place it where the entire assembly can see it. After the liturgy hang the poster in the children's gathering space and leave it there for the Advent and Christmas seasons.

2. As a reminder of today's liturgy of the word, give each child a figure similar to their figures on the poster. Have written on the figures the words "Oh, that you would come!"

3. Conclude the liturgy of the word by singing once again the Advent hymn which opened our celebration.

Other Possibilities:

1. Give the children written instructions for making and using an Advent wreath at home. Explain, especially to older children, details of its rich symbolism.

2. Pray in song and gesture for the coming of the savior Jesus. Use words of the long-ago people of Israel:
• Teach the children to sing the words "Oh, that you would come!" Use the following simple melody:

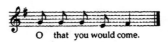

O that you would come.

Sing the verse with arms stretched upward.
• Then pray today's responsorial psalm, the leader singing the verses and the children responding in song with the words of Is 63 which they have just learned. Ask the children to bow their heads while the leader sings and to raise their arms heavenward as they sing.

3. To appreciate today's Old Testament reading, the leader would do well to read Is 63:7-64:11, the psalm of lamentation of which our reading is a part and which Carroll Stuhlmueller calls "one of the jewels of the Bible" (JBC). Post-exilic in origin, the psalm expresses both a confidence and an impatience that God will come and repeat in the present God's wonderful deeds of old. Share parts of the psalm with older children. Help them to appreciate its depth and its beauty, as well as the fitness of its choice for our contemplation on this First Sunday of Advent.

4. Expand upon the gospel:
• Ask little children to lie down and pretend to be sleeping. Tell them to keep their eyes closed until they hear a surprising sound. Sound the alarm on a clock, and then relate the experience to our being ready for Jesus at all times.
• With an older group, discuss the meaning of being ready and waiting:

Discuss some of the things for which we have to wait.

Discuss the difficulties and the value of waiting.

Then focus the attention of the group on Christmas. How do we use our waiting time? We use it, of course, to get ready. We plan our gifts, making them or shopping for them, plan decorations for our houses, find a Christmas tree, bring it home and decorate it, etc. How does all this enhance our celebration of Christmas? Or does it detract from our celebration of Christmas?
• Make a clock and mark on its face the days until Christmas. Attach one hand and move it from day to day as we do things to prepare ourselves for the coming of Jesus.

5. Talk with older children about the second coming of Christ. Much more urgent a possibility to the early Christians than it is to us, we, too, however, should live our lives mindful of its approach. Each year the church presents us with thoughts of the second coming of Christ on the First Sunday of Advent, and only after that does she turn our attention to John the Baptizer and the historical coming of Jesus. Proclaim to older children the beautiful words of Paul in our New Testament reading as a prayerful reflection on our wait for "the day of our Lord Jesus Christ."

6. To impress upon the children the merits and the difficulties of waiting, read them part of a book, and have them wait until next week to hear the rest of it.

Second Sunday of Advent

Lectionary for Masses with Children	Lectionary for Mass
**Is 40:3-5 Ps 85:8-9,10-11 ----- **Mk 1:1-8	**Is 40:1-5,9-11 Ps 85:9-10,11-12,13-14 *II Pt 3:8-14 **Mk 1:1-8

Focus: Our God is near! Prepare the way!

Gather the Children

1. Welcome the children joyfully. Remind them that we gather to listen to God's word and to think about how that word can touch and change our lives. Be sure the children know why we celebrate our children's liturgy of the word apart from the adult liturgy of the word.
2. The atmosphere of the children's worship space should be one of joyful and prayerful expectation, so that the children immediately sense the spirit of Advent. Use a purple gathering cloth and an Advent wreath. Play a quiet Advent hymn as the children enter the room.
3. Focus the attention of the children on the Advent wreath:
• Let the children speak briefly of what they know of the meaning of Advent, thus reviewing last week's liturgy with the group and at the same time orienting those children who were not present.
• Tell the children that the candles of our wreath remind us of Jesus, the light of the world and the light of our lives. Jesus is the savior who came to the people of Israel some two thousand years ago. We light the four candles of the wreath gradually to remind ourselves of the long historical wait of Israel for Jesus. We light two candles today because this is the second of our four weeks of waiting and preparing for the coming of Jesus into our hearts and lives at Christmas.
• Review the simple Advent hymn which the children learned last Sunday. Then light two purple candles of the wreath and sing the hymn.

Proclaim the Old Testament Reading

Note: The LMC shortens significantly today's well-known reading. The following suggestions are not limited to the shortened form.

1. Prepare the children for the reading by telling them of the historical situation prevailing at the time of its writing. It was written at a time when the people of God were living far away from their homeland and longing to return home. The writer of our reading comforted the sorrowful people with the assurance that God had not forgotten them and that God would soon send someone to help them. The writer told them to get ready for the coming of the one whom God was to send.
2. Share the images in the reading:
• The opening lines of the reading ask us to picture God as viewing the beloved people of God from heaven. With great compassion God sees their sorrow and knows that it is time to comfort them. They have suffered enough for their sins.
• A heavenly voice calls out that a straight path must be prepared for the Lord who will come in a glory that all people will witness.
• Finally the prophet himself calls out to Jerusalem that she should proclaim the nearness of God. The prophet describes the Lord as mighty, yet as caring as a shepherd who feeds the flock and gathers and leads the lambs.
3. Ask the children to listen carefully to the prophet Isaiah telling us of God's nearness and God's loving care. Proclaim the reading slowly and thoughtfully, yet joyfully.
4. Help the children savor the reading:
• The news that God was near was good. What must have been the reaction of the people as they heard it? Ask the children to close their eyes and think about the excitement and the happiness of the people of God at the message of Isaiah.
• Why does Isaiah ask the people to clear a path for the Lord and to make the difficult road easy to travel?
• Why does Isaiah image God as a shepherd? What does this image say about God's love? What does the image mean to us?
• Ask the children to spend a few moments in silent thanksgiving for God's love and care and for God's promise to send a savior. Play quiet reflective background music as the children pray.

Proclaim the Gospel

1. Prepare the children to hear the gospel:
• Ask the children to imagine that they are living at the time of Jesus but that they have not heard of Jesus. With their friends they are waiting for God to keep the promise to send them someone special to make them happy.
• Tell them about John the Baptizer. Describe John as Mark does in his powerful verse 6. Use a few props, such as a leather belt and a jar of honey. Then summarize John's message: John called the people to turn away from sin in preparation for the coming of someone far more important than he. John baptized people in the Jordan River.
2. Acclaim the gospel in song, and then proclaim it.
3. Apply the message of the gospel to our lives:
• Ask the children how people could have prepared for the one about whom John spoke. Ask them who they think the one announced by John was. John, of course, did not have Jesus in mind.

• Remind the children that we too are waiting for Jesus to come more fully into our hearts and lives. Discuss, in specific and not weak generic terms, what we can do to prepare for his coming.
• Give the children time for silent reflection to choose practical ways to prepare for Jesus in the coming week.

Make the Good News Our Own

1. Make a poster to share with the assembly the message of Isaiah:
• Before the liturgy, paint rugged hills and a hot desert sun on a piece of poster board. During the liturgy talk to the children about Isaiah's words to smooth the rugged road; and then, as the children watch, lay over the hills a gently sloping terrain.
• Give each child a paper human figure, upon which they may write their names.
• Ask the children to hold up their figures and respond "yes" to the questions:

Are you waiting with joy for the coming of Jesus?
Will you prepare your heart for his coming by acts of love?
Will you tell other people the good news that Jesus is near?

• Collect the figures and glue them quickly onto the poster as a symbol of our waiting to see the glory of the Lord. Younger children would like extra figures to take home.
• Carry the poster in the gift procession. After the liturgy hang the poster in the children's worship space and let it remain there throughout the Advent and Christmas seasons.
• If the children have the opportunity to prepare for the liturgy during the preceding week, allow them to participate more fully in the making of the poster. Children can paint the rugged hills and the desert sun; they can make the level terrain; they can cut out their own human figures.
2. Using ideas from the expanded Isaiah reading, make a poster to suggest the nearness of the promised one who comes with love and care.
• Have a piece of poster board on which are painted a mountain and the words "Here is your God!" As the children watch, glue a herald onto the mountain.
• Also have painted on the poster a sun breaking through clouds. Tell the children that the sun and the clouds remind us that we wait for Jesus who takes away the darkness in our lives.
• Give the children paper sheep to symbolize that we, like God's people of old, wait for the coming of Jesus who brings God's love and care.
• Complete and use the poster as above.
3. Conclude the liturgy by singing once again the opening Advent hymn.

Other Possibilities:

1. Talk with older children about prophets. A prophet is a person called by God to speak for God. Often the prophets of Israel called people from selfish, sinful lives to God-centered, socially responsible ones. Their words then were harsh, unwelcome, sometimes violently rejected. At other times Israel's prophets spoke words of hope and consolation, reminding the people of God's constant love and compassion even in the dark hours of their greatest sorrows.
• Ask the children what kinds of prophets we meet in our readings today. What kind of prophet would they like to meet? What kind of prophet would cause them to change their present lives for the better?
• Ask the children to think of who our contemporary prophets are. What is their message? Or are there no such men and women in the world today?
• In what ways should we ourselves be prophets? Or should we not be prophets?
• Since we will encounter two prophets again next Sunday, ask the children to find examples of prophets, contemporary or historical, during the coming week. Suggest that they read the newspaper for ideas.
2. Our first reading forms (most of) the prologue to the work of Second Isaiah, chapters 40-55 of the book of Isaiah. In his poetic writing the prophet tells of the glory of the messiah which all the world will witness. Our reading describes Second Isaiah's commissioning as a prophet during a convocation of the heavenly council. The reading is one of the most famous passages in the Old Testament, immortalized in Handel's "Messiah." Suggest to the children that they listen to Handel's work.
3. Involve older children more extensively in the proclamation of the first reading:
• Teach them to sing "Prepare the way of the Lord," from verse 3 of the reading. The leader might consider using the Taizé community's "Prepare the Way of the Lord."
• Choose one child to read verses 1-2 (God's words); a second, verses 3-5 (the words of "the voice"); and a third, verses 9-11 (the message of the prophet).
• Ask the first two children to read their parts. Next ask the entire group to sing "Prepare the Way of the Lord." Ask the third child to read his or her part, and then ask the entire group sing verse 3 once again.
4. Respond to the first reading by praying Ps 85:
• Teach the children to sing the psalm refrain, perhaps shortened if the children are very young. Enhance the song-prayer with gesture. The gesture may be as simple as a few movements of the arms.
• The leader should sing the psalm verses while the children listen prayerfully. The children should sing their refrain, accompanied by their gestures, at appropriate breaks in the leader's singing.
5. The second letter of Peter is perhaps the latest New Testament writing. Its primary purpose may have been to counter the difficulties caused by the delay of the second coming of Christ. Peter probably is not the author of the letter, since its concerns were not important ones during Peter's lifetime. Proclaim to older children the reading (omitted in the LMC), and then lead them in a discussion of how God's time is different from our time. How should that fact change our actions and our attitudes?

Third Sunday of Advent

Lectionary for Masses with Children	Lectionary for Mass

**Is 61:1-2
  Lk 1:47,49,53-54
**I Thes 5:16-24
**Jn 1:19-28
	**Is 61:1-2,10-11
	  Lk 1:46-48,49-50,53-54
	**I Thes 5:16-24
	**Jn 1:19-28

Focus: Joy forever is ours! Let us prepare for the coming of Jesus by giving joy to others.

Gather the Children

1. Arrange the gathering space so that the children immediately experience the joy of Advent. Use the purple gathering cloth again. Display prominently the Advent wreath and the lectionary.
2. Welcome the children with great joy. Remind them why we gather for our separate children's liturgy of the word. Be sure they know that our celebration, though physically removed from the adult celebration, is the same celebration of God's word.
3. Review briefly the meaning of Advent. As a sign of our Advent joy hang a banner filled with joyful faces or words or symbols. It would be ideal if the children made the banner in preparation for the liturgy.
4. Light the Advent wreath:
• Tell the children that we light three candles today because it is our third week of waiting and preparing for the coming of Jesus. We include the pink candle because of our joy that Jesus will come soon.
• Review the Advent hymn which the children have sung for the last two Sundays. Ask the children to listen carefully to its words and music, and to make the hymn a prayer that Jesus will fill our hearts with his love. Light three candles of the wreath, two purple and one pink, while the group sings the hymn.

Proclaim the Old Testament Reading

1. Prepare the children for the reading by discussing what makes people sad. Focus on broad problems such as hunger, homelessness, sickness, death, war. Show recent newspaper stories about sorrowful people.
2. Give the children background information about the historical situation of Israel at the time of Third Isaiah. The prophet spoke at a time when the people of God had returned from captivity to their own country. They were discouraged about the task of rebuilding their nearly devastated homeland. They faced many of the problems which we have just been talking about. The message of the prophet was one of hope and joy in the saving presence and action of God.
3. Plan simple action to accompany the reading:
• Choose three children, the first to represent the poor, the second to represent the brokenhearted, the third to represent prisoners. The first should kneel with hands cupped and extended and be prepared to say, "I am poor." The second should kneel with arms crossed over chest, head bowed, and be prepared to say, "I am brokenhearted." The third should kneel with arms held stiffly at sides, as if bound, and be prepared to say, "I am not free."
• Choose a fourth child prepared to ask, "Why are you sad?"
4. Proclaim the reading:
• The first three children assume their positions. The fourth stands a distance apart from them.
• The leader proclaims Is 61:1-2.
• The fourth child moves toward the first child and asks, "Why are you sad?" The first child replies, "I am poor." The fourth child repeats the action with the second child and the third child.
• The leader might conclude with appropriate parts of Is 61:7,10 from the expanded reading in the LM.
5. Respond to the reading:
• Impress upon the children the hope and joy that must have been the reaction of the people of God to the words of Isaiah.
• Relate the reading to our own lives. In our brokenheartedness and lack of freedom today, God still promises hope and joy. Refer to the newspaper stories which the children discussed earlier, and suggest how God might bring happiness into the lives of the suffering people we met. Do not focus exclusively on physical and material improvement. God heals and comforts and brings joy in many ways.
• Spend a few moments with the children in silent thanksgiving for God's promise of hope and joy.

Proclaim the Gospel

1. Prepare the children for the gospel by recalling last week's discussion of John the Baptizer:
• Remind them of the man John as Mark described him.
• Remind them of John's message that the promised one was coming.
• Remind them of John's advice to prepare for the coming of the savior by turning away from sin.
• Remind them of John's attitude of humility and service toward the one coming after him.
2. Ask the children to stand and listen to the good news about John and Jesus. Acclaim the gospel in song, then proclaim it. Because the symbolism of light is so prominent in our Advent and Christmas liturgies, the leader might include the first verses of the LM reading, which the LMC omits.
3. Conduct a brief discussion of the gospel. Who is the "light" about whom John the Evangelist speaks? Why does he call Jesus the "light"? How does John the Bap-

tizer describe the one who is to come? Why is this an appropriate gospel for Advent?

Make the Good News Our Own:

1. Encourage the children to share with others the good news we have heard:

• Have "joy stickers" for the children—circles cut out of colorful contact paper with the word "joy" printed boldly on them.

• Ask the children to proclaim their joy by responding "yes" to the questions:

Do you believe that the savior is coming soon?
Does the thought of his coming fill you with joy?
Will you share your joy with other people?
Do you accept your joy sticker as a sign that Jesus is your joy?

• Give out the stickers. Suggest that the children use them (with permission) as bumper stickers, or simply stick them in some prominent place at home.

• Next suggest to the children that we share our joy with the assembly in the church. Have prepared, but out of sight, a big "joy poster"—a yellow sunburst with "Joy forever is ours!" written on it in large colorful letters. Show the poster to the children and relate it both to the words of Isaiah and to the joy stickers. Carry the poster into the church during the gift procession. After the liturgy hang the poster in the children's worship space and leave it there for the remainder of Advent and during the Christmas season.

2. Bless the children with the blessing of the second reading:

• Ask the children to stand and practice the following gestures:

Begin with arms extended, palms upward at hip level. Bring arms together slightly while raising them high above head, palms still upward. Eyes should follow hands, then look upward.

Lower arms gracefully in front of body, then to sides, lowering eyes at same time.

Cross arms over chest, palms outward, fingers spread wide, turn head slightly to one side.

Extend left arm forward in a gesture of blessing and make a cross in the air with the right hand.

Bring hands together in prayer position, fingers pointed upward, and bow slightly.

• Ask the children to listen to a blessing which Paul, a devoted follower of Jesus, wrote in a letter to some of his Christian friends. Then proclaim I Thes 5:23.

• Ask the children to listen once again to the blessing, but this time to accompany the reading gracefully and prayerfully with the gestures. The leader should repeat the blessing and have the children simply follow his or her lead in fitting the gestures to Paul's words.

3. Pray the general intercessions, asking God to fill the lives of all people children with hope and joy.

4. Conclude the liturgy by singing once again the opening Advent hymn.

Other Possibilities:

1. Today, the Third Sunday of Advent, is traditionally "Gaudete Sunday." "Gaudete" is the Latin imperative "Rejoice!" Today's joyful readings surely impart to the liturgy a spirit of excited anticipation. We can hardly bear the wait for the promised one, even to find out who he will be! Our suspense will not end until next Sunday when we read Gabriel's announcement to Mary that she has been chosen to bear God's Son. Share these thoughts with older children, helping them to appreciate the magnificent crescendo of our Advent liturgies.

2. For a more detailed presentation of the first reading, one which involves preparation ahead of time, use the puppet show presentation described in Dick Hilliard's The Lord Blesses Me.

3. For an alternative poster:

• In an upper corner of a piece of deep pink poster board have painted a sun formed out of the letters of the word "joy," with rays emanating from the sun. Across the bottom of the poster have painted the earth with plants springing up from it and the words "forever is yours!"

• As the children watch, review the expressions of joy in the reading by gluing onto the poster the following figures:

A pair of figures, one stooped and rising, the other standing and reaching out to the first;

A standing figure dropping chains;

A standing figure dropping a pair of crutches.

• Carry the poster into the church in the gift procession, perhaps accompanied by crutches and chains.

4. Older children might enjoy deeper reflection on John the Evangelist's presentation of John the Baptizer. In how many different ways does John claim inferiority to Jesus? (It is almost humorous.) John is not the messiah, not Elijah, not even a prophet; he is only the "voice" of Is 40, the very voice we heard last Sunday. John's repeated self-effacement, climaxing in Jn 3:30, is a powerful example of ministry as it should be. It is an interesting historical possibility that the Evangelist might have been writing in part to counteract the influence of a cult of the Baptizer.

5. At the close of the liturgy the children might share with the entire assembly Paul's blessing of his Thessalonian friends. The leader should invite the children to stand at the front of the church. The leader should read the blessing and invite the assembly to accompany the children in making the gestures. Several older children should stand with the children to lead the group in the gestures.

6. Read the second reading carefully with older children. Encourage them to follow the advice of Paul to rejoice, to pray, to give thanks to God, to try their best to be good people.

7. Read younger children Irene Haas's lovely The Maggie B. The story tells of Margaret Barnstable, a little girl whose wish comes true to sail for a day "alone and free with someone nice for company." That someone nice is her brother, James, "a dear baby." Margaret spends her day keeping the ship tidy and her brother happy. The gentle, joy-filled story encourages children to show their love for their younger sisters and brothers.

Fourth Sunday of Advent

Lectionary for Masses with Children	Lectionary for Mass
-----	*II Sm 7:1-5,8-11,16
**Rom 16:25-27	Ps 89:2-3,4-5,27-29
Ps 47:1-2,7-8	**Rom 16:25-27
**Lk 1:26-38	**Lk 1:26-38

Focus: With Mary we say "Yes" to God.

Gather the Children

1. Once again decorate the children's gathering space so that the children immediately sense the spirit of the great season of Advent. Continue to use a purple gathering cloth and an Advent wreath. Display prominently all Advent posters and other seasonal objects the children have made. Have the lectionary in a place of honor. As the children enter the room, play quiet, joyful music.

2. Welcome the children happily and remind them why we gather for our special liturgy of the word.

3. Give glory to God in the words of Paul in his letter to the Romans:
- Prepare the children for the doxology by reminding them that, with Christmas nearly here, we stand on the brink of the fulfillment of God's promises through the ages. Let us, therefore, praise and thank God.
- Review the words of the Glory Be to the Father. Teach the children simple gestures to accompany the prayer:

For "Glory be to the Father": extend arms upward and forward, palms facing up;

For "and to the Son": lower arms to waist level, palms still facing upward;

For "and to the Holy Spirit": cross arms gracefully over chest, bowing slightly;

For "as it was in the beginning, is now, and ever shall be": move arms in circular motion by lowering them, raising them, finally bringing hands together in prayer position over head;

For "world without end. Amen.": bring hands, still in prayer position, to chest and bow.

- Proclaim the second reading, preceding and following the proclamation with the Glory Be to the Father and its gestures.

4. Focus the attention of the children on the Advent wreath:
- Ask the children what the candles of the wreath remind us of. Let them explain why we light all the candles today.
- Remind the group that Advent is the time of waiting and preparing for the coming of Jesus; thus, during the Sundays of Advent we have listened to the word of God spoken by his prophets:

We have listened to the words of the prophet Isaiah, who spoke comfort and hope to his people, assuring them that God would one day give them joy. Refer to the posters that symbolize the readings from Isaiah.

We have listened to the words of John the Baptizer, the cousin and the herald of Jesus, who made Jesus known when at last he came (using the lovely language of the sacramentary's second preface for Advent).

- Sing the Advent hymn which the children have used for the preceding Sundays of Advent, and light all the of the wreath.

5. Pray that we will prepare well for the coming of Jesus:
- Reflect silently for a few moments on how we are preparing our hearts for the coming of Jesus.
- Then read the following prayer as the children listen:

Loving God,
the whole world waits
for the coming of Jesus.
Without Jesus we live in darkness.
Just as the candles of our wreath
give light to this room,
Jesus gives light to our lives.
Hurry! Send Jesus to us soon!
We pray this, as we pray all things,
in the name of Jesus
and with your Holy Spirit.
Amen.

Proclaim the Gospel

1. Set the scene for gospel drama:
- Tell the children that today in the gospel we hear about God's "immediate preparation" to keep the ancient promise to send the savior. God loves us so much that God decided to send his own Son to be the savior. God wanted the savior to be as much like us as possible. So God planned for the savior to be born as a baby, just like each of us. Our gospel for this last Sunday before Christmas tells the story of how God chose someone to be the mother of the savior and asked her if she would be willing to do it.
- Ask the children: What was the savior's name? Whom did God choose to be the mother of Jesus? Whom did God send as a messenger to ask Mary if she would be the mother of Jesus? What did Mary say?

2. Ask the children to stand and listen to the story in the words of St. Luke. Acclaim the gospel joyfully in song, and then proclaim it.

3. Then retell the story with the children's help:
- Invite the children to pretend to be Gabriel as we listen again to the story of how God asked Mary if she would be the mother of the savior.
- Help the children practice their part:

Tell the children that they already know some of Gabriel's words. Then review the first lines of the Hail Mary: "Hail, Mary, full of grace! The Lord is with you. Blessed are you among women."

- Have the children repeat more of Gabriel's words:

  Do not fear, Mary.
  You have found favor with God.
  You shall have a son.
  You shall give him the name Jesus.
  The Holy Spirit will come upon you.
  The power of the Most High will come over you.

- Before the liturgy choose a child who is a good reader and let the child practice reading the gospel, omitting Gabriel's words. During the liturgy, the child should read the gospel, pausing before Gabriel's lines. The leader should say Gabriel's words and the children should repeat them. To delight little children give them tinsel "halos" to wear and take home.

Make the Good News Our Own

1. Pray that we, like Mary, will always say "Yes" to God:

- Explain that when Gabriel told Mary of God's plans for her, Mary accepted them humbly and wholeheartedly. To put it simply, Mary said "Yes" to God. Mary, in fact, said "Yes" to God not only at the annunciation but throughout her life.
- Ask the children if God ever asks us to do things. What are some things God asks us to do? How do we know what God wants of us? Help the children be practical.
- Acknowledge that it is not always easy to say "Yes" to God. Let the children, especially older children, discuss briefly some of the difficulties of accepting God's will.
- Pray silently with the children that, especially during this last week before Christmas, we will try our best to say "Yes" to God as Mary always did.

2. Make a poster as a reminder that Mary always said "Yes" to God:

- Have a light blue poster board with the words "I am the servant of the Lord" written across the bottom.
- As the children watch, glue on pictures of Mary, Gabriel and a dove, explaining that a dove is a common symbol of the Holy Spirit. The best pictures are pictures some of the children will draw in preparation for the liturgy. Continue to discuss the story and Mary's "Yes" during the assembling of the poster.
- Carry the poster into the church in the gift procession. Later hang the poster in the children's worship space and leave it there for the remainder of Advent and during the Christmas season.

3. Give the children symbols to take home that will remind them of our intention always to say "Yes" to God as Mary did:

Other Possibilities:

The following comments are for the leader who wishes to proclaim to the children the Old Testament reading from I Sm and then to pray the related, famous Ps 89, both of which the LMC omits:

1. The reading records the prophecy to David which forms the basis for Jewish expectation of a messiah from the house of David. David, favored and successful, indeed ideal king of Israel, offers to build a temple for Yahweh comparable in glory to his own palace. Yahweh, responding through Nathan the prophet, tells David that he has never had need for a temple, and then promises David that he will make David's house and kingdom last forever.

- The sense, the importance and the beauty of the prophecy are far more striking to the reader of the entire passage, I Sm 7:1-29. The leader should read it and learn from the word itself of David's proposal, of Yahweh's response and magnificent promise, and of David's "touching prayer of praise and thanksgiving" (JBC). The leader may then explain and proclaim the reading to the children with better facility and enthusiasm.
- In our selection from Ps 89 the psalmist recalls the Davidic covenant and praises Yahweh for Yahweh's kindness and faithfulness. It offers an excellent response to the first reading. Pray it with older children.
- Point out to older children that Gabriel informs Mary in our gospel that the covenant of Yahweh with David will find its fulfillment in her Son.

2. Help older children to appreciate the depth of Gabriel's description of Mary's son. He will be son of David, the one in whom all the messianic hopes of Israel will be fulfilled. He will be Son of God, knowing God completely and obeying God perfectly. Luke thus encapsulates his understanding of Jesus in Gabriel's words to Mary.

3. Following this outline is a simple reading in parts of the annunciation as told by Luke, today's gospel. The opening lines of the Hail Mary have been used for Gabriel's greeting of Mary. Readings in simple parts, such as this, have worked well in the author's parish.

The Annunciation
A Reading of Luke 1:26-38

Narrator:	The angel Gabriel was sent from God to a town of Galilee named Nazareth. He was sent to a young woman promised in marriage to a man named Joseph. Joseph was of the house of King David. The young woman's name was Mary. The angel said to Mary:
Gabriel:	Hail, Mary, full of grace! The Lord is with you. Blessed are you among women.
Narrator:	Mary was deeply troubled by the angel's words. She wondered what his greeting meant. The angel went on to say to her:
Gabriel:	Do not fear, Mary. You have found favor with God. You shall have a son and give him the name Jesus. He will be great. He will be called Son of the Most High.
Narrator:	Mary said to the angel:

Mary:	How can this be?
Narrator:	The angel answered:
Gabriel:	The Holy Spirit will come upon you. The power of the Most High will come over you. The holy child to be born will called Son of God.
Mary:	I am the servant of the Lord. Let it be done to me as you say.
Narrator:	Then the angel left her.

Christmas
The Birth of the Lord

Lectionary for Masses with Children	Lectionary for Mass
**Is 9:2-4,6-7 *Ps 96:1-2a,2b-3,11-12a *Ti 3:4-6 **Lk 2:1-14	**Is 9:1-6 *Ps 96:1-2,2-3,11-12,13 *Ti 2:11-14 **Lk 2:1-14

Focus: This very day a savior is born for you. He is Christ the Lord!

Gather the Children

1. As we begin our celebration of Christmas let the children's gathering space show restrained joy, a joy which we will augment as our liturgy continues. Use a white gathering cloth. In the center of the cloth have only the open lectionary and two white candles. Continue to display nearby any posters or banners which the children made during Advent. Darken the room and light the candles before the children assemble.

2. Speak quietly to the children, who are surely excited, about how we gather to celebrate the birth of Jesus and to pray that his peace and joy will fill the lives of all people. Join the children in a few moments of silent reflection on the meaning of this beautiful, much-loved feast.

3. Then open the liturgy formally by leading the children in a familiar Advent hymn.

Proclaim the Word of the Lord Spoken through the Prophet Isaiah

1. Remind the children of the meaning of Advent, the season during which we prepare for Christmas. With the whole world, indeed, with the whole people of God through the ages, we have been waiting and preparing to celebrate the coming of Jesus into the world and into our hearts and lives. It is as if the world were in darkness without Jesus. He comes to light up our lives and show us the way to our loving God.

2. Ask the children to listen to words spoken long ago by the great prophet Isaiah to people whose lives were so filled with fear of war and its accompanying suffering that they wondered if God had forgotten them. Isaiah's beautiful words were a source of hope to his people, and they should remain a source of hope to us today. Isaiah speaks of a wise and peace-loving king who will banish evil and bring joy to all people.

3. Proclaim the first reading to the children.

4. Comment on the description of the child and king. He is described as bringing light and joy and peace. With a red or green paint pen write these words, or draw symbols of them, on gold or silver poster board crowns. Then comment on the titles Isaiah uses to describe the king. Write these names on crowns also. Relate our magnificent reading briefly to the other four impressive Old Testament readings which we have heard proclaimed this Advent.

5. In response to the reading sing a hymn based upon the text, or at least the ideas, of the responsorial psalm, Ps 96. Or sing an appropriate Christmas carol, for example, "Unto Us a Child Is Born" (in *Worship III*).

Proclaim the Gospel

1. Introduce the gospel by asking the children whom we recognize today as the one who fulfills completely all the wonderful promises which God made through the prophet Isaiah. Tell the children that our thoughts focus on the meaning of the whole life of Jesus as we remember his birth in history.

2. Before reading the gospel prepare the children's worship space for a most joyful proclamation. Place a smaller red cloth on top of the white gathering cloth, or use a cloth which the children have made especially for Christmas. Bring out a wreath with red candles and red bows. It would be appropriate to use the Advent wreath with its greens refreshed, with its used candles replaced with new red ones, and with big red bows. Light all the candles. Place the crowns which describe the messianic king on the red cloth around the wreath. Ask the children to stand up, then lead them in a joyful alleluia. During the singing have one child carry the lectionary slowly and reverently to the leader. Then proclaim Luke's nativity narrative.

3. Respond to the gospel immediately by singing "Joy to the World."

4. Review the gospel story quickly, enhancing the interest of the children by showing them a picture of the nativity created by a great artist.

5. Focus on the words of the angel to the shepherds:

• Ask the children to think about why the angel called the news of the birth of the baby "good news of great joy" for "all the people" or, as the translation which the LMC uses simplifies, "good news . . . which will make everyone happy." Let the children suggest answers, then direct their attention to the most wonderful of all good news, that God is with us in Jesus. Jesus saves us from a life of sin and suffering and leads us to God. On this great feast of Christmas we thank God for the gift of Jesus our savior.

• Ask the older children what names the angel ascribed to Jesus. The angel called Jesus "Savior," "Christ" and "Lord." Thus Luke acknowledges Jesus as king and God, one who has come to save us and to fulfill all the promises of God through the ages. Quickly write on crowns, like the ones used earlier, Luke's titles of Jesus. Display them with the other crowns on the gathering cloth.

• Ask the children why Luke had angels go first to

shepherds with the news of the birth of the messiah. Why not go first to the king? Or to the religious leaders of the people? Or to friends of Mary and Joseph? Help the children to recognize the shepherds as poor, in fact mistrusted and even despised people, symbols of the very people to whom Jesus, in his later ministry, would turn again and again with special compassion and love.

• Ask older children to repeat the words of the heavenly host. Help them to understand that the song of the angels (it must have been sung!) gives magnificent praise to God and recognizes God's incredible act of gifting the people with mercy and love, or, to use Luke's expression, with God's gracious favor. Notice how Luke encapsulates the gift of God to humankind in the word "peace." Thoughts of peace between God and God's people and among people recur again and again in Luke's gospel.

Respond to the Readings

1. Ask the children what we should do in response to the message of our readings. Listen carefully to their suggestions. Gently lead them away from merely sentimental or "pious" thoughts, which so abound at this time of year, and encourage their heartfelt expressions of faith and love.

2. The aim of the following activity is to help the children grasp the important truth that their gifts of love make the life of Jesus and the love of God real in the world today.

• Talk briefly with the children about how the best gifts we give other people are not material gifts. Gifts of kindness, helpfulness, patience, encouragement, forgiveness and the like are wonderful and lasting, real Christmas gifts. These are the gifts which should occupy our attention during the Christmas season.

• Give each of the children a piece of white construction paper. Ask them to sketch quickly pictures of themselves doing kind and helpful things for others. Let them "wrap" their "gifts" by drawing big red bows on the backs of their pictures.

• Let the children take home their "gifts" and keep them as reminders of the real meaning of God's Christmas gift to us.

3. Quietly bring the children to attention. Then ask them to extend their arms, with upraised palms, and listen to the following prayer:

Loving God,
we rejoice today in the birth of Jesus.
Through Jesus you are with us.
Through Jesus we see your glory
and we delight in your gracious love.
May the birth of Jesus
fill us with joy and peace.
May the life of Jesus
call us to share our gifts from you
with all your children everywhere.
We pray as we always pray
through Jesus, your child,
and with your Holy Spirit,
who live with you forever.
Amen.

4. Conclude the liturgy by singing a Christmas hymn, one which the children know and love. Bob Dufford's "Children, Run Joyfully" (from *Gentle Night*) would be an excellent choice. Children love it and learn it quickly.

Other Possibilities:

1. Lead older children to deeper appreciation of our reading from the book of Isaiah.

• Many scholars see the passage as a liturgical hymn sung on the occasion of the coronation of a new king of the house of David. With the accession of each new king, hopes ran high that this king would be the ideal king promised to David. The king was hailed as an adopted son of God, hence the prophet speaks of the "child." The prophecy expresses the constant hope of the people of Israel for an ideal ruler who would bring lasting peace and justice; but, in fact, never did any historical king perfectly embody the qualities of which the piece speaks. Later Christian theology sees the fulfillment in Jesus of this prophecy, perhaps the most famous of all the messianic prophecies.

• The structure of the passage is straightforward. The prophet describes the king as one who brings light into the darkness of the lives of his people. Two images express the joy of the people which accompanies the great event: their joy is like that of a successful harvest, and their joy is like that of victory in war. The people acclaim the new king with a string of royal titles and describe his reign as one of peace and justice. Finally the prophet credits the whole wondrous happening to the Lord.

• Prepare the children to understand the reading, then proclaim it to them. Elicit their comments on whether it is possible for any human being to fulfill the prophecy. Discuss with them whether or not Jesus fulfilled it. Let them rephrase the prophecy with images and titles and descriptions which speak to today's average young Christian.

2. Teach a small group of older children the processional canon which Jack Miffleton describes to accompany "Grow Strong" (from *Promise Chain*). The quiet song and dance, complete with moving lighted candles, encourages prayerful reflection on our waiting for the coming of Christ. Use the procession to open the liturgy. Or teach a small group of children to do a simple liturgical dance to accompany the proclamation of the reading from Isaiah. Let them dress in white albs. Let them begin the dance in the back of the church, process to the front, and conclude their dance within the sanctuary.

3. Psalm 96 is "probably the most magnificent of all the enthronement psalms which celebrate the kingship of Yahweh" (Fuller, PNL). With Israel we are invited to "sing to the Lord a new song," a song announcing the Lord's salvation and telling the Lord's glory. From a Christian perspective, Ps 96 offers a wonderful hymn of praise to God for the salvation God works for us in Jesus, whose birth in time we commemorate on this great feast. The psalms are deeply beautiful, retaining their pertinence to human life even today, several mil-

lennia after their composition. There is urgent need for musicians to set to music the psalms themselves, and not merely thoughts based upon the psalms.

4. Use the LMC reading from the letter to Titus to help children appreciate the incomparability of the gift of God in Jesus and God's gracious kindness in giving us the gift.

5. Or use the LM Mass at Midnight reading from the letter to Titus to help older children see the feast of Christmas as a celebration anticipating the coming in glory of Jesus at the end of time. Let them extract from the reading some of the author's good practical advice for people like us who, while we celebrate the presence of God with us, also look to the full revelation of God's glory only in the future.

6. Enhance the proclamation of the gospel visually by accompanying it with a simple tableau of Mary, Joseph and Jesus, or by illustrating Luke's story with slides of great works of art, or by illustrating it with slides of pictures painted by the children.

7. Sing a Gloria with the children, ideally set to music which the assembly sings. Be sure the children realize that opening lines of the Gloria are the words of the heavenly host on the first Christmas. Or sing "Angels We Have Heard on High."

8. Encourage the children to bring to the liturgy wrapped gifts to give to the poor. Invite the children to place their gifts near the ambo when they rejoin the assembly.

9. Tell older children why we celebrate Christmas in late December. (No one knows exactly when Jesus was born, though there are scriptural indications it was in the spring.) Many scholars believe that our celebration of Christmas was chosen to coincide with ancient pagan celebrations surrounding the winter solstice, the point at which the lengthening night ceases to shorten the day. Christians celebrate the coming of the light of Jesus into the darkness of their lives at the same time that light triumphs over darkness in the natural order.

10. Introduce the children to the American Indian Christmas carol "Twas in the Moon of Wintertime," which the leader will find in *Worship III*. The lovely carol tells the story of the birth of Jesus in simple, gentle Indian thought. The carol was written by St. Jean de Brebeuf, a French Jesuit priest who came to North America and worked as a missionary among the Huron Indians. St. Jean and his companion priest and missionary Gabriel Lalemant were cruelly martyred in 1649 by a band of Iroquois, nearby Indians who were deadly enemies of the Hurons.

11. Many of the suggestions for this liturgy of the word may be easily adapted for a liturgy in which children and adults worship together. Surely on Christmas, particularly for an early celebration of the Mass at Midnight, children and adults should celebrate the entire liturgy together, with children involved as deeply as good taste and genuine liturgy permit. Such a celebration can only enhance the meaning of this great feast.

Sunday in the Octave of Christmas Holy Family

Lectionary for Masses with Children	Lectionary for Mass
*Sir 3:2-6	*Sir 3:2-6,12-14
*Ps 128:1-2,3,4-5	*Ps 128:1-2,3,4-5
*Col 3:12-17	*Col 3:12-21
Mt 2:13-15,19-21	**Lk 2:22-40 or 2:22,39-40

Focus: We rejoice in the family of Jesus. We strive to imitate its virtues.

Gather the Children

1. Today the children's gathering space should radiate Christmas joy. Use a white gathering cloth. Place on the white cloth a smaller red cloth. In the center of the red cloth arrange red or white candles in a cluster of evergreens. Or refresh the Advent wreath and transform it into a Christmas wreath by replacing its purple and pink candles with red ones and adding big red bows. Continue to display the liturgical banners and posters the children made during Advent.

2. After the children assemble, light the candles and remind the group that our celebration of Christmas continues. Ask the children to bow their heads and thank God quietly for the wonderful gift we have in Jesus. Then lead them in singing a familiar Christmas carol. Or teach them the refrain to Bob Dufford's "Children, Run Joyfully" (from *Gentle Night*). Children love the song and learn it easily.

Proclaim the Gospel

Note: The LMC omits the beautiful segments of the Lukan infancy narrative which the LM assigns to Holy Family Sunday in lectionary years B and C, and instead always uses the Matthean gospel of year A. The following suggestions, therefore, correspond to today's gospel reading in the LM. The leader who wishes to use the gospel in the LMC may consult the outline for Holy Family Sunday in Gather the Children, Year A.

1. Summarize the story of the birth of Jesus and the adoration of the shepherds. Illustrate the story with appropriate slides of great works of art. Or, more simply, use the flannel board.

2. The choice of the LM of a short form of today's gospel suggests that the emphasis of today's celebration is not on the presentation of Jesus (which we celebrate properly on February 2), but on his childhood with his family. Simply tell the children the story of the presentation of Jesus in the temple, once again illustrating it with slides or with the flannel board.

3. Then tell the children that Mary and Joseph soon took the baby Jesus back to their little town of Nazareth in Galilee. Although, with the exception of the story of the finding of the boy Jesus in the temple (the gospel for Holy Family Sunday in year C), the gospels are silent about the childhood of Jesus, it would be perfectly appropriate to initiate a discussion about some of the ordinary things that Mary, Joseph and Jesus must have done together as a family. Have some simple articles to illustrate the discussion, for example, a baby blanket, wooden toys, simple kitchen equipment, a hammer and nails. Mary and Joseph took care of their baby as all loving parents do. Jesus learned to walk and to talk. As a child he helped Mary with household chores and he helped Joseph with his carpentry work. Jesus learned to read and to write. Mary and Joseph told him about God and taught him how to pray. In short he grew and matured physically, mentally and spiritually just as any other child does. Today's feast celebrates the holiness of the little Jewish family that allowed the child Jesus to grow into the very special adult he was to be. The leader should picture the family of Jesus not simply as "pious," but as the model in goodness, in strength, in devotion to the will of God for all families who wish their children to respond perfectly in adulthood to the call of God.

4. Acclaim the gospel with a joyful alleluia and then proclaim its shortened form, simplified appropriately for very young children.

5. Ask the children to respond to the gospel by thinking quietly about the life of Mary, Joseph and Jesus together. During their meditation play a Christmas lullaby. Show the children a slide of the holy family.

Lead the Children in Reflection about the Holy Family

1. The leader must be extremely sensitive—extremely sensitive—in talking to the children about family life. Some of the children, of course, may not live with both their parents. It is always possible that there are serious problems in the families of some of the children, even problems which are not apparent from a casual acquaintance with the children. In discussing family life the leader must strive to present for emulation the highest Christian ideals, but at the same time take great care not to pass judgment on the parents of children in less than perfect homes or to develop a sense of guilt in children who are innocent victims in unhappy situations.

2. Help the children to know the holy family as a real family:

• Discuss good qualities of families today:

Take a large sheet of newsprint and write across the center "Families!" Invite the children to mention things they like about their parents. As the children respond, fill the paper with exclamations, such as "Thanks," "Wow," "Lucky me," "Great!"

Ask the children to mention good things their parents might say about their children. As the children talk, continue to fill the paper with exclamations.

• Talk about the life of the holy family:

Remind the children that the life of the holy family was in many ways different from the life of a modern American family. Mary, Joseph and Jesus lived in a small one room house. They had no car, of course. Mary spun and wove and made clothes. She kept the home fire going and cooked and baked. The family ate simple foods, usually bread and fruit and vegetables, sometimes fish, rarely meat. Joseph worked hard at his carpentry work and taught Jesus his trade. The family worshipped at the synagogue. Jesus learned to read and to write and to know the Hebrew scriptures at the synagogue school.

By referring to the children's list of good things about today's parents and children, help the group to realize that the life of the holy family was also much like our family life. Apply the appropriate family qualities to Jesus and his family. Glue onto the newsprint big pictures of Mary, Joseph and Jesus. The leader might engage several children to draw the pictures in advance of the liturgy. Or the leader might make very simple figures with triangles for bodies and circles for heads.

3. Remind the children that Mary, Joseph and Jesus must have tried hard to be loving and giving to each other. Talk gently with the children about how parents and children so often fail to love each other as they should. Encourage the children to do their best to imitate the virtues of the holy family.

Share the Advice about Christian Living which We Read in Our Second Reading

1. The leader should be mindful that there are good reasons for disclaiming Pauline authorship of the letter to the Colossians and claiming instead its authorship by a follower of the great apostle. It is not necessary, however, to burden children with scholarly debate, and the leader will not do wrong to speak of the letter as from the hand of Paul.
2. Tell the children that in today's second reading, we hear advice about how to live good Christian lives. The author wrote his advice in a letter to the Christians who lived in the city of Colossae in Asia Minor.
3. Ask the children to listen to part of the letter and to remember especially what it says that might help us in our relationships with the members of our families. Then proclaim the reading.
4. Lead the children in a brief discussion of the advice we have just heard proclaimed. Suggest that families would do well to take the advice to heart and strive to apply it to their lives together.

Pray for Families

1. Join the children in a few moments of quiet personal reflection and resolution concerning ways in which we can contribute to the happiness of our families.
2. Pray the general intercessions with the children. Include the needs of individual families as well as the needs of the whole human family. Encourage the children, especially older children, to participate in formulating the petitions.
3. The leader might visit a religious book store and purchase for the children small pictures, in good taste, of the holy family or of Jesus as a child. The "holy pictures" would make excellent remembrances of today's liturgy. Or give the children pictures of the holy family to take home and color.
4. Conclude the liturgy by singing a Christmas hymn.

Other Possibilities:

1. Today we have not followed the usual order of proclamation of readings, but have considered the gospel first and then the reading from the letter to the Colossians. For older children whose abilities to think abstractly are sufficiently developed, the leader should follow the traditional order of proclamation.
2. Share more of the gospel with older children:
• Luke's stories of the purification of Mary and the presentation of Jesus in the temple are beautiful stories. They tell us much about the spiritual atmosphere in which Jesus grew up, and they tell us about the child Jesus himself:

Luke states, even three times in his narrative, that Mary and Joseph fulfilled the prescriptions of the law of Moses concerning childbirth: Mary was ritually purified after the birth of her child, and the child, the first-born male, was consecrated to the Lord. Today's gospel is consistent with the whole of Luke's infancy narrative in insisting that the little Jewish family represented the best of Jewish piety. It is in the love and care of just such a family that we would expect God to place Jesus, the very Son of God, for his formative childhood years.

Through the prophecies of Simeon and Anna, Luke tells us about the identity and the destiny of Jesus. The child is the Lord's Anointed, the means of God's saving deed, a light to the Gentiles, the glory of Israel. He will call Israel to decision, he will be her deliverance. Luke describes Simeon (whose age is not indicated) and the old widow Anna in glowing terms. The two embody a living in God's presence and an openness to God's ways that all who love God should strive to imitate.

• After telling the children the stories, let several children read the gospel in parts. Choose two to read together as Mary and Joseph, choose one to be Simeon and one to be Anna. Let the children read the parts of the gospel that are about, or are spoken by, the people they represent.
• Invite the children to discuss the value of a family's being steeped in religious tradition, as Jesus's family obviously was. What religious traditions do we observe?

• Mary and Joseph "wondered" at the words of Simeon about the baby. How strange that Mary and Joseph should suddenly be so ignorant about the child, considering what they had already heard and seen about him! Was Luke confused? Or might he have been telling us something valuable about the childhood of Jesus?

3. The church uses Simeon's prayer, the "Nunc Dimittis," daily in her liturgy of the hours as part of night prayer. Give older children copies of the canticle to take home. Urge them to use it as part of their personal night prayer. Introduce mature children to the church's official night prayer.

4. In our first reading today the sage "Jesus, son of Eleazar, son of Sirach" (Sir 50:27), urges his fellow Jews to honor and care for their parents. Proclaim to older children the reading in the LM (to include its verses, which the LMC omits, about older parents) and use it as a springboard for a discussion about how modern society treats the elderly. Show some slides of old people. If there are children who are intimately involved with the care of failing relatives, let them share their personal experiences of frustration and of joy. Gently guide the children toward an attitude of loving concern for those older children of God whose minds or whose bodies are no longer whole and strong. Tomie de Paola's *Nanna Upstairs and Nanna Downstairs* and Mem Fox's *Wilfrid Gordon Mcdonald Partridge* are wonderful stories about understanding and loving concern for the elderly.

5. Psalm 128 describes in common biblical images the happiness of the one who walks in the way of the Lord. The psalmist pictures that happiness as consisting of a productive, healthy wife and a large, healthy family. Older children might like to read the whole psalm and "update" its images.

6. Our reading today from the letter to the Colossians is part of the author's description of the new life of the Christian. The first paragraph of the reading certainly describes what should be our reaction to the gift of God in Jesus, thus fitting perfectly the Christmas season. Share its thoughts with older children. The LM reading concludes with (and the LMC omits) advice which the author intends specifically for families. The reading must, of course, be interpreted in light of the social customs of its times. It is significant that what is here original about the thought is not its description of family structure and behavior, but its injunction to do all "in the Lord." (See PNL and JBC.)

7. Groups of older children might like to compose letters to the parish community describing family life as they would like it to be. Keep the letters anonymous and reproduce them for the children to give to their parents.

8. Note that today's feast is celebrated on December 30 in those years in which there is no Sunday between Christmas Day and New Year's Day.

Feast of the Epiphany

Lectionary for Masses with Children	Lectionary for Mass
**Is 60:1-6	**Is 60:1-6
Ps 72:1,2,10,11	Ps 72:1-2,7-8,10-11,12-13
- - - - -	Eph 3:2-3,5-6
**Mt 2:1-12	**Mt 2:1-12

Focus: Jesus was born for all of us. Let us adore him.

Gather the Children

1. The children's gathering space should be decorated today with all the splendor and joy of Christmas. Use a white gathering cloth with a smaller red cloth on top of the white one. Have a Christmas wreath. The leader might transform the Advent wreath into a Christmas wreath by refreshing its greens, replacing its used candles with red ones and adding red bows. Have figures of Mary, Joseph and the infant Jesus, even ones which the children have made. Have ready figures of the three kings, but do not let the children see them. As always display the lectionary prominently.
2. Welcome the children joyfully and remind them why we gather for our special liturgy of the word.
3. Proclaim the first reading:
• Ask the children why we use candles at Christmas.
• Then ask them to listen carefully to a few lines spoken by the prophet Isaiah a long time ago. Proclaim the reading, perhaps using only Is 60:1 for very young children.
• Light the Christmas wreath and sing "Joy to the World" or another favorite Christmas hymn.

Proclaim the Gospel

1. Talk briefly about the events of Christmas night, thus reviewing the narrative with the children. Use the figures displayed on the cloth, plus any additional figures of angels, shepherds and animals. Or use simple flannel board figures, which younger children always like. Or show appropriate slides of great works of art. Do not yet discuss today's story of the coming of the kings.
2. Ask the children if they know what great feast we celebrate today, a feast just as important as Christmas itself. Tell them that we celebrate the coming of Jesus to all people, even those far away from Bethlehem. Introduce to them the word "epiphany," whose root is the Greek word for appearance or manifestation.
3. Tell the gospel story, illustrating it with figures or slides. Do not confuse younger children with too much detail.
4. Acclaim the gospel with joyful song, and then proclaim it.

Respond to the Gospel

1. Point out to the children that the wise men are symbols of people like us, so far removed in time and space from the historical birth of Jesus.
2. Prepare a simple procession for the children to reenter the church after their liturgy of the word:

• Have ready three empty boxes and a supply of Christmas wrapping paper and ribbons. Remind the children that the wise men brought gifts to Jesus, then ask the children to suggest gifts that we can give to Jesus. Stress the value of gifts of love and service. Choose several particularly helpful gift ideas and cut out simple shapes to symbolize the ideas. Or write the ideas on stars or crowns. Put the shapes into the boxes and, with the help of the children, quickly wrap the boxes.
• Choose one child to lead the procession, holding high a large star. Choose three children to walk next in the procession, carrying the gift boxes. Give all the children crowns to wear. Instruct the children to follow the leaders into the church. When all the children have assembled near the altar, the leaders should lay the star and the gifts in front of the ambo. The children and the assembly might sing "O Come, All Ye Faithful" as the children process and place their gifts. Then all the children should return to their parents.
3. After preparing the procession, say a profession of faith with the children. Base it on the ideas of today's readings, perhaps as follows:

Leader:	Do you believe in God the Father, who sent Jesus, his Son, to live among us?
All:	I do!
Leader:	Do you believe that Jesus is King?
All:	I do!
Leader:	Do you believe that Jesus is God?
All:	I do!
Leader:	Do you believe that Jesus suffered for us?
All:	I do!
Leader:	Do you believe in the Holy Spirit, who is the presence of Jesus in the world today?
All:	I do!

4. If there are too many children for the leader to give all of them crowns for their procession, let just the three "kings" wear crowns. But give each child a star to take home. Suggest that at home the children draw pictures of Jesus on their stars to remind themselves that we want to follow the light of Jesus as the wise men did. Or give them each a picture to color at home of a star and three crowns, with an appropriate quotation from the day's readings.

Other Possibilities:

1. If the leader has opportunity to work with the chil-

dren before the liturgy, let the children themselves make simple figures of Mary, Joseph, Jesus, shepherds, angels and wise men: cut out, using one pattern only, enough simple figures for the children each to have one. Let the children draw features and clothes on the blank figures. Collect the figures as the children finish them, and add details to make the characters of the story: halos for Mary and Joseph, wings for the angels, staffs for the shepherds and cotton balls for their sheep, crowns and presents for the wise men. Have one small figure for Jesus, but do not complete it yet. During the liturgy of the word, bring out the figures. Complete Jesus by adding a halo, and then glue Jesus onto Mary, as if she is holding him. Use the figures to review the Christmas stories. After the liturgy let the children take their figures home. (If the children are not familiar with halos, simply tell them that through the centuries artists have used halos to indicate holiness.)

2. As an alternative to the gift ideas used earlier, give the children each a heart, ask them to personalize their hearts in some way, collect the hearts and wrap them in the gift boxes. Then, if time permits, teach the children the third verse of "O Come, Little Children":

Dear Christ Child, what gifts can we children bestow
By which our affection and gladness we show?
Our hearts, Lord, to you we will offer today.
We offer them gladly; accept them, we pray.

3. As gifts for the gift procession, older children might:
• Write out personal gifts of themselves to others;
• Or as a group decide on three things they can do for the parish community. Write their ideas on squares of poster board. Cover only the blank sides of the poster board with wrapping paper and bows, so that the gift ideas of the children will be visible.

4. Beautiful indeed is our reading today from Third Isaiah! And aptly chosen for our celebration of the great feast of the Epiphany. "The prophet sees Jerusalem as the one point of light in a world of darkness; as the light grows in intensity, it illuminates the dark world and attracts the nations" (McKenzie, AB, 20, p.177). The first three verses hail the return of the exiles to Jerusalem. The second three predict the gathering of the nations in Jerusalem in tribute to Yahweh. So close in spirit and vocabulary to Second Isaiah, these verses from Third Isaiah constitute a strong argument for Second Isaian authorship of Is 56-66 (JBC).
• Give older children copies of the reading. Explain it to them. Relate it to our Christian celebration today. God's great gift of salvation in Jesus far surpasses God's gift of the return of the exiles from Babylon. As the Gentiles streamed to the light of Jerusalem, so the magi symbolically represent the coming of all nations to the light of Jesus. Let the children proclaim the reading in unison.
• Help the children to see how the reading influenced Matthew's account of the revelation of Jesus to the world. Help them, further, to see how popular legend has taken over details of the reading and applied them to the Matthean story.

5. Pray Ps 72 both as a response to the first reading and in honor of the infant king whom the wise men came to adore. As an alternative response, the group might sing the refrain of "O Come, All Ye Faithful." Little children would enjoy following the leader's simple gestures during the singing.

6. Light, symbol of the presence of Yahweh and of salvation, dominates our Christian symbolism. We traditionally associate the five-pointed star with the magi, representatives of the Gentiles. (Why?) Show the older children how to fold and cut five-pointed stars. Then let them make big stars and write on the backs of their stars things they can do to spread Christmas love and peace to some, however small, part of our world.

7. January fifth is the twelfth day of Christmas; January sixth, the feast of the Epiphany (transferred, however, to Sunday). A delightful Twelfth-night/Epiphany custom, one which children of all ages enjoy, is the making of a king's cake. There are different ways to make a king's cake. A simple king's cake is an ordinary frosted cake on which a child can put a crown made of gumdrops or m&m's. A traditional king's cake is more complicated. It is a spicy yeast cake into which the cook bakes a bean. Whoever gets the bean when the cake is served is king for the day. In New Orleans (where the author grew up) it is traditional to begin the Mardi Gras season with a "Twelfth-night party" at which a king's cake is served. The person who gets the bean in the cake is king of the party, and must have another party soon with another king's cake. The new king must have the next party, and so on until each person has been king—and given a party. The round of parties ends by Mardi Gras day, when everyone is partied-out and ready for Lent. The following recipe for a king's cake is from the excellent Ursuline Convent cookbook Recipes and Reminiscences of New Orleans (P.O. Box 7491, Metairie, LA, 70010). The publishers of the cookbook have kindly given permission for the inclusion of the recipe in Gather The Children.

King's Cake

1 package yeast
1/4 cup warm water
6 tablespoons milk, scalded and cooled
4 cups flour
1 cup (2 sticks) butter
3/4 cup sugar
1/4 teaspoon salt
4 eggs
Melted butter

In a bowl, dissolve yeast in warm water. Add milk and enough flour, about 1/2 cup, to make a soft dough. In another bowl, combine butter, sugar, salt and eggs with an electric mixer. Remove from mixer and add soft ball of yeast dough. Mix thoroughly. Gradually add 2-1/2 cups flour to make a medium dough that is neither too soft nor too stiff. Place in a greased bowl and brush top of dough with butter. Cover with a damp cloth and set aside to rise until doubled in bulk, about 3 hours. Use remaining 1 cup flour to knead dough and to roll with hands into a "rope" shape. Place on a 14x17-inch greased cookie sheet and form "rope" of dough into an oval shape. The center should be about 7x12 inches. Connect ends of dough by dampening with water.

Cover with a damp cloth and let rise until doubled in bulk, about 1 hour. (A bean may be placed in cake if desired.) Bake in 325 F over, for 35 to 45 minutes, or until lightly browned. Decorate by brushing top of cake with corn syrup and alternating 3-inch bands of purple, green and gold colored granulated sugar. (To color sugar, add a few drops of food coloring to sugar, and shake in tightly covered jar until desired color is achieved.)

8. It is traditional to bless our homes on the feast of the Epiphany. The following ceremony is adapted from the one which appeared in *Share the Word*, Jan-Feb 1983. Mary's Canticle is from *Good News For Modern Man*. Bless the room in which the children are assembled. Shorten and simplify the service radically for little ones. Send the children home with copies of the ceremony for use in their own homes

Epiphany Blessing of a Home

All assemble by the front door (or outside, if weather permits).

Leader: Peace to this house.

All: And to all who enter here.

Leader: Wise men came from the east, to adore the Lord. Opening their treasures, they offered precious gifts.

All: Gold to the Great King!
Incense to the true God!
Myrrh for the day of his burial!

Reader: My heart praises the Lord!
My soul is glad because of God, my Savior!
He has remembered me, his lowly servant.
From now on all people will call me happy because of the great things the Mighty God has done for me.
His name is holy;
he shows mercy to those who fear him,
from one generation to another.
He stretched out his mighty arm
and scattered the proud with all their plans.
He brought down mighty kings from their thrones,
and lifted up the lowly.
He filled the hungry with good things,
and sent the rich away with empty hands.
He kept the promise he made to our ancestors,
and came to the help of his servant Israel;
he remembered to show mercy to Abraham and to all his descendants forever!

All: Our Father, who art in heaven . . .

Leader: Wise men came from the east, to adore the Lord. Opening their treasures, they offered precious gifts.

All: Gold to the Great King!
Incense to the true God!
Myrrh for the day of his burial!

Leader: All from Sheba shall come

All: Bearing gold and frankincense.

Leader: O Lord, hear my prayer.

All: And let my cry come to you.

Leader: Let us pray. (Moments of silence.) Father, you revealed your Son to the nations, by the guidance of a star. Lead us to your glory and our eternal home by the light of faith in Jesus Christ our Lord.

All: Amen.

With chalk or crayon, an inscription is made above the door:

19 + C + M + B + 94

The letters represent the Magi, traditionally named Caspar, Melchior, and Baltassar; the enclosing year represents the timeless God; each cross marks a point of the compass, or "all the nations."

Leader: Arise! Shine! Jerusalem, your light has come.

All: The glory of the Lord shines upon you.

Leader: Nations shall walk by your light.

All: Kings by your shining radiance.

Leader: Lord, Almighty God, bless this home. Let health and goodness abide here, humility and faith, and every triumph over sin. Let your word be obeyed and fulfilled here, and thanksgiving ever be made to you, Father, Son and Holy Spirit, now and forever.

All: Amen.

All then re-enter the home, while singing God's praises in a suitable Christmas/Epiphany hymn.

Baptism of the Lord

Lectionary for Masses with Children	Lectionary for Mass
**Is 42:1-2,4,6-7	**Is 42:1-4,6-7
**Ps 29:3-4,3,9-10	**Ps 29:1-2,3-4,3,9-10
*Acts 10:34-38	*Acts 10:34-38
**Lk 3:15-16,21-22	**Lk 3:15-16,21-22

Focus: Jesus was baptized as a sign that he wanted to do God's will. We have been baptized into God's family. We want to do God's will by following the example of Jesus.

Gather the Children

Note: When the feast of Epiphany is celebrated on January 7 or 8, the church observes the feast of the Baptism of the Lord on the following Monday.

1. Today's feast of the Baptism of the Lord brings our celebration of Christmas to a close and prepares us for reflection on the ministry of Jesus, which will occupy our attention from now until the First Sunday of Lent. Bring together the children in their gathering space, once again decorated with evergreens and candles in a way that speaks of the wonderful Christmas gift of Jesus. Have present signs of baptism: a bowl of water, a baptismal candle, a white garment.

2. Welcome the children and remind them why we come together for our special liturgy of the word. Have a brief discussion of things we're thankful for, including especially things related to Christmas. Light all the candles and sing a song of praise and thanksgiving for God's many gifts.

Prepare the Children to Hear the Gospel

1. The leader must adapt the following presentation to meet the needs of his or her particular parish. In parishes which celebrate liturgy of the word for children during all our Christmas Sunday and holyday liturgies, a summary of the events of the birth and childhood of Jesus might not be necessary.

2. Show a simple filmstrip, such as part one of *Jesus Our Brother* (from Ave Maria Press). Do not use the sound track. Or show appropriate slides of great works of art. Or show pictures or slides the children have made. The leader should keep his or her comments to a minimum, letting the children reflect quietly on the familiar story. Conclude the period of reflection by singing a joyful Christmas song, perhaps one which the children sang during their Christmas liturgy.

3. Talk about the early life of Jesus:

• As a child Jesus lived with Mary and Joseph in the little town of Nazareth in Galilee. He loved his parents and tried to make them happy. He helped his mother. Let the children make suggestions as to how he might have done this. Jesus helped Joseph, who was a carpenter. Have a wooden manger, wooden spoons, simple wooden toys. Help the children to realize that the life of Jesus with his parents was in many ways just like our own family lives. Be sensitive to the fact that some of the children may not come from happy homes, homes whose members strive continually to give and share unselfishly. Joseph must have died during these years of the "private" life of Jesus.

• Jesus gradually came to know what God wanted him to do with his life: God wanted Jesus to show all people how to live as brothers and sisters in one family. So, when Jesus was about thirty years old, he left his home and his mother to answer God's call.

4. Remind the children of the life-work of John the Baptizer to ready Israel for the promised one. The children should be familiar with John's work, including his baptism of the people, from our Advent liturgies.

Proclaim the Gospel

1. Tell the children about the baptism of Jesus, using the first two frames of part two of *Jesus Our Brother* or other pictures or slides. Mark, Matthew, Luke and John differ in their accounts of the baptism. Mark has Jesus baptized outright by John. Matthew has John baptize Jesus, but only after a discussion between the two men that makes it clear that Jesus did not submit to baptism because of his sinfulness. Luke puts John in prison immediately before Jesus is baptized (the lectionary reading omits this), and definitely directs attention away from the baptism and toward the revelation of God. The Evangelist John makes no mention at all of Jesus's baptism. The baptism of Jesus by John evidently was something of an embarrassment to the early church. The point of the synoptic accounts is that at Jesus's baptism God anointed Jesus with the Holy Spirit for messianic ministry and acknowledged Jesus as God's Son. Younger children cannot understand much of this, but the leader should speak to them at least of the presence of the Son, the coming of the Holy Spirit and the voice of the Father. The leader need not be overly concerned with details and explanation.

2. Acclaim the gospel joyfully in song, and then proclaim it. The leader will notice that the LMC uses the Lukan account of the baptism of Jesus in all three lectionary years, while the LM presents the three synoptic accounts successively. The leader of a group of older children might point out some of the differences in the gospel accounts, and then, following the LM, proclaim the Markan version of the narrative.

Make the Good News Our Own

1. Remind the children of their own baptisms. Tell them that at their baptisms their parents promised they would do their best to help them hear and heed God's word throughout their lives, just as Jesus did.

2. Next the leader should point out and explain, with a minimum of talk, the baptismal symbols which the children see on the gathering cloth. Finger the water. Show the white garment. Light the baptismal candle.

3. Focus especially on the baptismal candle. Remind

the children of the symbolism of candles, used so frequently and so prominently during Advent and Christmas. Candles remind us that God calls us to live by the light of Jesus. Discuss how we can do this. Help the children be practical. Record some of their ideas on a large paper flame and attach it to a large cardboard candle. Write the name "Jesus" on the candle. Write the date of the new year on the candle to encourage the children to live by the light of Jesus in the new year.

4. Lead the children in a renewal of our baptismal promises, perhaps as follows:

Leader: My brothers and sisters in God's family, today we remember and celebrate the baptism of Jesus. Let us profess our belief in God the Father, God the Son and God the Holy Spirit. And let us renew the promise of our baptism to live as Jesus did, always trying to do what God wants.

Do you believe in God the Father, who made heaven and earth, who made us and wants us to be happy?

All: I do!

Leader: Do you believe in Jesus, God's only Son, who always did God's will?

All: I do!

Leader: Do you promise to follow Jesus, who is the light of our lives?

All: I do!

Leader: Do you believe in the Holy Spirit, who lives in us and helps us follow Jesus to God?

All: I do!

Leader: Do you believe that after we die we will rise again with Jesus and live with God forever?

All: I do!

Leader: Loving God, you have given Jesus to live among us. Help us to follow him faithfully to you. We pray this, as we always pray, in the name of Jesus and with your Holy Spirit. Amen.

5. Let the children "light" and take home small paper candles with the year written on them: give each child a paper cylinder and a paper flame. If the flame is cut so that it remains attached to a horizontal strip of paper, then the candle may be "lit" by rolling up the strip and inserting it into the cylinder. Suggest that at home the children write their names on their candles and then display them as a reminder of our baptismal call to do the will of God as Jesus did.

6. Teach the children the simple song "You Have Put on Christ" by Howard Hughes (from the ICEL collection). Change the words to "We have put on Christ."

Other Possibilities:

1. The above outline highlights the symbolism of light, prominent in our Advent and Christmas liturgies and in the baptismal rite. The leader might prefer to concentrate on water, which is the primary baptismal symbol and which occurs in our gospel and our psalm. Water is life and salvation in biblical imagery. Water is even the primordial element (Gn 1:2), not enumerated among the works of creation, but presupposed (McKenzie, DOB, p.922). Talk with the children about

the necessity of water for life and growth, how common it is, its powers of renewal and destruction. Show them slides of water, of ice and snow, of tiny raindrops, of huge ships, of storms, of people enjoying water. Teach the children a song about water and its life-sustaining powers. Let them drink reverently from paper cups and take their cups home. Show the children how to make the Sign of the Cross with holy water.

2. As an alternative means of reviewing the early life of Jesus the leader might show the children episode three of the filmstrip *My Name Is Jesus* (from Roa Films). Rather than use the record, the leader might simply comment on the pictures.

3. Psalm 29, after a call to praise the Lord, "describes a magnificent theophany, the revelation of God's majesty in a tremendous thunderstorm" (notes in the Saint Joseph edition of the *New American Bible*). God's "voice" is the thunder, mighty, majestic, making the mountains tremble with fear, shaking the desert, stripping the forests. To help older children appreciate the church's frequent use of water symbolism, share all of Ps 29 with them. Explain its powerful imagery and then let them read it together, perhaps in parts.

4. Older children might benefit from reflection on our reading from the book of Isaiah. Verses 1-4 comprise the first of the four "Servant Songs." In verses 6-7, the so-called response to the poem, the ideas are repeated. In beautiful and moving poetry, the "Servant Songs" describe a mysterious "servant of Yahweh," chosen by God to gather Israel and to be a light to the nations, faithful to God through suffering and death. The Christian church sees the deepest meaning and the fulfillment of these prophecies in the life and death of Jesus.

• Help older children to see how the person and mission of Jesus are prefigured in the call of the servant and the description of his ministry in the reading. Discuss with the group how appropriate the reading is for today's celebration of the baptism of Jesus.

• Encourage the children to reflect upon the self-consciousness of Jesus. He was, of course, familiar with the scriptures. How was he influenced by passages such as our reading from Isaiah? Did the servant poems help Jesus to recognize God's plan for his life and death?

• Ask the children to imagine that they, like the evangelists, are writing the story of Jesus. Challenge them to think of how they might introduce the adult Jesus into their story. In this way, help them to understand that the appearance of the Spirit and the voice in the gospel function as God's introduction to us of Jesus, about to begin his public life and ministry. Our celebration of the baptism of Jesus forms a fitting introduction to our study of the public ministry of Jesus, upon which we embark next week when we return to "ordinary time."

5. Our second reading today is the first part of Peter's speech to Cornelius and his relatives and friends, immediately preceding the descent of the Holy Spirit upon them and their baptism. The story of Cornelius and Peter is important because it shows us that the Gentiles were to be accepted without qualification into the early church. The reading is appropriate today because it describes John's baptism as the beginning of the ministry of Jesus.

Second Sunday of the Year

Lectionary for Masses with Children	Lectionary for Mass
**I Sm 3:3-10,19 Ps 40:1,3,8,11 ----- **Jn 1:35-42	**I Sm 3:3-10,19 Ps 40:2,4,7-8,8-9,10 I Cor 6:13-15,17-20 **Jn 1:35-42

Focus: Call us, Lord, and we will respond.

Gather the Children

1. After the eager anticipation of Advent and the joyful celebration of Christmas, we return today to "ordinary time" and a systematic reading of the scriptures. Remove the Christmas decorations from the children's gathering space. Display the lectionary prominently.
2. Welcome the children enthusiastically and remind them that we gather to hear God's good news proclaimed and explained especially for children.

God Calls

1. Tell the children that our readings today speak of two things. Have several children cut out pre-traced letters to form the words "call" and "response." Arrange the letters into the words, glue the words onto colorful poster board, and help younger children to read the words.
2. Proclaim the Old Testament reading: God calls Samuel.
● For his or her own pleasure and in preparation for sharing the reading with the children, the leader should read the first three chapters of the first book of Samuel. Tell the children about Samuel's birth, his youth and his "job" in the temple.
● To help impart the spirit of today's reading, the leader should describe its setting. The call of Samuel took place "in the temple of the Lord where the ark of God was." Samuel, only a young boy when we meet him today, was sleeping in the temple, perhaps to tend the ever-burning lamp of God. Verse 3 implies that it was not yet morning. (See JBC.) The old priest Eli was asleep "in his usual place," which could not have been far away.
● Summarize the famous narrative of the call of Samuel, striving to capture its charm. Children love the story.
● Proclaim the reading.
● Briefly discuss with the children what made Samuel a good listener. Include his willingness to get up in the middle of the night and his eager and ready obedience to Eli and the Lord.
● Respond to the reading with Ps 40, shortening it and singing the refrain. Or sing the refrain to Dan Schutte's "Here I Am, Lord" (from Lord of Light).
● Conclude with a few words about Samuel's later life. The biblical writer claims that "the Lord was with Samuel, not permitting any word of his to be without ef-

fect," thus all Israel, "from Dan to Beer-sheba," came to know Samuel as an "accredited" prophet (I Sm 3:19-20). Without doubt the greatest spiritual leader of the Israelites since Moses (UOT, p.121), Samuel stands in biblical history as the last of the judges and the first of the prophets. During the period of his leadership Israel made the fateful shift from tribal confederacy to monarchy. Samuel was important in the selection of Saul as first king of Israel, and he functioned as Saul's advisor (mother-in-law style) and accuser for Yahweh during Saul's reign. Samuel also figures in the early history of David.
3. Proclaim the gospel: Jesus calls his first disciples.
● Remind the children of John the Baptizer's role as immediate forerunner of Jesus. The children should be familiar with John from last week's gospel and from our Advent liturgies. Tell the children that today's gospel shows John pointing out Jesus to others. Then summarize the gospel story, with its simple action and dialogue.
● Acclaim the gospel in song and then proclaim it. Today, the first Sunday after the Advent-Christmas season, would be a good day to teach the children a new gospel acclamation.
● Draw out the meaning of the gospel:
Talk of the significance of John's action in pointing out Jesus to others. Stress John's unselfish willingness to give up his friends to Jesus. (For John's attitude toward Jesus, see especially Jn 3:29-30.)

Talk of the invitation of Jesus to Andrew and the other disciple (traditionally John the Evangelist himself). What did Jesus really invite them to do? An overview of John's gospel enables us to understand Jesus's words as an invitation to the two to believe in him and to share his life.
● Talk of the response of the disciples. Ask the children what made the two disciples and Peter good listeners. Bring out such facts as their trust in John, their desire to know Jesus better, their openness to the invitation of Jesus.
4. Relate the gospel to our lives: God calls us.
● God calls us, too, and in many ways. Let the children suggest ways in which God calls us, such as through other people, through events in our lives, through the scriptures, etc.
● We must be good listeners if we are to hear the call of God in our lives.
Let the children suggest elements of good listening, such as thinking about listening, taking time to listen, praying to be good listeners.

- What are some of the things God asks us when God calls? Help the children to be thoughtful in their answers, not just to mouth clichés.
- Discuss why it is not always easy to respond eagerly and wholeheartedly to God's call.

Make the Good News Our Own

1. Give each child a slip of paper. Ask the children to write or draw on their papers ways of responding to the call of God in the coming week. Collect the papers and glue them in sunburst fashion around the words "call" and "response" on the poster. Very young children might simply write their names or draw their faces on paper figures of children who are running as if to answer a summons. In this case give each child a second figure to take home as a reminder of today's liturgy.
2. Spend a few moments in quiet prayer asking for help to answer God's call, just as Samuel and the first disciples did. Share and expand the prayers in the general intercessions.

Other Possibilities:

1. Groups of younger children might like to act out spontaneously the story of the call of the first disciples. They may also act out examples of how God calls us today.
2. Older children might be interested in deeper reflection on John's story of the call of the first disciples.
- John's gospel is quite unlike the synoptic gospels, and our reading today gives a good example of this. Andrew immediately recognizes Jesus as the Messiah. This is not so of the synoptic disciples who struggle with the problem for chapters. Are we more like the Johannine disciples or more like the synoptic disciples? Why?
- Jesus invites his new friends to "abide" with him, a term Jesus will use later to describe the relationship between God and himself. What further insight does John thus give us about the nature of discipleship?
- Mark's story of the call of the first disciples is our gospel for next Sunday. Encourage the children to read it during the week in preparation for our liturgy.
- That John and the synoptists differ radically should not be a source of consternation to the reader, but an invitation to look for the meaning of the stories and not simply for "the facts." John's gospel was the last of the four to be written. It is a product of more than half a century of reflection on the life of Jesus and the life of the Christian. We would be much the poorer if it were just another synoptic story of Jesus.
3. Enhance the appreciation of the older children for the story of the call of Samuel.
- With just a few words (some of which the LMC translation omits in its simplification), the sacred writer skillfully sets the scene for an important happening. Explain to the children some of the details of the reading. The "ark of God" (more commonly called the "ark of the covenant") was a small portable box, overlaid with gold inside and outside. It contained two tablets of stone believed to date from the Mosaic period. Later tradition, quite possibly not historical, added to its con-

tents a dish of manna and the rod of Aaron. The Hebrews carried it through the desert. It preceded them into battle. It was housed in the temple at Shiloh (where our reading takes place), later in Jerusalem, and probably was destroyed with the Jerusalem temple in 587 BCE. The ark was extremely important to the Israelites as a symbol of the presence of Yahweh. The young Samuel was sleeping in the temple, near the ark. His "job" might have been to keep burning "the lamp of God," another symbol of God's presence, much as a light in our own houses means that someone is at home. The lamp was never extinguished not only because of the importance of its light, but also because it was not easy to light. (See "Ark of the Covenant" and "Lamp" in McKenzie, DOB.)
- Our reading of the call of Samuel lends itself easily to a presentation in parts. Following this outline is a simple reading of the story, in parts, which has worked well in the author's parish. The leader or an older child should be the narrator. Younger children can take the parts of Samuel, Eli and the Lord.
- The careful reader will not fail to recognize in the story of the birth and youth of Samuel many details which are familiar to the Christian from Luke's infancy narrative. Elizabeth's condition before the birth of John resembles Hannah's. Mary's (some say Elizabeth's) "Magnificat" and Hannah's canticle are similar in several ways. The young Samuel resembles both John and Jesus (I Sm 1:22 and Lk 1:15, I Sm 2:26 and Lk 2:52). Luke must have known and loved the story well! Share some of these thoughts with older children.
4. Call and response are excellent topics for our reflection as Christians, particularly as we enter "ordinary time." It is to everyone's benefit to extend into our "ordinary" lives the peace and good will that are so unusually evident during the Christmas season. Let us consider it our call to do just that and focus on our response. Let older children make "T-shirts" to remind themselves of these things. For a pattern trace an ordinary T-shirt. Duplicate the pattern on newsprint for the children. Let them begin to plan pertinent catchy phrases and clever decorations for their "T-shirts" and finish them at home.

The Call of Samuel
A Reading of I Sm 3:3-10,19

Narrator:	Samuel was sleeping in the temple of the LORD, where the ark of God was. The LORD called to Samuel, who answered:
Samuel:	Here I am.
Narrator:	Samuel ran to Eli and said:
Samuel:	Here I am. You called me.
Eli:	I did not call you. Go back to sleep.
Narrator:	So Samuel went back to sleep. Again the LORD called Samuel, who rose and went to Eli.
Samuel:	Here I am. You called me.
Eli:	I did not call you, my son. Go back to sleep.

Narrator:	At that time Samuel was not familiar with the LORD, because the LORD had not revealed anything to him as yet. The LORD called Samuel again, for the third time. Getting up and going to Eli, he said:
Samuel:	Here I am. You called me.
Narrator:	Then Eli understood that the LORD was calling the youth. So he said to Samuel:
Eli:	Go to sleep, and if you are called, reply, "Speak, LORD, for your servant is listening."
Narrator:	When Samuel went to sleep in his place, the LORD came and revealed his presence, calling out as before,
The Lord:	Samuel, Samuel!
Samuel:	Speak, for your servant is listening.
Narrator:	Samuel grew up, and the LORD was with him, not permitting any word of his to be without effect.

Third Sunday of the Year

Lectionary for Masses with Children	Lectionary for Mass
**Jon 3:1-5,10	**Jon 3:1-5,10
*Ps 25:4-5,6-7,8-9	*Ps 25:4-5,6-7,8-9
-----	I Cor 7:29-31
**Mk 1:14-20	**Mk 1:14-20

Focus: We believe the Good News by following Jesus.

Gather the Children

1. Welcome the children to their special liturgy of the word. Lead them in joyful song to acknowledge the presence of God in the word. Ask one child to hold the lectionary high during the singing.

2. Ask the children to reflect quietly on our reasons for being here. If the children have not just celebrated the penitential rite with the adult assembly, the leader might pray now with the children as follows:

Leader: My brothers and sisters in God's family, as we prepare to listen to God's word, let us call to mind its power and its beauty. And let us remember with sorrow that we do not always listen well to that word.

Your word takes away the darkness of our lives: Lord, have mercy.

All: Lord, have mercy.

Leader: Your word takes away the weakness of our wills: Christ, have mercy.

All: Christ, have mercy.

Leader: Your word fills our hearts with love: Lord, have mercy.

All: Lord, have mercy.

Leader: May God's word always light our minds, strengthen our wills and fire our hearts. May God have mercy on us and forgive us for the times we have not listened to that word. May God's word lead us to life everlasting.

All: Amen.

3. To review our thoughts of last Sunday and to introduce our readings for today, let the children arrange again the large letters we used last week to form the words "call" and "response." Ask them to think for a few moments about how they heard the call of God and responded to it during the past week. Tell them that in today's readings we will continue to think about how we should respond to the call of God.

Proclaim the Old Testament Reading:
God Calls Jonah

1. Before telling the children about today's first reading see if they already know something about the well-known, wonderful story of Jonah. They may very well know about Jonah's adventure with the "whale," which, unfortunately, is not ever a part of the Sunday lectionary selection.

2. As background information for the children, summarize the first two chapters of the book of Jonah. God told Jonah to go to the great and wicked city of Nineveh and preach repentance to the people who lived there. But Jonah, whose own people hated the Ninevites, did not want the Ninevites to be saved. So he disobeyed God and ran away. He boarded a ship and set sail for the far west. But the Lord sent a violent wind, and such a furious storm arose that the ship was in mortal danger. Jonah realized that his disobedience was the cause of the storm and agreed that he should be thrown overboard. The raging of the sea subsided and the ship was safe. The Lord sent a huge fish to swallow Jonah. Jonah lived and prayed for three days in the belly of the fish, and then the Lord commanded the fish to spit Jonah upon the shore. Our reading today takes up the adventure at this point and reports the second call of the Lord to Jonah.

3. Ask the children to listen carefully for Jonah's response to God the second time God called him. Then proclaim the reading

4. Comment that both Jonah and the people of Nineveh had to learn the ways of the Lord. Respond to the reading, and pray that we too will learn God's ways, by praying Ps 25. Add simple gestures; for example, all could point gracefully to themselves as they sing the refrain, and then extend their arms forward and upward for the verses.

5. Or respond to the reading by listening quietly to, or by singing, Tim Manion's "I Lift Up my Soul" (from *A Dwelling Place*). The song is based on Ps 25.

Proclaim the Gospel:
Jesus Calls His Disciples

1. Ask the children to recall the details of the calling of the first disciples, the story we heard last Sunday from John's gospel.

2. Tell the children that today we will hear again the call of Jesus to his first disciples, but it will be as Mark recorded it and it is quite different from the way John recorded it.

3. Ask the children to stand and listen carefully to the gospel. Acclaim the gospel appropriately in song and then proclaim it.

4. Let older children comment on the differences between Mark's call of the first disciples and John's. Let them speculate about possible reasons for the differences. Briefly and simply explain that the New Testament is not so much concerned with "facts" as it is with the meaning for the early Christians (and for us later Christians) of what happened. Each evangelist told

about Jesus in his own special way, and we are richer in our understanding of Jesus because of their differences.

5. Focus on Mark's message:

• Turn the attention of the children to the words of Jesus at the beginning of our reading:

Have large letters spelling out the words "now," "turn back" ("reform" in the words of the LM) and "believe." Let the children arrange the letters to form the words. Lay the words on a large colorful poster board.

Share quickly and without excessive detail the meaning of Jesus's words: Jesus came to live among humans persons to assure us of the loving care and concern of God. Jesus asks that we believe and live that good news. In the weeks before Lent begins we will hear several stories about how Jesus embodied the love of God for us in his earthly words and actions.

• With an older group, overlay the words "turn back" with the word "shub."

Tell the children that "shub" is a Hebrew word very much like the Aramaic word Jesus must have used and which scholars translate as "turn back" or "reform." Its meaning is to turn around and face in the opposite direction.

Ask the children if they can think of a reason why Mark next told the story of the call of the first disciples. Help them see that the response of the disciples to the good news of Jesus was to turn their lives around, literally and otherwise, and follow him, to leave behind all that kept them from following Jesus completely.

Make the Good News Our Own

1. Unify today's readings by reminding the children that we have listened to several calls and heard several responses: of the first disciples, of Jonah, of the Ninevites. Suggest that the readings speak also to us of call and response.

• How do we hear God's call? What are some of the things we are called to do?

• What are the things that keep people—children and adults—from answering the call of God and following the way of Jesus completely?

2. Graphically illustrate our response to God's call with a long string of paper dolls. Write the names of the children on the dolls and tape the dolls to the wall. Add other paper dolls to represent Jonah, the Ninevites, the first disciples. At the head of the line add a larger leading figure to represent the calling of God. Give the children short strings of paper dolls to take home. Ask them to write or draw on the dolls the names or faces of people they know who try hard to answer God's call.

3. Pray in the general intercessions that all people will answer the call of God and make present God's reign here and now.

4. Younger children might enjoy the refrain to "Follow Me" as sung by John Denver.

Other Possibilities:

1. Today's stories of Jonah and the Ninevites and of the first disciples are active and interesting. If the leader prefers not to rely simply upon his or her own storytelling abilities, he or she might use the flannel board to illustrate the stories. Or the children might enjoy acting out the stories.

2. In preparation for telling the children about Jonah, the leader should read the entire (very short) book of Jonah. For an older group, give some background information about the story. The story is a humorous and deeply theological expansion of a single line in the Hebrew scriptures, II Kgs 14:25, written several centuries before the book of Jonah was written. The sacred author makes the prophet Jonah, merely mentioned in II Kgs, into the hero of a story whose purpose is to teach God's all-inclusive love. Nineveh was the capital city of hated Assyria, the country responsible for the downfall of the northern Israelite kingdom. It was abhorrent to the Israelite Jonah that God should have mercy on that wicked, foreign city. Since most people miss the point of the book of Jonah and know it only as a "call" story, suggest that the children share the story with their parents and their siblings and their friends during the coming week. Do we ever act like Jonah and try to limit God's love and mercy to those we deem worthy of it?

3. Discuss with older children how the response of the first disciples to the call of Jesus to repent and believe was not confession of sin, but attachment to the person of Jesus. What import does this response have for us? How does the call of Jesus to repent differ from John the Baptizer's call to repent?

4. As an alternative activity for older children, give them each a paper fish. Ask them to write on their fish things that keep them from following Jesus completely. Collect the fish and glue them in a clump on a piece of poster board. Cover the fish with a net. An orange or a grapefruit sack will do nicely for a net. Add the figure of a person walking away from the fish and toward the words "Follow Me."

5. Although Dan Schutte's "Here I Am, Lord" (from *Lord of Light*) is not based upon today's readings, the refrain highlights response to God's call. Sing it. Children enjoy it. Or teach the children Suzanne Toolan's "Two Fishermen" (in *Worship III*). The song tells of the call of Jesus to his earthly friends and, in the last verse, of his call to all Christians.

Fourth Sunday of the Year

Lectionary for Masses with Children	Lectionary for Mass
*Dt 18:18-19	*Dt 18:15-20
Ps 95:1-2,6-7	Ps 95:1-2,6-7,7-9
-----	I Cor 7:32-35
**Mk 1:21-28	**Mk 1:21-28

Focus: We respond with amazement to the authority of Jesus and ask, "What does this mean?"

Gather the Children

1. Welcome the children joyfully. Give them a few moments to reflect quietly on our reasons for being here, and then invite one or two of the children to share their thoughts with the group.
2. Lead the children in a prayer of thanksgiving to God for bringing us together to hear God's word.
3. Sing a song of praise to God in anticipation of the wonders of Jesus that we will witness as we read the first chapters of the gospel of Mark during the weeks until Lent begins.

Prepare the Children for Our Gospel Readings for the Next Few Sundays:

1. Refer to the posters or to the strings of paper dolls or to whatever the children made last Sunday, and help them recall the gospel message: the first disciples responded to the call of Jesus by reorienting their lives completely to follow Jesus.
2. Join the children in silent personal reflection on how well we responded to the call of Jesus to us during the past week.
3. Ask the children what they think the disciples saw in Jesus that made them respond so wholeheartedly and so totally to him. Help them to realize that the disciples did not know who Jesus really was, as we do, but they observed his actions and listened to his words and came gradually to the conclusion that he was someone special living among them.
4. Tell the children that in the first chapters of Mark's gospel, which we will read for the next few weeks, we learn much about who Jesus was. Ask the children to imagine that they also are disciples of Jesus, following him wherever he goes, listening to his words, watching what he does. Suggest that they keep asking with the disciples (quoting today's gospel), "What does this mean?" (or, as the LMC translation simplifies, "What is this?").
5. Begin a poster, which we will continue in the weeks ahead. In the center of a large green poster board, spell out with attractive letters the sentence "What does this mean?" Tell the children that we will add to the poster the things that we, with the disciples, learn about Jesus in the coming weeks.

Proclaim Today's Gospel

1. Briefly summarize the events of today's gospel. The story takes place in the synagogue of Capernaum. The synagogue is the place where Jewish people meet and worship, much like our church. The story is a report of the words and actions of Jesus one Sabbath in the synagogue, together with the reaction of the people.
2. Tell the children about "unclean spirits" (which the LMC translation renders "evil spirits"). In the time of Jesus people ascribed disease to the presence of evil spirits. The cries of the spirit in our reading indicate that the evil spirit had control over the man he possessed; in other words, the man's disease was serious. To "exorcize" a person means to free him or her of an evil spirit.
3. Ask the children to stand for the proclamation of the gospel. Acclaim the gospel with a lively sung alleluia and then proclaim it. For older children, use the more powerful translation of the LM, rather than that of the LMC, and ask the children to listen attentively for Mark's choice of vivid words.
4. Discuss the action of the story, bringing out the power of Jesus's teaching and the power he had over evil. With older children discuss Mark's remarkable choice of action words. Suggest that the story would make a good play.
5. Discuss the effect that the words and actions of Jesus had on the people who were present for the healing, including, we suppose, the disciples. What effect would they have had on us if we had been there?

Make the Good News Our Own

1. Begin to illustrate the answer to our question, "What does this mean?"
- With the children's help, summarize, in their words, the things we learn about Jesus in today's gospel: his teaching fascinated people and evil spirits obeyed him.
- Cut two interesting shapes from colorful construction paper. Write the words of the children on the shapes. Glue them onto the poster, beginning to form a circle of striking shapes and colors around the question on the poster.
- For younger children who cannot read well, do not use words on the poster, but let the children draw pictures to show the accomplishments of Jesus. The leader can then choose the pictures which are most suitable for the poster. In an ideal situation the children can draw their pictures as part of their preparation for today's liturgy.

• We will continue the poster in the coming weeks as we read the first part of Mark's gospel. Eventually we will have a ring of striking shapes reminding us of the words and deeds of Jesus which reveal who he is.

2. As a response of amazement at the power of God in Jesus, sing again our gathering song of praise to God.

3. Pray in the general intercessions that all people will be open to the teaching of Jesus, that all people will learn about Jesus from his actions and his words, that all people will reach out to help others as Jesus helped the sick man.

4. As a reminder of our liturgy give each child a paper on which is written, in big letters, the words "Jesus is amazing!" Let the children take their papers home and color the letters.

Other Possibilities:

1. With an older group consider the skill Jesus must have had as a teacher:

• Ask the children for their ideas about the qualities of a good teacher. Listen carefully to the children, then augment their description if necessary with such adjectives as knowledgeable, interesting, persuasive, caring, a model for his or her message.

• Discuss the extraordinary teaching abilities of Jesus, based on what the children remember of his life. With the children, prayerfully read and try to appreciate the remarkable compliment that Mark gives Jesus in today's gospel: "People were spellbound by his teaching."

• Pray that we will respond to the teaching of Jesus by a wholehearted acceptance of his message and a total surrender of our lives to him.

2. Help older children to look yet more deeply into our gospel:

• Though at first sight we might think of our gospel as a report of two separate events in the life of Jesus, his teaching in the synagogue and a miracle, Mark has intimately interrelated the two events. Notice first that Jesus's entrance into the synagogue (verse 21) and his departure from it (verse 29) "frame" our gospel. In this way Mark asks us to consider what happens in the synagogue as a unit. Notice also that the crowd interprets the exorcism as an illustration of the teaching authority of Jesus. In short, the effect of Mark's report of what happened in the synagogue is to shine the spotlight on the teaching authority of Jesus and not on his spectacular miracle. Share some of these thoughts with the children to help bring them to a deeper appreciation of Mark's literary and theological artistry.

• Although Mark presents less of the content of Jesus's teaching than do Matthew and Luke, he un-questionably sees the teaching of Jesus as vital to his mission and as characteristic of his activity. Furthermore, Mark knew that some people saw Jesus primarily as a wonder worker. Our gospel is a striking example of how Mark attempted to balance the picture of Jesus as wonder-worker with the picture of Jesus as teacher. Share these thoughts with the children.

3. Beginning today and continuing for the next several Sundays, the lectionary presents us with a series of miracles performed by Jesus. If the leader will read the larger section of Mark's gospel from which our readings come (1:14-3:6), he or she will learn the effect that the miracles and words of Jesus had on his contemporaries: the common people were amazed and flocked to him; the religious leaders were angered and began to plot against him. By means of our poster we will try to identify with the crowds of people who observe the actions and hear the words of Jesus and come to some conclusions about who he is. We will work on the poster through the seventh Sunday of the year or until the gospel readings are interrupted by the readings of Lent.

4. Introduce older children to Thomas Troeger's "Silence! Frenzied, Unclean Spirit" (in *Worship III*). The poem is a masterpiece, both preserving the theology of Mark's powerful story and capturing its tone. Have the children read the first verse together several times until they enter its disturbing mood, until its words fill their mouths, until its thoughts grip their minds. Read the remaining verses and let their words and thoughts act upon mind and heart. Carol Doran's music, which fits the poem skillfully, is difficult and needs the keyboard accompaniment, but give it a try.

5. Proclaim to older children today's reading from the Old Testament:

• Reflect briefly on the importance of Moses as a prophet. Through Moses more than through any other Old Testament person, God made the divine nature and will known to the Israelites. Ask the children to support this statement from what they know about Moses.

• Proclaim today's reading from the book of Deuteronomy. Then discuss how it indicates the stature of Moses as a man who spoke for God.

• Relate the reading to the gospel by focusing on the role of Jesus as teacher and law-giver surpassing even Moses in importance. Some Israelites interpreted Dt 18:15 to mean that God would send one final prophet before the consummation of history. Christians see Jesus as this great prophet.

• Use parts of Ps 95 as a prayer that we will not "harden our hearts" to the voice of God.

Fifth Sunday of the Year

Lectionary for Masses with Children	Lectionary for Mass
**Jb 7:1-4,6-7	**Jb 7:1-4,6-7
*Ps 147:1,4,5,7	*Ps 147:1-2,3-4,5-6
I Cor 9:16-18	I Cor 9:16-19,22-23
**Mk 1:29-39	**Mk 1:29-39

Focus: By his healing and his preaching Jesus proclaims the good news. We rejoice!

Gather the Children

1. Welcome the children with joy and remind them why we gather for our special liturgy of the word. Join them for a few moments of silent prayer that God will help us hear and understand the word we hear today.

2. Lead the children in song to acknowledge the presence of God in the word. Ask one child to hold the lectionary high during the singing. Enthrone the lectionary in a place of honor in the children's gathering space and light candles near it.

Proclaim the Old Testament Reading

1. Unfortunately we read from the magnificent book of Job only twice during the entire three year cycle of Sunday liturgies of the word (today and once next summer). Supply some background information about the book:

• Let the children share what they already know of the story of Job.

• If necessary, supplement their recollections about the story:

The story of Job is based on an ancient folktale. Pious and upright, Job suddenly loses his possessions, his family, his health. Plunged into the most drastic suffering of body and spirit Job curses the day he was born and tries to understand what has happened to him. Three friends come to console him. They insist that his suffering is punishment for sin and they beg him to seek God's forgiveness. But Job maintains his innocence and rejects the traditional wisdom of his friends as inadequate. Finally he calls upon God to explain. In thrilling verse God answers Job "out of the storm," speaking of divine wisdom and power and calling Job to task for thinking that he can fathom the ways of the almighty. Job is content with God's answer. In the end God restores the prosperity of Job. Read the book! The story is a literary masterpiece and a fascinating tale as well as a theological discourse of deepest merit.

Describe for the children briefly and vividly the troubles of Job, his complaints and the attempts of his friends to help him understand his sufferings.

2. Proclaim the reading:

• Tell the children that our first reading today is from the early part of the book and offers part of Job's complaint about his condition.

• Proclaim some of Job's words, shortening the reading appropriately for very young children.

• Allow older children to comment on Job's depression. How would they console him?

3. Continue with Job's story. Describe the response of God and tell of the happy ending of the story. Encourage older children to read parts of the story in their own bibles.

4. Show the children a picture or a slide of a great artist's conception of some aspect of the story of Job.

5. Respond to the reading with Ps 147. Suggest that the children put themselves in the place of Job and pray the psalm in praise of God for restoring their happiness. Shorten the psalm somewhat so that the children can grasp its meaning more easily. Sing the refrain. Add gestures to enhance the effect of the verses.

6. Use our selection from the book of Job to prepare the children for hearing the gospel. Job's complaining thrusts us into the heart and soul of a suffering and depressed person of Old Testament times. The gospel presents a multiplicity of Jesus's healings. The first reading thus helps us to contemplate and appreciate the sufferings of the people whom Jesus will heal in our gospel.

Proclaim the Gospel

1. To introduce the gospel, help the children recall the most important ideas of last week's liturgy. If the children began a poster, use it to remind them of our thoughts:

• We were struck by the teaching power of Jesus.

• We were amazed at his power over evil spirits.

• With the people who lived at the time of Jesus, we ask, "What does this mean?"

2. Show the flow of today's gospel selection from last week's selection:

• Explain that the first part of today's gospel, together with the gospel we heard last week, gives us Mark's account of what Jesus did in a "typical" day. The gospel then continues with what Jesus did early the next morning and during the next day.

• Ask the children if they remember where last week's gospel story took place. Tell them that today's gospel begins as Jesus leaves that place, the synagogue.

3. Acclaim the gospel with a joyful alleluia. During the singing conduct an informal procession with the lectionary. Then proclaim the gospel.

4. Refer to Ps 147 again and suggest that the sick people who came to Jesus and experienced his healing power might have prayed the psalm as Job did in praise of God who heals the sick and mends the brokenhearted.

Give older children copies of the psalm to take home and pray when they are hurting.

Make the Good News Our Own

1. Continue the poster we began last week:
- Remind the children that we are recording on our poster things Jesus did that make us believe he is special.
- Review the scenes of the gospel and, using the children's words or drawings, add to the poster these things that Jesus did: he cured Peter's mother-in-law, he cured crowds of sick and possessed people, he spent time praying.

2. In response to the healing power and compassion of God in Jesus, sing a song of joyful praise to God.

3. Pray in the general intercessions that all people will let Jesus touch their lives with his good news and his healing power. Pray that we will follow the example of Jesus in showing care for those who suffer.

Other Possibilities:

1. Once again Mark places the miracles of Jesus at the service of his mission to proclaim the good news of God's presence and love. Jesus's miracles are indeed spectacular, but Mark has Jesus state clearly in today's gospel selection that he did not "come" primarily to work miracles. Help older children to understand the important but not sovereign place of miracles in the life-work of Jesus.

2. Talk about the prayer life of Jesus:
- Point out Mark's reference to the prayer of Jesus. When and where does Mark say Jesus prayed? Ask the children why they think Jesus prayed and with what result. How often does Mark refer to the prayer of Jesus?
- Mark does not record the Lord's Prayer, but today would be a good day to remind the children that the Lord's Prayer is the prayer that Jesus himself taught us. Encourage the children to pray the prayer of Jesus with special attention during today's liturgy of the eucharist.
- To encourage little children to pray, give them the following papers to take home and color: have drawn on the papers the rising sun, the noonday sun, and the moon and the stars. Have written in big letters the words "Pray often."

3. To continue with our observation of last week that this section of Mark's gospel is full of action and would make a good play, ask older children to divide today's gospel passage into (three?) scenes. What is the climax of the action? How would they stage the play with a contemporary Jesus?

4. Suggest to older children that they imagine they are Jesus and write a journal entry covering his activity for the two days about which we have been reading in Mark's gospel.

5. The book of Job probes the mystery of suffering, one of the deepest problems of human existence. Present to older children examples of people who suffer, physically and otherwise, in the world today. What does the book of Job teach us about how to comfort the sorrowful? What does it teach us about how to bear suffering ourselves?

6. Read Archibald MacLeish's "J.B." It is a drama in verse which tells the story of Job in terms of modern American life.

Sixth Sunday of the Year

Lectionary for Masses with Children	Lectionary for Mass
- - - - -	**Lv 13:1-2,44-46
I Cor 10:31-11:1	*Ps 32:1-2,5-11
*Ps 32:1,5,11	I Cor 10:31-11:1
**Mk 1:40-45	**Mk 1:40-45

Focus: Jesus touched a leper and healed him. We rejoice in the compassion and the power of Jesus.

Gather the Children

1. Welcome the children happily to our celebration of God's word. Remind the group that we are together to listen to God's word, just as the adult assembly is doing. Join the children in quiet prayer that God will fill our minds and our lives with the word.

2. Have one child hold the lectionary high while all the children sing a lively song of praise to God. Then enthrone the lectionary in a place of honor and light candles near it.

3. If the children have not already celebrated the penitential rite, pray it now, focusing on our failure to treat others with the compassion of Jesus:

Leader: My brothers and sisters in God's family, let us pray to listen well to God's word and live by it faithfully every day.

You ask us to hear the cries of others: Lord, have mercy.

All: Lord, have mercy.

Leader: You ask us to be there when others need us: Christ, have mercy.

All: Christ, have mercy.

Leader: You ask us to reach out and touch those who are in pain: Lord, have mercy.

All: Lord, have mercy.

Leader: May almighty God look upon us kindly and forgive us when we fail to imitate the compassion of Jesus. May God enfold us in love and care and fill us with the joy of salvation.

All: Amen.

4. To review the gospel message of the last few Sundays, call the attention of the children to the poster they have been making. Remind the group that we have joined the contemporaries of Jesus in spirit, and we are wondering about the meaning of the things that Jesus says and does.

5. Tell the children that today we will hear more about the power and the love of Jesus. Ask them to be thinking during our discussion of the next few minutes about what we should add to our poster today.

Proclaim the Old Testament First Reading

Note: The LMC omits today's Old Testament reading, in spite of its relationship with the gospel. The leader who wishes to proclaim the reading may find the following suggestions helpful. The leader who chooses not to proclaim the reading might adapt the suggestions to familiarize the children with the disease leprosy.

1. Acquaint the children with leprosy:

• Let the children talk about what, if anything, they already know of the disease.

• Tell the children that the term "leprosy" in biblical literature covered a variety of skin diseases, some mild, some very serious. The biblical laws regarding leprosy, which we read in Lv 13-14, and some of which are included in our reading, were an attempt to control the spread of the disease.

• Supply a few facts about the physical aspect of the disease. Use the first paragraph of our reading and supplement it with information from an encyclopedia or a good dictionary. Then, drawing upon the remainder of our reading, focus on the social terrors of the disease. People have always feared leprosy because it disfigures the body. In biblical times (and even later) lepers were social outcasts, forced to live apart from society and to warn others of their approach by calling out, "Unclean, unclean!" The rules may have been necessary to safeguard the health of the community as a whole, but they caused untold suffering for those who had the disease. When a person's leprosy had healed he or she could perform certain elaborate ritual actions after which the priest would declare the person clean and so able to take part once again in ordinary communal life. (See Lv 14:1-32.)

• Make sure the children know that modern medical science has made great advances in the treatment of leprosy and other skin diseases.

2. Proclaim the reading.

3. In response to our considerations, ask the children to reflect silently on the suffering of lepers, especially in the days before medical science understood much about contagious diseases.

Proclaim the Gospel

1. Introduce the gospel by telling the children that Jesus will cure a leper. Ask older children to listen carefully during our reading for these things:

• How Jesus cured the man;

• What Jesus asked the man to do;

• What the man did;

• What happened to Jesus on account of what the man did.

2. Ask the children to stand and listen to the gospel as if they were there when the events it describes were happening. Acclaim the gospel in joyful song, and then proclaim it.

3. Discuss the above points with older children. The

story has the (form-critical) traditional form of a miracle story: the statement of the problem (here coupled with an appeal for help), the solution, the proof that the solution worked. It is always interesting to see how the evangelists adhere to a form or diverge from it. What has Mark added to the basic miracle-story structure of the account?

Make the Good News Our Own

1. With the children's help and using their wording or pictures add to the poster that:
• Jesus cured a leper by word and touch; and
• People followed Jesus everywhere he went.
2. Lead the children in reflection on what we have witnessed about Jesus in the last few weeks. As all listen prayerfully, have several children read slowly the phrases or describe the pictures we now have recorded on the poster.
3. Lead the children in a question-answer profession of faith which includes the things about Jesus on the poster; for example:

Leader: Do you believe in God, who sent Jesus to live among us?
All: Yes! Amen!
Leader: Do you believe that Jesus proclaimed in word and action the good news of God's saving love?
All: Yes! Amen!
Leader: Do you believe that Jesus healed a leper by touching him and speaking to him?
All: Yes! Amen!
Leader: Do you believe in the Holy Spirit who helps us to be the hands and the voice of Jesus in the world today?
All: Yes! Amen!
Leader: Do you believe that after we die we will live again in joy with God?
All: Yes! Amen!

The leader or the children may add other things about Jesus that we have witnessed in recent gospel readings. The leader and the children might like to sing to each other their profession of faith:

Other Possibilities:

1. Have a child or an adult draw pictures to illustrate the gospel. Or use the flannel board. Or, since the gospel is an action story, let the children dramatize it.
2. Encourage the children to imitate the compassion of Jesus toward the leper by telling them about St. Francis of Assisi and the leper he met and kissed. Or tell them about Father Joseph Damien, a nineteenth century Belgian priest who spent sixteen years as pastor and physician to the lepers of Hawaii. He himself contracted the disease, but refused proper treatment because it would have required leaving his lepers.
3. Jesus touched the leper to heal him. Focus on this gentle, powerful gesture:
• Talk with the children about how we use our hands. We use our hands for good: to help, to forgive, to comfort those who hurt, to give peace. We can also use our hands to hurt: to push, to fight, to slam doors, to destroy property. Ask the children to pray for strength to use their hands kindly.
• Sing a song about using our hands kindly. During the singing let the children take turns laying their hands gently on each other, unless, as may well be the case with older children, the group is uncomfortable with the gesture. Ask the children to think of people who are not present but who need their healing touch. Then invite them to lay their hands symbolically on those hurting people. Remind them that the sign of peace during the liturgy of the eucharist gives us opportunity to touch each other in loving concern.
• Make a poster with the hand prints of all the children. Superimpose on the poster the words "Our hands are your hands."
• Ask the children to go home and trace their own hands and think of all the ways they will touch others with love. Or give them paper hands to take home.
• Send the children to the library to find and read the *The Emperor and The Kite* by Jane Yolen. It is a story of how a tiny princess saves her father, the emperor, by the work of her hands.
• Talk with older children about the love and compassion of Jesus which enabled him to touch a repulsive leper, to reach out to a person with an ugly exterior. Would we do the same?
4. Introduce an older group to Mark's "messianic secret" to explain the mysterious injunction of Jesus to the leper that he not say a word to anyone about his cure. Mark did not want his readers to misunderstand Jesus, whose life found its ultimate meaning only in the cross.
5. Tell an older group that leprosy in the bible is a symbol for sin. Then pray Ps 32 in thanksgiving to God for taking away our sins.
6. Ask the children to thank God for the wonders of modern medicine.

Seventh Sunday of the Year

Lectionary for Masses with Children	Lectionary for Mass
**Is 43:22-25 Ps 41:1-2,3,13 - - - - - **Mk 2:1-12	**Is 43:18-19,21-22,24-25 Ps 41:2-3,4-5,13-14 II Cor 1:18-22 **Mk 2:1-12

Focus: We believe in Jesus who has the power to heal us in body and spirit.

Gather the Children

1. Welcome the children happily to their gathering space, and ask them to assemble quietly in a circle. Invite one child to hold the lectionary high while all sing a song of joyful praise to God. Enthrone the lectionary and light candles near it.
2. Remind the children why we come together for our special liturgy of the word. Join the children for a few moments of quiet prayer that God will fill our hearts and light our minds with the words of scripture.
3. With the help of the poster the children are making, review the events in the life of Jesus which we have heard proclaimed in the last few weeks—his teaching, his healings and his exorcisms, his prayer, his increasing popularity. Ask the children to imagine that we are disciples of Jesus and that we have witnessed all these things. What would the words and actions of Jesus mean to us?

Proclaim the Old Testament Reading

1. Introduce the first reading by telling the children that it reminds us of something wonderful about God, the same wonderful thing that Jesus will demonstrate in today's gospel.
2. Lead the children in prayerful meditation based upon the reading:
• Ask the children to think of times when they have needed forgiveness. Give little ones help to focus gently on some of their failings. Without help, little children often think of their accidents as personal failings, or of unpleasant things others have done to them. Play quiet reflective music while the children think.
• Then ask the children to listen to a reading from the book of the prophet Isaiah, a reading which assures us that God is forgiving. For younger children, proclaim verses 24-25, reading the verses slowly and prayerfully. For older children, proclaim more of the reading, including verses 18-19, which the LMC omits.
• Respond in prayer, acknowledging both our sins and the forgiving love of God. Ask little children to repeat the following prayer, line by line:

> God of mercy,
> we love you very much.
> Sometimes we do things that hurt people.
> Sometimes we say things that make people sad.
> We are sorry for these things.
> We know you forgive us.

> Thank you for forgiving us.
> Thank you for forgetting our sins.
> We know you always love us.
> We will always love you.
> Amen.

• Older children will consider beneath them repeating a prayer after the leader. The leader of an older group might say the prayer alone, asking the children to listen.
• Ask younger children to show that they forgive each other, as God forgives us, by the following simple ritual. The leader turns to the nearest child, places his or her hands on the child's head and says, "Forgiveness and peace!" That child should extend the same gesture to the next child, and so on around the circle of children. Older children may not respond positively to the ritual. Do not insist on any ritual action that makes children uncomfortable or overly self-conscious.
• Remind the children that when we give each other the sign of peace during the liturgy of the eucharist, we are expressing our willingness to forgive those who offend us.

Proclaim the Gospel

1. Tell the children that in our gospel today we will hear about another healing by Jesus, this time of a paralytic. If necessary, give the meaning of "paralytic." Then tell the children Jesus will do something else for the sick man that will cause quite a stir in the crowd of onlookers.
2. Acclaim the gospel with joy in song and gesture and then proclaim it.
3. Discuss the gospel:
• Where did the story take place? It took place at the home of Jesus. Tell the children a little about houses in Palestine at the time of Jesus. They were usually one story structures with flat roofs. The roof was often of straw, which covered wooden planks and branches. The roof was easily accessible by ladder. People slept on the roof when the nights were hot. Thus it was quite possible to let down the paralytic through the roof to the room below.
• What was the first thing that Jesus said to the paralytic?
• What was the reaction of some of the people? Why did the words of Jesus so anger them?
• What did Jesus do then? Why did he do it? (He tells us directly.)
• What was the reaction of the crowd?
4. Continue the discussion, focusing on the meaning of the story for Christian life:
• Ask older children what the story tells us is the rea-

son for the miracles of Jesus. Point out that both our reading from the book of Isaiah and our gospel impress upon us that God is willing and anxious and able to forgive our sins. It is appropriate indeed to read of the forgiveness of our sin as we approach Ash Wednesday and the season of Lent.

• Ask younger children what they think of the friends of the paralytic. How might we imitate them?

Make the Good News Our Own

1. Continue the poster the children have been making for the last several Sundays. Add colorful shapes which proclaim in the children's words or pictures that Jesus healed a paralytic and that Jesus forgave sins.

2. Follow the activity with a profession of faith. Use a question-answer ritual, basing the questions on the information about Jesus recorded on the poster.

3. Sing a lively song of praise to God in response to the wonders of Jesus that we have read about during the past few weeks.

4. As a reminder of our liturgy today, give the children papers which say, "We have never seen anything like this!" Ask the children to decorate their papers at home by tracing over the letters in color and adding exclamation points, stars, and other signs of joyful surprise to show their amazement at the power of Jesus.

Other Possibilities:

1. With a younger group, have children prepare in advance pictures to illustrate the gospel. Show the pictures during the liturgy of the word. A group of older children would also enjoy seeing the work of younger children.

2. The children, especially younger ones, would enjoy dramatizing the gospel story.

3. Ask older children to imagine that they are living at the time of Jesus and so, unlike people today, do not know that Jesus is the Son of God. Have one child pretend to be a television newscaster (definitely an anachronism) and report to the group, with much excitement, all the amazing actions of Jesus which are recorded on our poster. Then the newscaster should "interview" willing children concerning their conclusions about who Jesus is and what his words and actions mean.

4. To enlarge on the theme of friendship, which is so prominent in the gospel:

• Read to the children a story about friendship. Younger children will enjoy *That's What Friends Are For* by Florence Parry Heidi. Any group (including a group of adults) will enjoy *The Giving Tree* by Shel Silverstein.

• Let the children draw pictures of people who help them. Make a collage of the pictures and superimpose on the collage the words "Be a friend!"

• Pray for those who help people who cannot help themselves. Inspire the children with stories about such people, modern or historical.

5. Read to the children "Jesus Heals a Sick Man" from Augsburg's *What the Bible Tells Us Series*. The text is simple, yet faithful to the gospel account. The pictures are beautiful and rich in meaning.

6. As we have remarked on several occasions during the last few Sundays, one of Mark's goals in writing his gospel was to counter the image of Jesus as a mere miracle worker. Mark has reported an exorcism as an illustration of the teaching authority of Jesus. He has shown that the power of Jesus to heal is subordinate to his mission to proclaim the good news. And today we read that Mark's Jesus views his healing power as a sign that he has authority to forgive sins. Share these thoughts with older children, at the same time summarizing our recent discussions about Jesus and his miracles. No more than Mark's first century readers should we think that the most amazing thing about Jesus was his extraordinary power to work miracles.

7. The unknown poet-author of our Old Testament reading, whom we call Second Isaiah, probably wrote during the latter part of the Judaean exile in Babylon. Our reading today is taken from a poem which deals with the redemption and restoration of Israel. In the passage the Lord promises to do something new for Israel, something better than even the exodus. Israel has "burdened" her Lord with her sins and "wearied" her Lord with her crimes, and yet the Lord will completely blot out her past offenses from memory. It is wonderful indeed that Yahweh, who created us and knows our names, who knows us better than we know ourselves, who will never forget us, does not remember our sins! Many regard the poem as Second Isaiah's "finest poem and richest presentation" (JBC). The leader should read and reflect upon the entire poem (43:1-44:23) and then draw upon personal experience to share with older children today's beautiful reading (much of which the LMC omits).

First Sunday of Lent

Lectionary for Masses with Children	Lectionary for Mass
**Gn 9:8-15 Ps 25:4-5,6,7 - - - - - **Mk 1:12-15	**Gn 9:8-15 Ps 25:4-5,6-7,8-9 *I Pt 3:18-22 **Mk 1:12-15

Focus: We believe the Good News of Jesus and we try hard to live as God wants.

Gather the Children

1. The great penitential season of Lent began just a few days ago on Ash Wednesday. The atmosphere of the children's gathering space should convey the spirit of the season. Remove all posters, banners and other materials the children made to enhance their previous liturgies. Use a brown or purple burlap gathering cloth and brown or purple candles. Have a simple crucifix. Display the lectionary appropriately. Play quiet reflective music as the children enter the room.
2. Welcome the children with joy and ask them to gather in a circle. Remind them why we come together for our special liturgy of the word. Join them in quiet prayer to hear God's and to live our lives according to that word.
3. Teach the children a gospel acclamation appropriate for use during Lent, that is, an acclamation that does not use the word "alleluia." Compose gestures to accompany the acclamation. Little children usually respond eagerly to gestures.
4. Conduct a simple procession with the lectionary to recognize the presence of God in the word proclaimed to the faithful. Choose two children to carry the candles, one to carry the crucifix and one to carry the lectionary. The four children should walk around the circle of children, then lay the candles, the crucifix and the book on the cloth. Meanwhile all the children should sing the gospel acclamation. Finally the leader should light the candles. (Although the symbolism of unlighted candles is inadequate, it is simply not safe for young children to carry lighted candles.)

Talk about the Season of Lent

1. Ask the children to comment on the decor of the adult gathering space. How does it differ today from that of last Sunday? How does the decor of our children's gathering space differ from last Sunday's? Help the children to grasp the simplicity of our decorations, to realize that this is a special season and to become properly thoughtful.
2. Ask the children if they know what season of the liturgical year began last Wednesday. Show them a purple card with "Lent" written on it in dark purple letters. Ask them what great feast comes at the end of Lent. Show them a card with "Easter" written on it in colorful letters. Point out the crucifix on the cloth. Let the children tell each other what else they know about Lent.

3. Summarize and augment the discussion by telling the children that Lent is a time to prepare for Easter, our great celebration of new life, by trying hard to draw closer to God. It is a special, holy time during which we pray especially often and try especially hard to be good.

Proclaim the Old Testament Reading

1. Today Noah makes his only appearance in our entire three-year cycle of Sunday readings. Introduce Noah by telling the children that Noah was a man who lived long ago, long before Jesus, long before even Moses and Abraham. Noah was a man who lived God's way of love when most people were wicked. God rewarded Noah because he was so good, and through Noah God blessed all the living beings of the earth.
2. In preparation for the liturgy the leader should refresh his or her memory of the story of Noah by reading Gn 5:28-10:52. Quickly tell the children the story of the ark and the flood, of God's promise never again to destroy the earth by flood, of the rainbow. Draw simple pictures to accompany the story. Or use a library book with good pictures, for example, *Noah and the Great Flood* by Warwick Hutton. Give the children rainbow "pins" to wear home.
3. Pray the responsorial psalm, remembering Noah's faithfulness to God and praying to imitate it. Teach the children to sing the refrain. Add simple gestures.

Proclaim the Gospel

1. For little children we concentrate on the experience of Jesus in the desert, a time of close communion with God, and Jesus's ensuing proclamation of the nearness of God's reign. Mark tells us also that Jesus encountered evil in the desert, but we will not talk to little ones today of the temptations of Jesus.
2. Prepare the children for the gospel proclamation by talking with them about the desert. Tell them about its barrenness, its quiet and its peacefulness, its beauty at night. Show them slides of the desert, of animals who live in the desert. Show them sand and a desert plant.
3. Tell the children that Jesus went to the desert to be alone with God and to talk to God in prayer, to discover what God wanted him to do. Jesus stayed in the desert for forty days. At the end of his stay in the desert he began to preach the good news of God's love. He asked all those who heard him to believe in God's love and to try hard to be good.
4. Acclaim the gospel in song and then proclaim the reading.

5. Respond to the gospel:

• Let the children share ideas about how they will try during Lent to be good and to believe the good news of Jesus. Help them to be practical and positive. Then give them a few quiet moments to choose specific things to do during the next week.

• Conduct a brief discussion of the importance of prayer in the life of Jesus and in our own lives. Then pray with the children that we will live well the season of Lent. Ask willing older children to share their prayer aloud with the entire group. Ask little children to bow their heads and repeat, line by line, a prayer such as the following:

Loving God,
look upon us, your children,
with kindness and mercy.
Feed us with your word.
Help us during Lent
to grow in love for you
and in love and care for each other.
Give us happiness and life forever
with you in heaven.
We ask this in the name of Jesus.
Amen.

Make the Good News Our Own

1. Give each of the children a paper with "Lent" written on it in large letters. Ask them to color the letters, at home, in brown and purple to remind them of the season. They may add small pictures of the story of Noah and of Jesus in the desert. Tell the children to display their pictures in their homes to remind them to pray and be good during the days Lent.

2. Pray in the general intercessions that God will help us and all people to be good, that God will protect us and keep us from harm, that God will draw us close.

Other Possibilities:

1. On this First Sunday of Lent the church always offers for our contemplation the story of the temptations of Jesus in the desert. Today we read Mark's description of the story, a description much less detailed than those of Matthew and Luke who supplement their use of Mark's material from their common non-Markan source.

• If the leader wishes to tell younger children the story of the temptations of Jesus, he or she should not do so with the detail of Matthew and Luke, but rather use the story to show the children that God was with Jesus to care for him and to protect him from harm. Angels in scripture symbolize the presence and the protection of God, and their presence with Jesus assures us that God was with him. Tell the children that God is with us also, as God was with Jesus, to care for us and to protect us from harm. Sing a song that celebrates God's love and protection, for example, the spiritual "He's Got the Whole World in His Hands." Give the children paper angels to take home as reminders of God's care and protection.

• Share with older children more of the remarkable symbolism of Mark's powerful, two-verse account of the testing of Jesus by Satan. Mark pictures the desert as the "home turf" of Satan, the great contender of Jesus, and it is in the desert that Jesus first meets his powerful enemy and triumphs over him. Thus the story offers us in drama a symbol and a foretaste of the ministry and death of Jesus. Mark tells us that Jesus "was with the wild beasts." The imagery is uncertain, but could the "wild beasts" be the wolf, the leopard, the lion, the bear, the cobra of Is 11? Is Mark telling us, once again in symbolic drama, that the peace and harmony of the long-awaited messianic age are reality in Jesus? Jesus's stay of forty days in the desert evokes memories of the Israelites' forty years of wandering in the desert. The Israelites were tested in the desert and failed, but Jesus does not fail his test. Thus, says Mark, Jesus is the new Israel.

2. During the Sundays of Lent the Old Testament readings call our attention to some of the great figures in Israelite history: Noah, Abraham, Moses, the prophets in general, Jeremiah and Second Isaiah in particular. Because our time with the children is so limited during their Sunday liturgy of the word, we cannot possibly do more than touch briefly upon these readings. Leaders who see the children during the week should make every effort to present great Old Testament stories during their Lenten religion classes. Younger children especially are extremely impressed by well-told stories of our biblical heroes. Help develop in older children a sense of biblical history by marking on a time line the great people and events of Israelite history. Draw upon the children's growing knowledge of secular history to add familiar figures and events to the time line.

3. Augment the story of Noah:

• Make a big rainbow as a sign of God's care. Help the children compose a prayer which calls to mind the signs all around us of God's love and care. Write the prayer on the rainbow and use it during the Sundays of Lent.

• Noah's passage through the flood waters is a symbol of Christian baptism. Today's New Testament reading, which the LMC omits, points out that, just as Noah and his family passed through the waters of the flood to life, so we Christians pass through the waters of baptism to eternal salvation. Bless water and sprinkle the children with it. Or let them make the Sign of the Cross using the blessed water.

• Make a banner to use during Lent. From newspaper backed with something stiff, cut out big letters to spell "Believe the good news!" Glue the letters onto a long purple cloth or paper. Hang it in the children's gathering space for all of Lent. Use the banner to lead the procession of children from the church as they assemble for their liturgy of the word.

5. To focus upon the penitential spirit of the season, teach the children the traditional "Attende Domine" or its English, "Hear Us, Almighty Lord," which the leader may find, for example, in *Worship III*. Invite willing children to offer spontaneous prayers of sorrow for their wrongdoings, and sing the invocation after each prayer.

Second Sunday of Lent

Lectionary for Masses with Children	Lectionary for Mass
- - - - -	**Gn 22:1-2,9,10-13,15-18
Ps 103:1-2,8,11	Ps 116:10,15,16-17,18-19
*Rom 8:31,38-39	Rom 8:31-34
**Mk 9:2-10	**Mk 9:2-10

Focus: We praise Jesus, the glorious Son of God, and we resolve to listen to him.

Gather the Children

1. Once again the children's gathering space should convey visually and audibly the spirit of the great penitential season of Lent. Continue to use a purple or brown gathering cloth, purple or brown candles and a crucifix. Display the lectionary prominently. Play quiet reflective music as the children enter the room.

2. Welcome the children joyfully to our celebration of God's word. Remind them that our liturgy of the word focuses upon the same readings as the adult liturgy of the word, but our liturgy is planned especially for children to understand and enjoy.

3. Comment on the Lenten decor. Tell the group that today is the Second Sunday of Lent. Let the children recall for each other the meaning of Lent. Show them the cards we used last week with the words "Lent" and "Easter" written on them. Ask the children to examine themselves quietly as to how seriously they are trying to live well the season of Lent by doing God's will.

4. If the children have not just celebrated the penitential rite with the adult assembly, lead them now in the prayer, perhaps as follows:

Leader: My brothers and sisters in God's family, let us prepare ourselves to listen to God's word by thinking about God's love and compassion.

Lord Jesus, you show us the way to the Father: Lord, have mercy.

All: Lord, have mercy.

Leader: You call us back when we turn from the way: Christ, have mercy.

All: Christ, have mercy.

Leader: You promise us forgiveness and peace: Lord, have mercy.

All: Lord, have mercy.

Leader: May almighty God, whose word we await, forgive us our sins and lead us to life forever.

All: Amen.

Proclaim the Old Testament Reading

Note: The LMC omits today's reading from the Old Testament. The following suggestions are for the leader who wishes to include this reading in today's liturgy of the word.

1. We meet Abraham occasionally in our liturgy of the word, and so the children should not be totally unfamiliar with this famous and important man of Hebrew history. Tell the group that Abraham lived long after Noah (whom we heard about last week), but still many centuries before Jesus. Abraham was God's friend, obedient to God and faithful to God always. God promised to give Abraham a wonderful land and to make him the father of many generations. Abraham waited many years for God to keep the promise. Isaac was the long-awaited child of Abraham and his wife Sarah, born in their old age and source of great joy to them.

2. The story of the near sacrifice of Isaac is frightening, but we never wish to frighten the children in our care. The leader should introduce today's reading to children as God's plan for testing Abraham's loyalty. Younger children should be told explicitly that God did not want Abraham to kill the boy Isaac.

3. Tell the story vividly, at the same time remaining true to the account in Genesis. The leader may wish to include other details found in the complete account, Gn 22: 1-18.

4. Proclaim the reading, perhaps using only verses 15-18, and simplifying them appropriately for younger children.

5. Let the children comment on Abraham's great love for God and his faithful obedience to his divine friend.

Proclaim the Gospel

1. Prepare the children for the proclamation of the gospel:
• Attach to fireplace matches cardboard cutouts of a light bulb, the sun, a star, a candle and other objects related to light. Create a "stabile" by inserting the objects into styrofoam or florist foam. Talk with the children about the use and the beauty of light.
• Or have the cardboard cutouts in a bag covered with bright red and orange and yellow stripes. Tell the children that the bag is a bag of light. Let them pull out the objects. Little children especially will enjoy the element of surprise.
• Have an empty bottle of bleach and some stained white clothes. Talk with the children about bleaching clothes to make them white. Show them some clean, bright white clothes.

2. Remind the children that Peter, James and John were some of Jesus's best friends. Remind them also that Moses and Elijah were holy men who lived long before Jesus and who were important to the Jewish people. Have flannel board figures of the five and Jesus and show them to the children. Tell the children that our gospel is about Jesus and all of these people.

3. Ask the children to stand for the gospel. Acclaim the gospel suitably for Lent and them proclaim it.

4. With the help of the children retell the gospel story using the flannel board figures. In addition to the five figures above, have a mountain, a cloud and a second figure of Jesus, but this one completely white.

5. Sum up the meaning of the gospel by telling the children that the three special friends of Jesus had the wonderful privilege of seeing for a few moments the glory that Jesus had because he was God, a glory that was usually hidden when he lived on earth.

Respond to the Gospel

1. Ask the children to recall other ways in which Jesus showed that he possessed the glory of God during his life on earth. Draw upon the gospel readings of the last two months, mentioning the love and compassion of Jesus for the sick and disabled, his great teaching authority, his power to forgive sins, his ability to see into the hearts of people and understand them. Help the children to realize that the revelation of the glory of Jesus at his transfiguration was a dramatic confirmation to his friends of what he was continually revealing by his earthly words and actions.

2. Direct the attention of the children to the "voice" from the cloud:

• Whose was the voice? Where else have we heard a similar voice in Mark's gospel?

• What did the voice call Peter, James and John to do? What did it mean for their lives?

• What good advice might Mark be giving to us also? When do we listen to Jesus? Relate the command to listen to Jesus to our efforts to live well the season of Lent.

3. Ask the children what Jesus ordered his disciples not to do after the transfiguration was over. Help especially the older children to see that Jesus knew that his friends could not understand what his divinity really meant until they had witnessed his death and experienced his resurrection.

4. As reminders to the children of our liturgy today give them white candles to take home. Tell them to burn their candles during mealtime and to think of the glory of Jesus and of our privilege and obligation to listen to him.

5. Conclude today's liturgy with a profession of faith. The leader might invite willing children to express aloud their personal faith in God.

Other Possibilities:

1. Older children might benefit from a deeper consideration of the transfiguration:

• We obtain more information about Mark's evaluation of the transfiguration by looking at the story in its context. As the gospels for the opening "ordinary" Sundays of the year have made clear, Jesus is an authoritative teacher and preacher and a powerful healer.

People have observed the words and works of Jesus and have begun to ask, "Who can this man be?" Shortly before he records the transfiguration, Mark has Peter make his great confession of faith to Jesus: "You are the Messiah!" Then Jesus predicts his passion, death and resurrection to his disciples, reprimands Peter for his rejection of the idea, and tells his disciples and the crowds that they too must follow the way of the cross. The transfiguration story follows with the command of Jesus to be silent about it until after his death and resurrection. The transfiguration thus serves two purposes. It confirms and supplements Peter's belief in Jesus: Jesus is indeed the anointed one of God, but, more than that, he is the glorious Son of God. But the transfiguration also underscores the necessity of accepting the suffering and death of Jesus in knowing his true identity. Share some of these thoughts with older children.

• The story of the transfiguration is appropriate for Lent, since it asks us to focus our attention on the cross of Jesus as an essential part of his identity. Ask older children to symbolize this aspect of the identity of Jesus with gold or silver foil for the radiant glory of Jesus and pieces of wood for his cross. Enlarge the most provocative symbol and display it in the children's gathering space during the rest of Lent.

2. The story of the testing of Abraham is theologically and psychologically very powerful. Perhaps it arose in part to explain the origin of the Hebrew prohibition against human sacrifice. Give older children copies of Gn 22:1-18 and ask them to list the elements of the story that make it so dramatic. Comment especially on Abraham's willingness to sacrifice in faith the very reward of his faith (JBC). Let the children act out the story, enlarging imaginatively upon the conversation that Abraham and Isaac might have had as they walked toward the place of sacrifice. Why is Isaac a "type" of Jesus?

3. There are two excellent children's stories related to the testing of Abraham. *Two Crabs and the Moonlight* by Tohr Yamaguchi tells a similar story in simple, beautiful fiction. The little crab Ake is willing to sacrifice his life to the moonlight to save his mother. In *The Binding of Isaac* Barbara Cohen imagines plausibly yet tenderly how Isaac might have told his story to his grandchildren.

4. The LMC refocuses today's LM New Testament reading, from the letter of Paul to the Romans, by omitting most of it and adding verses 38-39. Proclaim the new reading as a profession of faith and joy in God. How appropriate is the reading for Lent? For this Second Sunday of Lent? Have a calligrapher write out the magnificent verses 38-39, and give the children copies to take home and decorate with festive borders. Challenge the children to memorize the verses.

Lectionary for Masses with Children	Lectionary for Mass
**Ex 20:1-3,7-8,12-17	**Ex 20:1-17 or 20:1-3,7-8,12-17
Ps 19:7,8,9-10	Ps 19:8,9,10,11
-----	*I Cor 1:22-25
**Jn 2:13-22	**Jn 2:13-25

Third Sunday of Lent

Focus: God gave us the ten commandments because God loves us. God asks us to respond to the commandments with love, but also to see beyond them.

Gather the Children

1. Gather the children in their separate space, decorated appropriately for Lent. Use a brown or purple burlap gathering cloth. Place brown or purple candles beside the open lectionary.
2. Welcome the children with joy and remind them why we come together each Sunday for our special liturgy of the word.
3. Ask the children to extend their arms, palms upward, and repeat the response to the psalm, "Lord, you have the words of everlasting life." Then teach them to sing the verse.
4. Remind the children that we continue to celebrate Lent. Ask them to reflect on how well they have tried, during the past week, to pray, to be good and to draw closer to God and to other people in love. Ask for a volunteer to pray aloud that God will help us do these things during the coming week. If no child volunteers to pray aloud, simply encourage the children to speak to God in their hearts.

Proclaim the Old Testament Reading

1. Prepare the children to hear the reading:
• Begin with a brief discussion of the necessity of law for orderly life. Joanne Stover's *If Everybody Did* is a playful illustration of what the world would be like if we all did as we pleased and no one paid any attention to laws. The leader might read the story for ideas and examples to use with the children.
• Let the children talk about what they know of the ten commandments. Help them include such things as:

According to tradition, God gave the commandments to Moses after the Israelites had escaped from Egypt and while they were wandering in the desert.

They are part of the covenant between God and God's chosen people. God promised to take special care of the people and they promised to keep God's commandments.

Some of the commandments involve our relationship with God; the rest involve our relationship with each other. Give examples.

• Have two clay tablets with Roman numerals on them, I-III on the first, IV-X on the second. (Not all religious traditions divide the commandments thus.) Tell older children that there is evidence that the commandments were originally each one word. For this reason the ten commandments are sometimes called "God's words" or "the decalogue."
2. Proclaim the reading. Perhaps ten older, prepared children could proclaim the reading to the group, each of the ten reading one of the commandments.
3. Discuss the commandments briefly:
• Ask why God gave the people the commandments. Lead the children to realize that the commandments were meant to assist people in their efforts to live as God wanted, and they were very helpful. Thus the commandments were a sign of God's love.
• Tell older children that the ten commandments were only the first part of an extensive set of laws that the Israelites recorded in their Pentateuch. It required much study to know and much effort to keep all the laws. The scribes, by post-exilic times, were a class of professional exponents and teachers of the law.
• Ask older children if they know how Jesus viewed the commandments. Help them see that he considered the commandments simply as the starting point for a good life. He also tried to free men and women from the burden that the law had become.
• Let the children share briefly their ideas about the relationship of the commandments to our life today. The leader should be prepared to supply practical and interesting examples.
4. Respond to the reading:
• Tell the children that the Israelites came to love the law as the expression of God's will for them. They believed that to live the law perfectly was to live just as God wanted and would bring them happiness.
• Pray the responsorial psalm as a prayer of thanks to God for the law.

Proclaim the Gospel

1. Today's gospel is a difficult one for children (even adults) to understand. For little children, the leader might use the following approach:
• Tell the children about Jesus and the merchants and the money changers in the temple. Tell them that Jesus saw their lack of reverence for the house of God and their greed. He became justifiably angry and acted out of love and respect for God. He knocked over the tables of the money changers and drove the animals out of the temple precincts.
• The Jewish leaders responded by asking, in effect, "Who are you that you can get away with such actions?" They wanted a sign of the authority of Jesus. Jesus gave them a sign to watch for: he told them what would happen to his own body, which he called a tem-

ple. He told them that his body would be destroyed and raised up again in three days. To maintain the interest of the children, the leader might "destroy" a "temple" made of blocks. Then tell the children that when Jesus was talking about the temple of his body, he was really thinking about his death and resurrection. We will celebrate these great events at the end of Lent.

• Acclaim the gospel suitably for Lent, then proclaim it.

• In response to the gospel allow the children some time to thank God for the gift of Jesus whose body was destroyed and raised up again for us.

2. For older children the leader might:

• First tell them the story of the cleansing of the temple. Include, as John does, that the merchants and money changers apparently were not doing anything wrong. (See JBC.) Let the children react, and thus bring out the point that to obey the letter of the law is often inadequate.

• Then summarize the rest of the gospel, focusing on the prediction of the death and resurrection of Jesus and the difficulty people had in believing in him.

• Finally acclaim and proclaim the gospel.

Make the Good News Our Own

1. Profess our faith. It is especially appropriate to do so today because the gospel tells of so many who had difficulty believing in Jesus.

2. As a sign that we want to respect the law and respond to it in its fullness:

• Give each older child a paper cut in the shape of two stone tablets. Each child should write on the paper one way that he or she can obey the law, even go beyond the law, in his or her everyday actions. Give a few practical example, such as setting the table without being asked and without complaining, taking care of your little brother just to be nice to your mother, talking with your father pleasantly when he wants to talk with you. Relate these kind works to our efforts to be good during Lent. Then collect the papers and place them on the open lectionary.

• Give each younger child a lump of "play dough" to take home and use to make "stone tablets" like the ones on which God wrote the law for Moses and the people.

Other Possibilities:

1. In year A we read John's gospel accounts of the Samaritan woman at the well, the cure of the man born blind and the raising of Lazarus on the third, fourth and fifth Sundays, respectively, of Lent. These readings relate significantly to Christian initiation, and for this reason may be used in place of the readings for the corresponding Sundays in years B and C. The year A readings are especially appropriate if there are catechumens in the assembly. The leader should find out well in advance which gospel readings the parish will use on these three Sundays of Lent and plan accordingly. If the parish plans to use the Year A readings, the leader may consult *Gather the Children* for Year A for suggestions.

2. For very young children, the leader might wish to ex-

pand the story of the giving of the commandments to Moses and, if necessary, shorten the presentation of the gospel:

• Conduct a brief introductory discussion of laws children know about: obey traffic lights, keep off new grass, don't pick the flowers, don't run in the house, don't play with matches, don't jump on the bed, eat healthful food, etc. Talk about why these laws are good and necessary for our safety and happiness.

• Introduce Moses as the one to whom God gave the laws which we call the ten commandments. God gave the commandments to Moses to help people live good and happy lives.

• Proclaim parts of the reading, perhaps just several laws the children can understand.

• Explain that God's laws are not always easy to keep. Sometimes we would rather forget them or give up trying. Pray for strength to keep God's laws.

• Do some role-playing to illustrate positive and negative behavior with regard to the commandments, for example, stealing, then returning a valuable to its owner; fighting, then playing nicely with others; lying, then telling the truth.

3. As an alternative activity, make paper symbols of things the children might do to keep the commandments, especially in the broad sense of loving God and each other. A broom, for example, may be a sign of helping at home; a toy may be a sign of playing nicely with a younger sister or brother; a bible may be a sign of listening to God; a letter may be a sign of reaching out to someone who is lonely. Let several children compose prayers suggested by the symbols, and then lay the symbols on the open lectionary. Give the children random symbols to take home.

4. Record the first reading. Enhance the recording with imaginative sound effects. Play the recording to proclaim the reading.

5. The *Sadlier Scripture Series* includes a good presentation of the giving of the commandments in "God Takes a People." If there is time, show appropriate parts of the filmstrip, or even the whole filmstrip.

6. There are several excellent children's books which deal with the subject of breaking a law because of a higher good. Mary Perine's *Salt Boy* and Margaret Greaves's *A Net To Catch the Wind* are provocative stories about children who disobey their parents. Either story will form the basis of an excellent discussion among older children.

7. On the first Sunday of Lent, in each of the three lectionary years, the church asks us to consider the temptations of Jesus, and on the second Sunday, his transfiguration. For the next three Sundays during year B the church offers us selections from John's gospel that turn our attention to the passion and death of Jesus and his future glorification through these events. On Passion Sunday we will read Mark's account of the passion. Help the children to visualize the unity of the gospel readings of the next few weeks by showing them pictures of different kinds of crosses or pictures of different artists' representations of the crucifixion. The leader might consider borrowing paintings from the local public library.

8. John's placement of the cleansing of the temple in the

second chapter of his gospel is interesting. The synoptics place it at the end of Jesus's ministry, which seems more probable historically in view of the violent reaction that such an affront to temple worship would have caused among the Jews. John's placement, however, is theologically motivated. In the words of Reginald Fuller (PNL), John has Jesus "lay out all his cards on the table right at the outset" of his ministry. Jesus brings Jewish public worship to an end and replaces it with worship centered on his revelation of God. Share these thoughts with older children who are interested in the structure of the gospels.

9. Share with older children our reading from Paul's first letter to the Corinthians. Illustrate the demand of the Jews for "signs" by their demand in the gospel. Ask the children what demands people make on God today to lead them to belief in Jesus.

Fourth Sunday of Lent

Lectionary for Masses with Children	Lectionary for Mass
- - - -	*II Chr 36:14-17,19-23
*Eph 2:4-10	*Ps 137:1-2,3,4-5,6
Ps 25:4-5,6,7	*Eph 2:4-10
**Jn 3:16-17	**Jn 3:14-21

Focus: We see in the cross the deepest manifestation of the love of God for us.

Gather the Children

1. The atmosphere of the children's gathering space should convey the thoughtfulness of the penitential season of Lent. Use a purple or brown burlap cloth and purple or brown candles. Display the lectionary prominently and tastefully. Have a crucifix present, one which will attract the attention of the children.
2. Welcome the children with joy and remind them why we gather for our special liturgy of the word.
3. While one child holds the lectionary high, lead all the children in song to acknowledge the presence of God in the word. Enthrone the lectionary and light the candles.
4. Pray quietly with the children that we will listen well to God's word today and always.

Talk about the Season of Lent

1. Point out the Lenten decor and let the children talk briefly about the meaning of Lent. Show the card with "Lent" written on it, which we have used earlier in the season. Remind the children that Lent is a time to think, to pray, to try hard to be good, to draw closer to God and to each other.
2. Ask the children if they know which Sunday of Lent it is today. Hold up a big "4" and tell the group that today marks the half-way point in the season. Ask them what joyous event we will celebrate in three weeks. Show them the card with the word "Easter" on it.
3. If the children have not celebrated the penitential rite with the adult assembly, celebrate it now with them, perhaps as follows:

Leader: My brothers and sisters in God's family, before we listen to God's word, let us thank God for being constantly willing to forgive us, no matter what our sin.

You forgive us when we forget your gifts of love: Lord, have mercy.

All: Lord, have mercy.

Leader: You forgive us when we are ungrateful to our parents and to others who love us: Christ, have mercy.

All: Christ, have mercy.

Leader: You forgive us when we fail to be gentle and peace loving: Lord, have mercy.

All: Lord, have mercy.

Leader: We know that God loves us. The signs of God's love are all around us. May God help us to recognize those gifts of love and to re-

turn that love by living the way God wants us to live. May God forgive us for the times we do not return that love. May God bring us to life everlasting.

All: Amen.

The leader and the children might sing the invocations:

Lord Jesus...gifts of love. Lord, have mer-cy. Lord, have mer-cy.

Lord Jesus... love us. Christ, have mer-cy. Christ, have mer-cy.

Lord Jesus...peace lov-ing. Lord, have mer-cy. Lord, have mer-cy.

Proclaim the Old Testament Reading

Note: The LMC omits today's Old Testament reading. The leader who wishes to proclaim it to the children may find the following suggestions helpful.

1. Prepare the children for the reading by reminding them of the Old Testament stories we have heard this Lent: a story of Noah, a story of Abraham, a story of Moses. These stories show God's great love for the people, and speak of how God asks in return their love and trust and that they love each other.
2. Today's Old Testament reading is from one of the lesser known historical books of the bible. The reading tells of how the people did not listen to God and did not respond to God's love with their love and trust. It tells of how God punished the people to help them learn to obey and to be good people, just as a parent punishes a child to teach the child how to live. The punishment of God's people was a sad one: they were conquered by their enemies and made to leave their homeland and to live for years in exile in a foreign land.
3. Proclaim the reading.
4. Discuss briefly:
• The sadness of the people in exile, far away from their homeland; and
• That God's punishment of the people showed that God loved them.
5. Some of the children may have seen "Godspell." Ask if they remember the lovely, haunting song "On the Willows." The song is based upon the LM responsorial psalm, Ps 137. (The LMC, however, has replaced Ps 137 with Ps 25.) Explain the song, telling the children that it

expresses the sorrow of the people of God in exile and evokes wonderful memories of their homeland. Play the song. Ask the children to listen quietly and to think about the times we have not been as good as we could have been. Ask them to think also about how much God loves us and wants us to be good. If time is short or if the song is not available, simply pray Ps 137.

Proclaim the Gospel

1. Tell the children that several hundred years after the exile, God sent someone special to show the world how to live. God sent Jesus, the very son of God, to live among the people. Emphasize that for God to send Jesus was the greatest thing God ever did to show love for the people. In today's gospel we hear how John the Evangelist says just that.
2. Acclaim the gospel appropriately for Lent, and then proclaim Jn 3:16.
3. Discuss what it means to say that God "gave his only Son." Stress that God gave us Jesus completely, even to his death on the cross.

Respond to the Good News of God's Great Love

1. Focus on the crucifix:
• Turn the attention of the children to the crucifix in their gathering space. Ask them what thoughts a crucifix brings to their minds.
• Ask if any of them has a crucifix at home.
2. Lead the group in a simple veneration of the cross:
• Have ready a large cardboard cross and place it in the center of the gathering cloth. Give each child a paper heart.
• Ask the children to think quietly for a few moments about the great love of God for us. Then ask them to lay their hearts on the cross to symbolize their acceptance of that love.
• Glue the hearts on the cross and superimpose on the hearts letters spelling "God so loved the world." Carry the cross into the church in the gift procession.
3. Profess our faith. State explicitly that we believe in God who loves us so much that "God gave his only Son" to live among us. State further that we believe in Jesus who loved us enough to die on the cross for us.
4. Tell the children that Jn 3:16 is perhaps the best-known verse in the New Testament. Ask them if they have ever seen a bumper sticker with "John 3:16" on it. Give them bumper stickers to take home. Make the bumper stickers of contact paper and write on them with a paint pen.

Other Possibilities:

1. The leader should recall that a parish may choose today to use the readings for the Fourth Sunday of Lent of lectionary year A. For suggestions concerning the proclamation of these alternate readings, the leader may consult the volume of *Gather the Children* for year A.
2. With an older group of children and more time, introduce Nicodemus as one who came to Jesus at night. Talk briefly about light and darkness as symbols of good and evil. Proclaim the appropriate parts of the gospel.
3. For the Old Testament proclamation, tell the story of the brazen serpent, Nm 21:9ff. Talk about the power of the serpent raised high to save the Israelites, then about the power of the crucified Christ to give life. Proclaim the appropriate parts of the gospel. Teach the children the refrain to Dan Schutte's "Behold the Wood" (from *A Dwelling Place*). Listen to the song's second verse because it speaks of the Son's being lifted up on a tree.
4. Let the children cover the cardboard cross, mosaic style, with pictures of, or words about, how they can show love for others, especially at cost to themselves.
5. Show the children slides of various artists' conceptions of the crucifixion. Play reflective background music. Suggest to older children that they create their own pictures, perhaps abstractions, of the crucifixion as a sign of God's love.
6. Using the ideas from our beautiful second reading from the letter to the Ephesians, make placards proclaiming signs of God's love. Carry them in the gift procession. Or make a mobile illustrating the same thoughts.
7. Little children will enjoy the story *Do You Know What I'll Do?* by Charlotte Zolotow. It will give them good ideas about how they can show love for others, as Jesus showed us his love.
8. Psalm 137, as it describes the feelings of the Jews during their exile in Babylon, also offers a description of our own situation in Lent. The Jews found hope in the memory of Jerusalem, their wondrous homeland. We find our hope in the Easter triumph of Jesus. (See Fuller, PNL.) Invite older children to compose a new psalm in which the Christian community prays to God to let thoughts of Easter joy console its members and give them hope during their Lenten journey.

Fifth Sunday of Lent

Lectionary for Masses with Children	Lectionary for Mass
**Jer 31:31-34 *Ps 51:1,10,12 - - - - - **Jn 12:24-26	**Jer 31:31-34 *Ps 51:3-4,12-13,14-15 *Heb 5:7-9 **Jn 12:20-33

Focus: It is only by dying to ourselves that we find life.

Gather the Children

1. The children's gathering space should be decorated to encourage the thoughtful, penitential spirit of Lent. Use a brown or purple burlap gathering cloth and brown or purple candles. Have a crucifix on the cloth.
2. Ask one child to raise high the lectionary. Ask the other children to extend their arms toward the lectionary as though reaching to receive the book. All should listen reverently while the leader proclaims in song the wonders of God's word:

All glory and all praise to you!
Your word, O Lord, is old, yet ever new!
Your word, O Lord, gives life that's true!
All glory and all praise to you!

3. Ask the children to reflect quietly on our reasons for being here at our special liturgy of God's word. Pray that God will help us listen well to the word.

Reflect on the Meaning of Lent

1. Hold up a big "5" to remind the children that today is the Fifth Sunday of Lent. Ask the group how many more weeks it is until Easter.
2. Tell the children that with only two more weeks of Lent, now is a good time to renew and strengthen our Lenten efforts to pray, to be good, to draw closer to God and to each other in love. Let the children think quietly for a few moments about how they can increase their efforts to do these things.
3. Pray together to give thanks to God for the season of Lent and the encouragement Lent gives us to improve our lives. If the children have not already celebrated the penitential rite with the adult assembly, the leader might lead the children now in prayer as follows:

Leader: My brothers and sisters in God's family, let us praise God for the help God gives us to live good lives.

You teach us your ways: Lord, have mercy.
All: Lord, have mercy.
Leader: You give us joy in doing your will: Christ, have mercy.
All: Christ, have mercy.
Leader: You keep us in your presence: Lord, have mercy.

All: Lord, have mercy.
Leader: May God be near us always. May God make us more and more like Jesus, who taught us by his life and death how to live. May God make us happy when we are good. May God forgive us all our sins and give us everlasting life.
All: Amen.

The leader and the children might sing the invocations as they did on the Fourth Sunday of Lent.

Proclaim the Old Testament Reading

1. Tell the children that the first reading today is a promise that God made to the people when they were frightened and sad. They were living in exile in a land far away from their beloved homeland. God's promise, spoken through the great prophet Jeremiah, was that better times would come.
2. Ask the children to listen quietly to the beautiful words of God's promise. Proclaim the reading, perhaps using only Jer 31:33 for very young children.
3. Explain that the promise meant that one day the people would love God and each other so much that it would not be hard to keep God's law. Comment on how wonderful it would be if God's love and God's law were always in our hearts. It would be as if we had new hearts, so full of God's love would they be.
4. Ask the children if they know how God finally kept the promise. Draw from them that Jesus is the fulfillment of the promise, because by his life and death he showed us how to live just as God wanted.

Proclaim the Gospel

1. Prepare the children for the proclamation of the gospel:
• Have a few large seeds for the children to look at. Comment that seeds look dry and lifeless, as if they are dead.
• Put a seed in a small flower pot. Then discuss what would happen if we kept it warm, watered it occasionally and gave it plenty of fresh air and sunshine. Would it grow? Why not? Lead the children to say that the seed must be buried in the ground or it will not grow.
• Fill the pot with soil, then plant the seed. Ask the children if it will grow now, given the proper temperature, water, sunshine, fresh air, etc.
• Summarize and conclude the activity by pointing out seeds seem to die, but then, after they are buried, they come to new life.

2. Relate the above discussion to the gospel:
- Tell the children that Jesus, like the seed, died and was buried. Tell them that the death of Jesus, like the death of the seed, caused new life.
- When did Jesus die? When did he rise to new life? When do we and the whole church celebrate these great events in the life of Jesus? Be sure the children realize that this will happen soon.
- In our gospel today Jesus himself tells us that it is necessary for us, too, to die before we can have new life.

3. Acclaim the gospel appropriately for Lent and then proclaim it.

4. Lead the children gently to see that Jesus meant his words about dying and rising to apply to us too. Be practical and sensitive, especially with little children. The words of Jesus, who is love, should help children and never frighten them. For example:
- Ask the children what Jesus meant when he said that if we love our life, we will lose it. Let the children respond, though little ones will not be able to understand this concept.
- Tell the children that Jesus was talking about how we sometimes think only about ourselves and what we want, and forget about others and what might make them happy. Ask the children to think of times when they made others unhappy because they were thinking only of themselves. The leader should not insist on the children's sharing, but should be ready with suggestions: "Maybe you wouldn't set the table before dinner. Maybe you did set the table, but you complained so much that you made your mother unhappy. Maybe you were selfish with your things or mean to your sister or brother. Maybe you made a big mess in the house and were very unpleasant when you had to clean it up." Admit that grown-ups also are selfish, that we're all selfish sometimes. Jesus was reminding us not to be selfish, but to think of others first. Agree, with the children, that it's hard not to be selfish. That's why Jesus said it was like dying, dying to ourselves.
- Ask the children what they think Jesus meant when he said that if we hate our life, we will keep it forever. This time let the children respond and give examples of how we can be unselfish. Perhaps after the above discussion, the children will begin to understand the words of Jesus, but they carry very difficult concepts for little ones.
- Suggest that we all ask Jesus quietly, in our hearts, to help us to think of others first, as Jesus always did. Join the children in a few moments of quiet, personal prayer.

Make the Good News Our Own

1. To reinforce the idea of dying to ourselves, let the children plant seeds:
- For younger children, have a broad, shallow, dirt-filled container and let each child put in a pinch of grass seeds. Grass seed, if kept warm and moist, will sprout quickly, quite possibly even in the next two weeks before Easter. Ask the children to think about acts of unselfishness as they plant their seeds. Give the children hardy seeds to take home and plant. Tape the seeds to cards that explain the activity and relate it to today's liturgy.

- Give each older child a large paper seed. Ask the children to write on their seeds ways children can die to selfishness and sin. Collect the seeds and put them in a flower pot. Put a sign on the pot with a few words to explain what it is and let the children place the pot before the ambo when they rejoin the adult assembly.

2. Pray in the general intercessions that all people will die to the selfishness and sin within them in order to have life as Jesus promises it.

3. Conclude the liturgy by listening to Dan Schutte's "Behold the Cross" (from *A Dwelling Place*). The song is based in part upon today's gospel, citing in particular the grain of wheat analogy. Teach the children to sing the refrain.

Other Possibilities:

1. The leader should be mindful of the fact that parish liturgy planners may choose to use today the readings of lectionary year A. For suggestions as to how to present the year A readings to children, the leader might consult *Gather the Children*, Year A.

2. Lead older children into deeper thought about our reading from the book of Jeremiah:
- Tell them of its place in Jewish history. Jeremiah is prophesying to the Jews in exile in Babylon. He interprets the exile as punishment for lack of faithfulness to the Mosaic covenant. Jeremiah envisions a new covenant, but this time one which God will write not on tablets of stone, but in the hearts of people. Christians see the fulfillment of Jeremiah's prophecy in "the covenant which was established by the blood of Christ and which led to the outpouring of the Spirit into the hearts of the believers" (PNL). This is the one passage in the Old Testament which refers explicitly to the New Testament.
- Talk with the children about the Babylonian captivity and the sufferings of the Jewish people when they lived away from their beloved homeland. Perhaps the children will remember something about this from our last two Sunday liturgies. Ask how they think the Jewish people responded to words such as Jeremiah's during their suffering. In this way lead the children to appreciate how Jeremiah consoled his people during times of sorrow. Give the children copies of some of Jeremiah's words to take home and decorate. Or put them on a big poster during the liturgy.
- To relate the feelings of the Jewish people in exile to the experience of the children, talk about some of the many political exiles who live in our midst today. What hope might the leaders of the world hold out to them?

3. Psalm 51, the most famous of the penitential psalms, follows Jeremiah's prophecy well because it is a prayer for a renewed heart. Sing the psalm with the children. Ask older children to rewrite the prayer as it might come from the heart of a modern exile. Or respond to the Jeremiah reading by listening to Bob Dufford's "Father, Mercy" (from *Neither Silver Nor Gold*), which is based on Ps 51. Ask the children to pray for a "new heart," that is, a heart that is happy with the things God wants.

4. With younger children develop the theme of "promise." We have reflected during Lent upon several of

God's promises to the people—promises through Noah, through Abraham, through Moses and today through Jeremiah. By using examples of promises that have meaning for the children, help them see that God's promises to the people gave them hope and comfort when they were very sad.

5. To introduce the gospel, instead of planting seeds show the appropriate parts of the filmstrip "The Little Grain of Wheat" (from the Seabury Press series *Little People's Paperbacks*). After proclaiming the gospel show the whole filmstrip. If the filmstrip is not available and there is opportunity beforehand, have the children draw pictures of planting seeds. Older, neater children might enjoy drawing their pictures on transparencies.

6. Little children might like to pantomime the death and rebirth of a seed.

7. Although it changes the symbolism of our gospel, the leader might focus on the life of a butterfly. Have a large paper butterfly. Let the children decorate the wings, mosaic-style, with pictures of ways they die to themselves, by acts of unselfishness, to show their love for others. Put the butterfly into a paper or papier-maché cocoon and take it out on Easter.

8. The reading today from the letter to the Hebrews (omitted in the LMC) offers us opportunity to meditate on the sufferings of Jesus. Talk with the children about how it was difficult for even Jesus to accept his sufferings. But because of his obedience "he became the source of eternal life for all those who obey him."

There are many children's books related to the theme of dying to ourselves in order to make someone else happy. *Josefina February*, by Evaline Ness, tells the story of a little Haitian girl who makes a big sacrifice to give her grandfather a birthday present. *Two Crabs and the Moonlight*, by Tohr Yamaguchi, is a powerful story of a little crab who is willing to die to save his mother. The leader may have used the latter story with the children on the Second Sunday of Lent, to complement the Old Testament reading of the sacrifice of Isaac, in which case the focus would have been on the mother crab. To complement today's readings, we view the story from the perspective of the little crab.

Passion Sunday

Focus: Jesus was obedient for us even to death on a cross.

Lectionary for Masses with Children	Lectionary for Mass
**Mk 11:1-10	**Mk 11:1-10 or Jn 12:12-16
Is 50:6-7	Is 50:4-7
Ps 22:7-8,16-17-18,19,20	Ps 22:8-9,17-18,19-20,23-24
- - - - -	Phil 2:6-11
**Mk 15:1-39	**Mk 14:1-15:47 or 15:1-39

Gather the Children

1. Bring the children together in their separate gathering space, decorated suitably for Passion Sunday. Continue to use a brown or purple burlap gathering cloth and brown or purple candles. Display the lectionary prominently. Have present a large wooden or cardboard cross and a few palm branches.
2. Remind the children that we come together to listen to the word of God and think about what it means for our lives.
3. Light the candles. While one child holds high the lectionary, all should sing to greet the Lord, present in the word.

Reflect on the Meaning of Passion Sunday

1. Tell the children that today is the last Sunday of Lent and the last Sunday before Easter. The church asks us to reflect today upon the things that happened to Jesus during the last days of his life on earth. We know that Jesus suffered much during those days, and so, because "passion" means "suffering," we call today Passion Sunday. We call this whole next week Holy Week. The leader might hold up cards with "Passion Sunday" and "Holy Week" written on them in large letters.
2. If the children have not just celebrated the penitential rite with the adult assembly, lead them in prayer as follows:

Leader:	My brothers and sisters in God's family, let us give praise for God's constant love and forgiveness.
	Lord Jesus, you lived and died to show us how much God loves us. You forgive us when we forget that love: Lord, have mercy.
All:	Lord, have mercy.
Leader:	You lived and died to show us how to do what God wants. You forgive us when we do not do what God wants: Christ, have mercy.
All:	Christ, have mercy.
Leader:	You lived and died to show us how to love others. You forgive us when we do not love others as we should. Lord, have mercy.
All:	Lord, have mercy.

Leader:	May God almighty help us always to follow the example of Jesus and to live in love as he did. May God forgive us our many failings to give love to others. May God give us a share of the new life of Jesus, a life of everlasting happiness with God.
All:	Amen.

The leader and the children might sing the invocations as they did on the Fourth Sunday of Lent.

Celebrate the Events Recounted in the Gospel Readings

1. Entry into Jerusalem:
• Tell the children what happened on Palm Sunday: Jesus's reputation as a teacher and healer had spread even to Jerusalem. When the people in the city heard that Jesus was coming, they went out to meet him with great excitement. Jesus rode on a donkey. The people cut palm branches to hold and wave. They entered the city in a parade, singing and very happy that Jesus was with them.
2. Teach the children to sing the words of the joyful crowd:

Hosanna in the highest!
Blessed is he who comes in the name of the Lord!

Suitable music to accompany the acclamation is not hard to find. Ask the children where they often hear those very words. (The leader will notice that the LMC translation, in its efforts to simplify the scriptural readings, renders the words of the crowd differently from the familiar words of the preface acclamation.)
• Proclaim Jn 12:12-16, simplified appropriately for younger children.
• Have a procession:

Ask one child to take the part of Jesus and to carry the large cross, a symbol of Jesus.

Give each child a palm branch. The branches may be of green paper, but it would be better for the leader to reserve a portion of real palm branches from the supply which the assembly will use.

Let the children process around the room waving their palm branches and led by the child carrying the cross. All should sing the words of the crowd several times.

Have the children lay their palm branches in a pile on the gathering cloth and return to their places around the cloth. Place the cross on top of the pile of palms.

If a procession of all the children is not practical, simply let a few of the children process. All can still hold palm branches and sing.

2. The last supper:

• Tell the children briefly what happened at the last supper: Jesus knew that he was soon to die and was anxious to eat a last special meal with his special friends. During the meal he blessed bread and wine and gave them to his friends to eat and drink as his own body and blood. We call this special meal the last supper, and the day on which we celebrate the last supper, Holy Thursday. Encourage the children to come to church with their parents on Holy Thursday evening for the parish Liturgy of the Lord's Supper.

• Ask the children if they know when the parish assembly does the same thing Jesus did at the last supper. Teach them to sing the memorial acclamation:

When we eat this bread and drink this cup
we proclaim your death, Lord Jesus,
until you come in glory.

• Have a simple presentation of the events of the last supper:

Clear the gathering cloth and cover it with a new white cloth. Replace the candles and the lectionary. Place the large cross on the cloth, and some bread and a goblet on the cloth near the cross.

Choose one child to take the part of Jesus and ask the rest of the children to be the disciples. Direct the one child to hold up the bread and the goblet at the appropriate times during the reading.

Proclaim Mk 14:17,22-25.

All sing the above memorial acclamation.

If the group is small, the child who has the part of Jesus might pantomime breaking and distributing the bread and passing the goblet. The rest of the children might then pantomime eating the bread and drinking from the cup. As an alternative way of conducting the pantomime, a child who is a good reader might proclaim the gospel and the leader take the part of Jesus. In either case, the children should not really eat or drink anything, for fear of their confusing what they are doing with a real eucharist.

3. The death of Jesus:

• Tell the children briefly what happened on Holy Thursday night and Good Friday: after the last supper, Jesus went to a garden to pray. He was frightened by what he knew was about to happen to him and he prayed to God for strength to do God's will. The enemies of Jesus came to the garden and captured him. They tried him as a criminal and decided that he should be put to death on a cross. Many of the same people who had welcomed Jesus into Jerusalem with such joy just a few days before now shouted out that he should be crucified. Many people made fun of Jesus and made him suffer greatly. They put a crown of thorns on his head and gave him a heavy cross to carry. Jesus carried the cross out of the city to the place where he was to die. Soldiers nailed Jesus to the cross and raised it high. After three hours of suffering on the cross, Jesus died. Later that evening some friends of Je-

sus took his body down from the cross and placed it in a tomb of rock. We call the day on which Jesus died Good Friday. We call it "good" Friday because Jesus died on that day to show us how much God loves us.

• Teach the children to sing the memorial acclamation:

Dying you destroyed our death,
rising you restored our life.
Lord Jesus, come in glory.

• Have a simple presentation of the events of Good Friday:

Remove the bread, the goblet and the white cloth, leaving the lectionary, the candles and the large cross on the Lenten gathering cloth. Place on the cloth a crown of thorns, made of real or paper brambles and large enough to fit over the top of the cross, several nails, real or cardboard, and two flashlights.

Ask one child to take the part of Jesus and to hold up the cross. Ask several children to take the parts of the soldiers, and give them the crown of thorns and the nails. Ask two children to hold the flashlights. Ask the remaining children to kneel. Let the children put the crown of thorns on the cross, then put the nails in precut holes in the cross, then spotlight the cross with the flashlights.

Proclaim Jn 19:1-2, 17-19, 30, simplified appropriately for children.

Sing the above memorial acclamation together.
Turn off the spotlights and all kneel in silence for a moment.

4. Suggest, but do not dwell upon, the happy events of Easter to come by removing the crown of thorns and the nails from the cross and laying them and the cross on the cloth. Tell the children that Good Friday is not the end of the story. We'll celebrate the wonderful new life of Jesus on Easter.

5. Encourage the children to spend some time on Good Friday thinking quietly about all that Jesus did for us. Suggest that they draw pictures of Jesus's suffering and dying for us. Encourage older children to participate in the parish celebration of the Passion of the Lord on Good Friday.

Make the Good News Our Own

1. Pray the general intercessions. Pray especially for all those who, like Jesus, suffer innocently.
2. Give each child a cross to take home as a reminder during the coming week of the great love of Jesus for us and for God, a love so great that Jesus suffered and died to teach us how to love each other and to make us happy.
3. Replace the crown of thorns and the nails on the large cross and let the children carry it into the church, when they rejoin the assembly, and place it near the ambo.

Other Possibilities:

1. For older children, in place of the above dramatization of the passion narrative:
• Have a dramatic reading of the gospel with all the children participating. Following this outline is a sim-

ple reading of the passion in parts which has worked well in the author's parish.

• Or choose several capable readers who can prepare beforehand and let them read appropriate sections of the passion narrative.

2. The leader should consult the parish minister of music for musical renditions of the acclamations suggested in the presentation of the passion.

3. Separate the scenes of the passion with music. The music of the Taizé community offers several possibilities. "Adoramus Te Domine II" or "Jesus, Remember Me" are appropriate. The refrain to Dan Schutte's "Behold the Wood" (from *A Dwelling Place*) is also appropriate, particularly if the children have sung it on the past two Sundays.

4. Modern New Testament scholars agree widely that the beautiful reading from Paul's letter to the Philippians is a pre-Pauline hymn representing an early profession of Christian faith. For older children a profession of faith based on the reading would be most appropriate. For example, ask the children to respond "I do" to each of the following questions:

Do you believe that Jesus had the nature of God but was willing to be born in the likeness of a human person?

Do you believe that Jesus humbled himself, obediently accepting death, even death on a cross?

Do you believe that God exalted Jesus and gave him the name which is above all names?

Do you believe that at the name of Jesus every knee should bend and every tongue confess, "Jesus Christ is Lord!"?

Or listen to Roc O'Connor's "Jesus the Lord" (from *Lord of Light*) or to John Foley's "I Will Sing of the Lord" (from *Neither Silver Nor Gold*). Both songs are based upon the lovely and deeply theological hymn which Paul incorporated into his letter to his beloved Philippian friends.

5. Have an older group prepare the general intercessions in advance. Ask them to look through current newspapers for situations in which people are suffering innocently, as Jesus did.

6. A younger group would like to prepare a large mural depicting scenes from the passion for display during the liturgy and during the coming week.

The Passion of Our Lord Jesus Christ

A Reading of the Passion of Jesus Based on the Gospel Accounts

Palm Sunday

Boys: When Jesus and his disciples were near Jerusalem, he sent two of them of ahead and told them:

Jesus: Go into the village and you will find a donkey. Untie it and bring it to me. If anyone says anything to you, tell him that the Master needs it.

Girls: So the disciples went off and did what Jesus asked. They brought the donkey back to Jesus. They laid their coats on him, and Jesus mounted the donkey and rode on toward Jerusalem.

Boys: Great crowds of people had gathered and were waiting to welcome Jesus. They spread their coats on the road in front of him to do him honor so that he might ride over them. Others cut branches from the trees and spread them on the road, too.

Girls: The crowds all around Jesus were shouting:
"All praise to the Son of David!
Blessed be he who comes in the name of the Lord!"

Holy Thursday

Boys: On the first day of the feast of Unleavened Bread, when the Passover Lamb was sacrificed, Jesus said to Peter and John:

Jesus: Go and prepare our Passover supper for us.

Peter: Where do you want us to get ready?

Jesus: Just as you enter the city, you will come upon a man carrying a pitcher of water. Follow him into the house he enters, and say to the owner, "The Teacher asks you, 'Do you have a guest room where I may eat the Passover meal with my disciples?'" That man will show you a large upstairs room furnished with couches for the feast. Prepare everything for us there.

Girls: Peter and John went off. They found everything just as Jesus had said and they prepared the Passover supper.

Boys: When evening came, Jesus arrived with the Twelve. During the meal he said:

Jesus: I have wanted very much to eat this meal with you before I suffer.

Girls: During the meal Jesus took bread, blessed it, broke it, and gave it to his disciples.

Jesus: Take this and eat it. This is my body.

Boys: Then he took a cup, gave thanks, and gave it to them.

Jesus: All of you drink from it. This cup is the new covenant in my blood, which will be shed for you.

Girls: Later Jesus said to Peter:

Jesus: Peter! Peter! I have prayed for you that your faith in me may never fail. You, in turn, must strengthen your brothers.

Peter: Lord, I will never turn away from you.

Jesus: I tell you, Peter, three times this day you will say that you do not even know me.

Peter: Even though I have to die with you, I will never say that I do not know you.

Boys: All the other disciples said the same.

Girls: After singing songs of praise to God, they left the room and walked out to the Mount of Olives to pray.

Jesus: You stay here. Keep awake and pray. I am going farther into the garden to pray. I am very sad.

Boys: Jesus walked away from his disciples and prayed:

Jesus: My Father, if it is possible, take away what will happen to me. But let it be what you want, and not what I want.

Girls: Jesus went back and found his disciples sleeping. Three times he went off to pray and came back to find his friends sleeping.

Boys: Later Judas, one of the disciples, led a crowd of people to Jesus. Judas kissed Jesus, so that the crowd would know who Jesus was. They captured Jesus and took him to the court. All the disciples ran away in fear, but Peter followed him at a distance.

Girls: The religious leaders told lies about Jesus. They made fun of him. They spat in his face and hit him. They said he should be killed.

Boys: Peter was sitting in the courtyard nearby. When some people asked him if he was a friend of Jesus, he said:

Peter: I don't even know the man!

Girls: Three times Peter insisted that he didn't even know Jesus. But then Peter remembered that Jesus had known he would deny him, and he ran out and cried bitterly.

Good Friday

Boys: The next morning the religious leaders led Jesus to Pilate. Pilate talked to Jesus and did not think he should be put to death.

Girls: The leaders stirred up the crowd of people to ask for the death of Jesus.

Boys: "Crucify him! Crucify him!" shouted the crowd.

Girls: Pilate was afraid, and so he did what they asked and ordered Jesus to be beaten and crucified.

Boys: Soldiers tore off Jesus's clothes and put a crown of thorns on his head. They called him "King of the Jews" and made fun of him. When they had finished making a fool of him, they dressed him in his own clothes and led him off to his death, carrying his own cross.

Girls: They nailed Jesus to the cross between two robbers. People continued to make fun of him.

From noon until three o'clock Jesus hung on the cross. It was dark over all the land.

Boys: Toward mid-afternoon Jesus cried out in a loud voice:

Jesus: My God, my God, why have you left me all alone?

Girls: Once again Jesus cried out in a loud voice and then he died.

Boys: After Jesus died, the earth shook and people were afraid. Many then believed that Jesus was the Son of God.

Girls: When evening came, some friends of Jesus took down his body from the cross and laid it in a new tomb cut out of rock. Then they rolled a huge stone across the entrance of the tomb.

Easter Sunday

Lectionary for Masses with Children	Lectionary for Mass
**Acts 10:34,37-43 Ps 118:1-2,15-17,22-23 Col 3:1-4 or I Cor 5:6-8 Jn 20:1-9	**Acts 10:34,37-43 Ps 118:1-2,15-17,22-23 Col 3:1-4 or I Cor 5:6-8 **Mk 16:1-8 or Jn 20:1-9

Focus: The Lord has been raised up! Let us rejoice and be glad!

Gather the Children

1. The decoration of the children's gathering space should be especially joyful today, standing in sharp contrast with the serious, reserved atmosphere of Lent. Introduce a new white or brightly colored gathering cloth, perhaps one which the children have made. Use one big new white candle. Hang large alleluia banners from the ceiling. Have present symbols of new life, for example, spring flowers and butterflies and brightly colored eggs in an Easter basket.
2. Welcome the children with obvious happiness. Teach them a joyful Easter song. Add a few simple gestures.
3. Let the children comment on the new cloth and the decorations. Tell them that the word "alleluia" is a Hebrew word that means "Praise the Lord!"
4. Ask the children if they know why we are so happy today. Let them share their thoughts with the group. Remind them briefly of the sad events of Good Friday, then tell them that the death of Jesus on the cross only seemed to be the end of the life of Jesus. On Easter Sunday Jesus rose to new life, never to suffer or die again. And, even more, he wants us to share that new life.
5. Light the Easter candle and sing once again our Easter song of praise and thanks to God for the new life we celebrate.

Proclaim the Good News

1. We exercise the option of using the gospel reading from the Easter vigil in place of the gospel proper to Easter Sunday. John's story is a confused amalgam of tradition. The synoptic accounts are easier to follow.
2. Ask the children to listen to the story of how the friends of Jesus discovered that he was no longer dead but alive again. Then tell the story of Mk 16:1-7, supplying whatever background information is helpful to aid the children's understanding. Enliven the story for younger children with a simple flannel board presentation.
3. Acclaim the gospel with several joyful alleluias and then proclaim it.

Make Our Own the Good News of the New Life of Jesus

1. Have ready a large cardboard cross, ideally the one used last week on Passion Sunday. Tell the children that we will decorate the cross as a sign that Jesus is no longer dead but alive with new life.
2. Let each child make two paper flowers by gluing paper candy cups to one-and-a-half-inch-wide strips of green construction paper folded in half lengthwise (for strength). Or staple yellow stars to the stems and let the children draw the centers of their flowers or glue on yellow tissue paper centers. Because our time is so limited, the leader obviously must have all supplies completely ready. It is wise to distribute glue on squares of wax paper and not to give children bottles of glue. Ask the older children to help the younger ones.
3. Have pre-cut letters spelling "alleluia." Or have pre-traced letters and let older children cut them out.
4. Collect one flower from each child as a sign of the child's joy in the new life of Jesus. Glue the flowers in a cluster at the base of the cross. Glue the letters across the crossbeam. Let the children take the cross into the church when they rejoin the assembly and place it near the ambo.
5. Let the children take home their second flowers as reminders of our Easter liturgy.

Profess Our Faith

1. Proclaim the first reading:
- For older children who know well the story of the resurrection of Jesus, it would be best to proclaim the first reading before proclaiming the gospel, thus maintaining the traditional order of liturgical proclamation. The first reading, however, will make more sense to younger children after they have already reflected upon the events recounted in the gospel.
- Before proclaiming the reading, tell the children that we will listen to part of a speech that Peter made. Peter was so full of love and joy that he wanted to share the wonderful good news of Jesus with people who knew nothing about him.
- Proclaim the reading. Perhaps a good young reader, who is well-prepared, might proclaim the reading today.
2. Renew our baptismal promises:
- Tell the children that Easter is a wonderfully appropriate day to profess our faith in God. Ask the group to answer the following questions by saying, "I do! Alleluia!" Better, teach them to sing their response:

Leader: My brothers and sisters in God's family, today we celebrate the new life of Jesus and ask God that one day we, too, may have that new life. Let us together proclaim that we believe in God and let us promise to live as God wants.

53

	Do you believe in God, the Father almighty, who made heaven and earth?
All:	I do! Alleluia!
Leader:	Do you believe in Jesus Christ, God's only Son, who lived and died for us and rose to new life?
All:	I do! Alleluia!
Leader:	Do you promise to follow Jesus who leads us to God?
All:	I do! Alleluia!
Leader:	Do you believe in the Holy Spirit, who lives in us today to help us follow Jesus to God?
All:	I do! Alleluia!
Leader:	Do you believe that after we die we will rise again with Jesus to live with God forever?
All:	I do! Alleluia!
Leader:	God, the Father of Jesus and our Father, has given Jesus new life. God promises us new life, too. May God help us follow Jesus faithfully all our lives.
All:	Amen.

3. Conclude the renewal with a water rite to recall our baptismal life, the new life of Jesus in us. The leader might use a pine branch or a sprig of boxwood for the sprinkling. Sing an appropriate acclamation, perhaps Howard Hughes's "You Have Put on Christ," changing the words to "We have . . ." Or sing the acclamation "Springs of water, bless the Lord . . ." from the Easter vigil liturgy of baptism:

Other Possibilities:

1. The leaders of the parish children's liturgy of the word program and the parish staff might consider celebrating an entire liturgy for children on Easter Sunday, and not just the usual children's liturgy of the word. In addition to pleasing the children, to have a separate children's liturgy on Easter Sunday provides extra space in the adult assembly to help accommodate the large crowds of people who celebrate Easter by coming to church.

2. With time to practice and the help of a musician, a group of children might learn a traditional Easter hymn and sing it to open or to close our Easter liturgy of the word.

3. The gospel lends itself well to simple dramatization:
• After the proclamation of the gospel, the leader might reread it and have several children pantomime the action.
• Or older children who have time to prepare might present the gospel as a play. Let one child be the narrator and read a prepared script. Let two children be the women and learn their simple words. Let a child be "the angel of the Lord" and have the child learn the angel's words. Less formally, give the child a copy of the angel's words to read. Use a few simple props and costumes. Props and costumes, even very simple ones, help put young actors at ease.

4. Older children should reflect more deeply on the meaning of the resurrection:
• If there is opportunity to prepare the liturgy with the children, it would be helpful to have them look at the four gospels which the church presents to us on Easter: Mt 28:1-10, Mk 16:1-8, Lk 24:1-12 (the Easter vigil gospels) and Jn 20:1-9 (the Easter Sunday gospel).

Not one of the evangelists describes the resurrection itself. Rather the evangelists bear witness to the empty tomb and recount the post-resurrection appearances of Jesus. Were there any witnesses to the resurrection? Would scientific proof of the resurrection make a difference in our faith?

The best friends of Jesus were completely surprised and even reluctant to believe the good news that Jesus was yet the "living one."

The gospel writers do not agree on the details surrounding the finding of the empty tomb, and it is useless to try to harmonize their accounts. Unlike so many of us today, they simply were not interested in what we consider factual precision.

• Through a consideration of the above, help the children to realize that the importance of the resurrection does not lie in the after-death condition of the body of Jesus but in the difference that the life and death of Jesus make in the life of the church.

5. Mark's gospel ends with today's gospel passage, and ends strangely and abruptly with the fearful women fleeing from the tomb, afraid to tell anyone what they had experienced at the tomb. The so-called "longer ending" of the gospel, Mk 16:9-20, offers a summary of Jesus's resurrection appearances, but it differs so in vocabulary and style from the rest of Mark's gospel that most scholars think it was composed by someone other than Mark. Surely Mark knew that Jesus had been raised from the dead. He makes numerous references to the event in his gospel. He has the young man at the tomb report it (in our reading today). Why, then, did Mark not include any resurrection appearances? Was his original ending lost? Is he emphasizing that the earthly career of Jesus climaxed in his death and cannot be understood apart from it? Is he suggesting that the mystery of Jesus cannot be solved until the parousia? And thus that the word remains for his followers "Watch!"? (See Achtemeier, *Mark*, p.110.) Discuss these possibilities with older children. Perhaps they can suggest others.

6. It is generally accepted that the speeches in Acts are Lucan compositions reflecting the preaching of the early church and not actual accounts of what Peter and Paul and other early Christian leaders said. Proclaim the entire first reading to older children, and let them comment on how the early church summarized the life and significance of Jesus. It is interesting to note that the setting of the resurrection appearances was, at least sometimes, a meal. Our eucharistic meal commemorates not only the last supper Jesus had with his friends, but also the meals they had together after he rose from the dead. (See PNL, p.23.)

7. A sequence is a hymn sung or recited in the liturgy between the alleluia and the gospel. It was originally a long, drawn-out series of notes, called a "jubilatus," extending the final syllable of the alleluia. Texts were added to the jubilatus, forming a rhymed, metrical poem. Sequences were popular in medieval times.

There are thousands of sequences, some very famous, some very ornate. Today the western church retains only four sequences: the "Victimae Paschali Laudes" on Easter Sunday, the "Veni Sancte Spiritus" on Pentecost Sunday, the "Lauda Sion Salvatorem" on the feast of Corpus Christi and the "Stabat Mater Dolorosa" on the feast of Our Lady of Sorrows on September 15. The "Dies Irae," another famous sequence, was used until recently at requiem masses and on All Souls' Day.

• Give older children copies of the sequence for Easter Sunday. Give them a few moments to read it to themselves and then ask them to read it aloud together. Or invite a cantor to sing the sequence for the group. Perhaps some of the children would like to prepare a simple dramatization to accompany the reading or the singing. Discuss the meaning of the prayer. Ask the children to illustrate the sequence and to read it every day during Easter week, as the church used to do. A translation of the sequence follows this outline. Because it seems suitable for children, we use the translation of the *Daily Missal of the Mystical Body*, edited by the Maryknoll Fathers (New York: P.J. Kenedy and Sons, 1961). The leader might also consider the translation of Peter Scagnelli along with the musical setting which *Worship III* suggests.

8. With older children develop the Easter theme of the victory of light over darkness:

• Before the liturgy and with the help of some of the children, decorate a large white Easter candle with a cross, the numerals of the current year and various symbols of new life. Have the candle in a central position in the children's gathering space.

• Talk with the children about the light of Jesus that shines upon us and destroys the darkness of sin forever. Tell them briefly about the "Exultet," the magnificent Easter Song of the church, in which our joy in Christ our light and our freedom bursts forth exuberantly. Light the candle and say—better, sing—the opening verses of the "Exultet."

• Describe and explain the Paschal candle. Tell the children to look for it after they return to the church.

• Instead of decorating a cross, let older children decorate candles to take home. Have a supply of paint pens and suggest that the children draw on their candles flowers or other signs of Easter and write "Alleluia!"

• Charlotte Zolotow's *When the Wind Stops* is a short story, suitable for little children, which, on a natural level, treats the subject of life coming from death.

Sequence for Easter

The Holy Paschal work is wrought,
    The Victim's praise be told,
The loving Shepherd back has brought
    The sheep into his fold.
The Just and Innocent was slain
To reconcile to God again.

Death from the Lord of life has fled:
    The conflict strange is o'er;
Behold, he lives that was dead,
    And lives forevermore.
Mary, you sought him that day;
Tell what you saw on the way.

"I saw the empty cavern's gloom,
    The garments of the prison,
The Angel guardians of the tomb,
    The glory of the Risen."
We know that Christ has burst the grave,
Then, victor King, your people save.
          Amen. Alleluia.

Second Sunday of Easter

Lectionary for Masses with Children	Lectionary for Mass
*Acts 4:32-35	*Acts 4:32-35
*Ps 118:2-4,22-24	*Ps 118:2-4,13-15,22-24
I Jn 5:1-6	I Jn 5:1-6
**Jn 20:19-29	**Jn 20:19-31

Focus: We rejoice because we believe in Jesus, even though we have not seen him.

Gather the Children

1. Gather the children around a white Easter cloth. Continue to have present Easter symbols of joy and new life—butterflies, spring flowers, eggs, alleluia banners, large white candles, a cross decorated on Easter Sunday during the liturgy of the word. Point out that we still use our Easter decorations because we continue to celebrate the wonderful new life of Jesus.

2. Remind the children that the candle is a symbol of the presence of Jesus, the risen Lord, in our midst. Tell the group that we will certainly light the candle, but not yet.

3. Express our continuing joy in the new life of Jesus by singing the same Easter hymn we sang on Easter Day.

4. Tell the children that our celebration of Easter lasts for fifty days (even longer than Lent). During all this time we will celebrate joyfully the new life of Jesus.

Proclaim the Gospel

Note: The leader will notice that in its simplification of the gospel the translation used by LMC omits Jesus's words of greeting to his disciples "Peace be with you." The following suggestions presume the retention of this greeting.

1. Involve the children in the events described in the gospel:

• Remind the children of our gospel story of last week: some women had gone to the tomb of Jesus. A young man dressed in white had told them that Jesus was alive and that his disciples would see him in Galilee. The women had run from the tomb, frightened and confused, and had told no one what they had seen and heard.

• Ask the children to imagine that we are the disciples of Jesus and that it is Easter Sunday evening. The only thing we can think about is Jesus and what happened to him just a few days before.

• Ask the children to think about how they would feel in such a situation. Talk about such feelings as fear, disappointment, sadness, loneliness, worry, confusion. As the children share their thoughts, draw a big sad face.

• Ask the children to imagine that we are so sad and afraid that we have all gathered together in this room and locked the doors and the windows. Send a child to the doors and the windows to "check" that they are tightly closed and securely locked.

• Ask the children to imagine that all of a sudden Jesus is present with us. Light the Easter candle. Let the children react, expressing their feelings of surprise and fear and joy and wonder.

• Tell the children that the first word Jesus said to his disciples showed that he understood how they felt and that he wanted to help them. Ask if they can guess the word. Have ready large pre-cut, scrambled letters spelling out "Peace." Let the children arrange the letters properly and glue them in the middle of a piece of poster board.

• Continue the story by telling the children about Thomas:

Thomas was not present when Jesus appeared to the disciples on Easter Sunday evening. When the disciples told Thomas what had happened, Thomas couldn't believe it. Thomas said that he would not believe unless he could touch Jesus's hands and side.

A week later all the disciples, including Thomas, were together again in the same room, again with the doors locked. Jesus came to them once more. He again greeted them with the words, "Peace be with you." Then he talked to Thomas, inviting him to touch him and encouraging him to believe.

Thomas next said some beautiful words to Jesus which showed that he then believed firmly in Jesus. He said, "My Lord and my God!"

• Finish the story by quoting Jesus's final words to Thomas. Then ask the children if they know anyone who has never seen Jesus but who believes in him. Help them to realize that the words of Jesus apply to us.

2. Acclaim the gospel with several joyful alleluias and then proclaim it.

Make the Good News Our Own

1. Discuss with the children the meaning of the words of Jesus "Peace be with you."

• What did it mean to the disciples and to Thomas?

• Jesus wants to give all of us also his peace. What does the peace of the risen Christ mean to us? Include such ideas as the following: Jesus wants to take away our fears and our sadness, as he did for the disciples, to free us from struggles and quarreling and fighting, to forgive us, as he forgave Thomas for not believing, and to help us be forgiving to others.

• Ask the children if they can think of a time when we share a sign of peace with other people. Show them the proper way to exchange the greeting of peace and then encourage them to offer the sign of peace joyfully and sincerely at the proper time during the liturgy of the eucharist.

• Complete the "Peace" poster:

Give the children each a paper hand. For a more attractive poster use a small child's hand, and not an adult's hand, for the pattern. Let the children write their names on the hands, the older children helping the younger ones.

To symbolize that we would like to have the peace of the risen Jesus and to share that peace with everyone, have the children lay their hands on the poster surrounding the word "Peace." Then glue the hands onto the poster.

Let the children carry the poster into the church when then rejoin the adult assembly and place it near the ambo.

2. Say or sing a profession of faith. One used on Easter Sunday would be ideal.

3. Pray in the general intercessions that all people will know the good news of the new life of Jesus, that we will all share the peace of the risen Lord, that we will all one day have life in his name.

4. Give each child another paper hand to take home. Have written on these hands "Peace" in broad letters so that the children can color the letters. Ask the children to display the hands in their homes as a reminder of the Easter gift of peace which Jesus, our risen Lord, wants us to have.

5. "We Walk by Faith" by Marty Haugen would be an excellent hymn to teach the children, in fact, to teach the entire assembly. It is simple in thought and easy to sing. It expresses the longing of those who cannot see and touch the Lord, as Thomas and his friends could, to see the Lord one day "in full and endless sight."

Other Possibilities:

1. Explore the gospel more deeply with older children:

• We have not discussed Jesus's bestowal of the Holy Spirit on the disciples. John presents this event on Easter Sunday, the same event which Luke reserves for Pentecost Sunday, the fiftieth day after Easter. John represents the return of Jesus to the Father as a single spiritual reality, while Luke separates it chronologically into the resurrection, the ascension and the coming of the Holy Spirit in order to focus our attention separately on the various aspects of this great event. (The liturgy for Pentecost Sunday presents both accounts of the coming of the Holy Spirit: John's account, Jn 20:19-23, and Luke's account, Acts 2:1-11.) The specific gift which John associates with the coming of the Holy Spirit is the forgiveness of sin. Catholics have traditionally found in this passage the scriptural basis for the sacrament of reconciliation. Discuss with older children John's insight in presenting the Easter gift of the Holy Spirit as the power and the mission to forgive sin. Relate the forgiveness of sin to the spreading of the gospel, the power and the mission more often associated with the presence of the Spirit.

• Discuss with the children why the disciples were fearful, so fearful that they locked the doors of the room where they gathered. Scholars make the quite reasonable suggestion that the disciples were fearful that they might face the same horrible death as their master. It is also possible that they were afraid the authorities were after them for stealing the body of Jesus from the tomb in order to fake his resurrection. The locked doors appear again the next week when Thomas is present with his friends. Their function is quite different here. They serve as a witness to the resurrected Jesus: no ordinary living human being could pass through locked doors.

• Let us not be too hard on Thomas, whose very name and action survive in our phrase "doubting Thomas." Some scholars suggest that the story of Thomas was created by John to dramatize the doubt of the disciples at the appearance of the risen Jesus, a fact that the other evangelists, especially Luke, report, but which is strangely missing in the account of John. It is possible that an expression of doubt was originally a part of John's story, immediately preceding the otherwise not quite logical statement that Jesus showed his disciples his hands and his side, and that John transformed the doubt into a separate incident and attributed it to Thomas. (See Raymond Brown, AB, 29A, p.1031-2.) At any rate the final words of a disciple in the gospel of John are those of Thomas, and they constitute a magnificent expression of faith in Jesus. (Chapter 21 was probably not part of John's original gospel, although quite possibly the gospel never circulated without it.)

• Note that, although Jesus declares blessed those who do not see him and yet believe in him, such a condition is not the only source of joy. The disciples also rejoiced at the sight of the Lord. Their joy, though arising from a different source, was no less real than ours.

• Read to the children the last paragraph of the gospel (which the LMC omits) to help them appreciate the purpose of the gospels.

2. Among the literary devices which Luke uses in the Acts of the Apostles to keep the attention of his readers focused on the main purposes of his narrative are the three major summary passages which we read on this Second Sunday of Easter, one during each of the three years of the lectionary cycle. The passages present a beautiful picture of the early Christian community, though a picture which must surely color the real with the ideal. Today's reading, the second of the summary passages, describes the sharing of the early Christians. Encourage the children to live their lives as faithful followers of Jesus by discussing the sharing and then thinking about how we can imitate the early Christians in ways that are practical for our lives today.

3. To help older children understand the humiliation and exaltation of Jesus and how the Christian community shares the new life of Jesus, use the vivid and well-known imagery in Ps 118:22:

The stone which the builders rejected
has become the cornerstone.

Psalm 118 is perhaps the first psalm that the early Christian community used to describe the death and resurrection of Jesus. Introduce and discuss Peter's analogy of the Christian community as a building of living stones with Jesus as the living cornerstone (I Pt 2:4-7). Peter applies the words of Ps 118:22 to the risen Christ "who was rejected, but whose precious quality in God's sight is found in the new life he shares with those who come to him" (JBC, p.365).

Third Sunday of Easter

Lectionary for Masses with Children	Lectionary for Mass
**Acts 3:13-15,17-19	**Acts 3:13-15,17-19
Ps 4:1,3,6-7	Ps 4:2,4,7-8,9
- - - - -	I Jn 2:1-5
**Lk 24:35-48	**Lk 24:35-48

Focus: We rejoice in what we have hear about Jesus. We ask help to turn to God because of what we hear.

Gather the Children

1. Gather the children in their separate worship space, still dressed in all its Easter finery, and welcome the group with joy.
2. Remind the children why we come together for our special liturgy of the word: we gather to proclaim the word of God joyfully, to listen to it carefully and to think about its meaning for our lives.
3. Tell the children that today is the Third Sunday of Easter, and that we continue to celebrate the triumph of Jesus over sin and death. Be sure the children notice that our Easter decorations remain. Light the Easter candle and sing again the Easter song we have used for our previous Easter celebrations.

Proclaim the Gospel

1. Introduce the gospel by telling the children that we will hear once more about how Jesus showed himself to his disciples after his resurrection to help them believe the good news that he was really alive again.
2. Summarize Lk 24:36-43. A flannel board presentation would interest younger children.
3. Continue the gospel story:
• Jesus reminded his disciples that he had told them, before he died, that he would suffer and die and rise again, but they had not believed that something so terrible and so wonderful could happen to him.
• Then Jesus told his disciples that they should proclaim to all people what they had seen and heard, so that all people would turn to God because of what had happened.
4. Acclaim the gospel by singing several joyful alleluias. During the singing have one child pick up the lectionary reverently, hold it high, walk slowly to the leader and present the book. Then proclaim the gospel.

Make the Good News Our Own

1. Reinforce the gospel message by asking the children to restate what Jesus told the disciples to do.
2. Have ready a big paper with these words written on it in large letters:

> You have ... and ... Go ... others.

Fill in the spaces with pictures of an eye, an ear and a mouth for "seen," "heard" and "tell."
3. Ask the children what the disciples would want to tell others about Jesus. List their ideas on the paper, surrounding the sentence. Then arrange the ideas quickly into logical order and read them as a profession of faith in Jesus.

Share the First Reading

1. For older children who know well the story of Jesus the leader should preserve the traditional order of proclamation of readings and proclaim the first reading before proclaiming the gospel. Younger children, however, will follow today's liturgy of the word more easily if they hear the gospel first.
2. In preparation for sharing the first reading, the leader should read the entire, very interesting third chapter of the Acts of the Apostles.
3. Let the children share what they remember about Peter. Then remind them that Peter was the one whom Jesus chose to be the leader of his disciples after his death.
4. Tell the children that Peter spoke to the crowd about Jesus and did many wonderful things in his name.
5. Summarize quickly the story of Peter's cure of the crippled man, Acts 3:1-12,16, the event that occasioned the speech of Peter of which our reading is a part. Tell the children that Peter then told the crowd about who Jesus was, that it was trust in him that had given the crippled man perfect health and that they, too, should believe in Jesus.
6. Proclaim Peter's speech, simplifying it appropriately for younger children.

Respond to the Readings

1. Ask the children to think quietly of the wonderful things we have heard about Jesus.
2. Lead the group in praying the general intercessions. Pray that all people will hear the wonderful good news of Jesus and live better lives because of the life of Jesus among us.
3. Give each child a sticker that says "I've heard about Jesus!" Make the stickers of cheerful contact paper. Write on the contact paper with paint pens or permanent magic markers.

Other Possibilities:

1. Concentrate on the appearance of Jesus to his disciples (though it is essentially a repetition of last Sunday's gospel). Draw a parallel between the food and the words which Jesus and his disciples shared and our own sharing of word and food during our liturgy of word and eucharist today.
2. The most persistent theme of today's readings is that the scriptures show us that it was necessary for Jesus to suffer and die. Little children cannot understand this

fact, neither will it interest them; but an approach such as the following might interest older children:

- Focus their attention on the importance of the scriptures in the minds of the disciples and the early Christians:

Remind the children of the great sadness and the bitter disappointment of the friends of Jesus when he was crucified.

Tell the children that Jesus wanted his friends to know that his suffering and death and resurrection were always part of God's plan. In the gospel which we read today Jesus reminds his disciples that he had told them before his death that he would suffer and die and rise, but they had not been able to believe that such things could happen. Jesus also reminds his friends in today's gospel that God had told all the Jewish people in their scriptures, God's written word, about the suffering and rising of the promised one, but none had believed it would happen.

- Proclaim the appropriate parts of the gospel.
- Discuss briefly why God planned for Jesus to suffer and die and rise. Include both God's great love for us and the example of Jesus to us of perfect obedience to God's will.
- Respond to the gospel:

Give thanks for God's great love, a love so deeply expressed in the suffering and death of Jesus.

Pray that we will respond to the suffering and rising of Jesus by turning to God.

Pray that those who suffer innocently today will find hope and strength in the suffering of Jesus. The leader might bring along the newspaper and give specific examples of human suffering.

Sing Honeytree's "Father, Lift Me Up" or "Jesus, Lift Me Up" as a prayer that we will rise with Jesus.

3. An alternative approach to the readings, again best suited to older children, would be to move from the fact that the scriptures show us that the messiah had to suffer to the fact that we must open our own minds and hearts to God's word as found in the scriptures. If the leader uses this approach, the children might compose a profession of faith and write it on a scroll. Then one child can proclaim the children's profession of faith to the whole group, as Peter proclaimed his belief in Jesus to the crowd who gathered after Peter cured the crippled man.

4. Focus on the thought, stated in Peter's speech and repeated in the gospel, that the disciples were witnesses of what happened to Jesus. Lead into our own responsibility to be witnesses to Jesus today.

Fourth Sunday of Easter

Lectionary for Masses with Children	Lectionary for Mass
**Acts 4:8-12	**Acts 4:8-12
*Ps 118:1 and 21, 22-23	*Ps 118:1,8-9,21-23,26,21-29
*I Jn 3:1-2	*I Jn 3:1-2
**Jn 10:11-16	**Jn 10:11-18

Focus: Jesus, our good shepherd, saves us and cares for us. We rejoice in the wonderful love of God.

Gather the Children

1. Gather the children in their worship space, still decorated in all Easter joy. Tell the children explicitly that we continue to celebrate Easter. Then, as for the last three Sundays, light the Easter candle and sing an Easter hymn.
2. Let the children share their thoughts about why we gather for our special liturgy of the word. Join them in a few moments of silent prayer, asking God to help us listen well to the word.

Prepare the Children for the Proclamation of the Gospel

1. Show the children a large cardboard shepherd's staff. Let them identify it and then share what they know about shepherds.
2. For little children have ready a simple visual display of sheep and a shepherd. For example, have sheep cut from stick-on name tags, a shepherd, a fence of construction paper, a pond of aluminum foil, and green poster board on which to lay out the display. If possible, use as many sheep as there are children present. Move the figures around as the discussion progresses, the sheep following the shepherd and the shepherd taking care to see that none is hurt or lost.
3. Focus on the qualities of a good shepherd: a good shepherd knows the sheep, loves them, cares for them and protects them.

Proclaim the Gospel

1. Introduce the theme of the gospel by writing "Jesus" on the shepherd in the above display. Tell the children that Jesus calls himself the good shepherd. Then ask the children who the sheep are. They will know! Unless the number of children precludes it, write the names of the children on the sheep.
2. Ask the children why Jesus describes himself as our good shepherd. Help them relate the qualities of a good shepherd to the love of Jesus for us.
3. Ask the children to stand and listen to the beautiful words that Jesus used when he told us that he is our good shepherd. Ask the children to imagine that Jesus himself is here, speaking these words to us.
4. Acclaim the gospel appropriately in song and then proclaim it slowly and prayerfully.

Respond to the News of God's Wonderful Love

1. Ask the children to sit down again and to think quietly about how much Jesus, our good shepherd, loves us. Then lead them in a prayer of thanksgiving for the wonderful love of Jesus. The leader might pray as follows:

> Gentle Jesus, our good shepherd,
> thank you for your loving care.
> We love you very much.
> We will follow where you lead us.
> We are safe and happy with you.
> We give our lives to you,
> because you gave your life for us.
> Protect us now on earth,
> and one day take us home forever
> to live with you, the Father and the Holy Spirit.
> Amen.

2. Symbolize our willingness to follow Jesus, our good shepherd:
- Have ready several large paper sheep. (Sheep are easy to draw—a curly outline, four straight lines for legs, and a big eye will do.) Let the children suggest ways we can follow Jesus. Help them to be practical. Record the ideas on the sheep in simple pictures or in words.
- Choose children to carry the large staff and the sheep when the group rejoins the adult assembly, and lay them near the ambo.
3. Give each child one of the small sheep to stick on his or her clothing and wear home. Or let each child take home a picture of a sheep with enough space around it to add later a picture of the good shepherd, Jesus.
4. To conclude the liturgy teach the children a song which sings of God's shepherd-like love for us.

Other Possibilities:
1. Proclaim the reading from the Acts of the Apostles:
- To prepare for today's liturgy, the leader should read and enjoy Acts 3:1-4:31. The story is action-packed and the children will love it.
- The children should remember some things about Peter from our last few Sunday liturgies of the word. Let them remind each other of what they know about the great apostle.
- Help the children realize that Peter was a person who believed strongly in the great love of God for us. He was so happy in that love that he wanted to tell eve-

ryone about it. Because of his strong faith and love, God gave Peter the power of Jesus to do some of the wonderful things Jesus had done and to speak boldly about Jesus.

• Let the children recall what they remember, from last Sunday's reading from Acts, about Peter's cure of the crippled man and his speech to the crowd of amazed witnesses.

• Summarize the story of what happened to Peter and John after Peter's speech to the crowd: the two men were thrown into prison for the night, questioned the next day by the religious leaders of the people, released because so many people had seen the remarkable cure, but ordered never again to mention the name of Jesus. Peter and John returned to their own people and prayed to God for the strength to continue to speak and heal in the name of Jesus.

• Explain that our reading today tells us what Peter said to the religious leaders when they questioned him. Ask the children to imagine that they were there and to listen carefully to Peter's words.

• Proclaim the reading.

2. Pray Ps 118 in response to the first reading:

• Suggest that, after their release from prison, Peter and John might have praised God in the words of our responsorial psalm. Ask the children to imagine that we are with Peter and John and to join them in their praise of God.

• Teach the children to sing the psalm refrain, then pray the psalm with the children. If there are good readers in the group, let them read the verses. With very young children, the leader should read—better, sing—the verses.

3. For older children, in place of the display of sheep and shepherd described above, have a large cardboard staff and one or two large cardboard sheep. Write on the staff the qualities of Jesus that lead us to call him our good shepherd. Write on the sheep suggestions from the children about how we can follow Jesus in our lives today.

4. From the discussion of Jesus as our good shepherd, lead into the role of Peter and the apostles as the shepherds of the early church, and then into the role of bishops and pastors as shepherds of the church today. Tell the children the names of their bishop and their pastor.

5. Little children would enjoy Golden MacDonald's *Little Lost Lamb*. The story tells of a shepherd boy who returns to the mountain pastures at night to seek his little lost lamb. It will interest the leader who is familiar with children's literature to know that "Golden MacDonald" is the same person as Margaret Wise Brown. The lovely story *Little Lost Lamb* has all the simplicity and all the gentleness for which we so love Margaret Wise Brown's children's books.

6. With older children, discuss the importance of the name Jesus, both to the early Christians, as we learn from the first reading, and to us today.

7. See the outline for the Second Sunday of Easter for comments on Jesus as "the stone rejected by the builders" which "has become the cornerstone," a description which the author of the our first reading took from Ps 118, our responsorial psalm.

8. Our reading from the first letter of John is surely one of the most beautiful passages in the New Testament. Proclaim the reading, and let it spark a discussion of Christian hope and the unspeakable joys of our life to come. Tell the children that the reading is often used at masses for the dead.

Fifth Sunday of Easter

Lectionary for Masses with Children	Lectionary for Mass
*Acts 9:26-28	*Acts 9:26-31
Ps 22:27,30-31	Ps 22:26-27,28,30,31-32
*I Jn 3:18	*I Jn 3:18-24
**Jn 15:1-5,7-8	**Jn 15:1-8

Focus: "I am the vine. You are the branches." We rejoice in the life of Jesus within us and pray that his life in us will grow.

Gather the Children

1. Gather the children in their worship space. Once again use Easter decorations, light the Easter candle, sing an Easter song, and remind the children that we continue our Easter celebration.
2. Remind the children why we gather for our special liturgy of the word and ask them to pray silently that the word of God will live and grow in our minds and our hearts.

Proclaim the Gospel

1. Prepare the children for the gospel by helping them to understand the analogy of the vine and the branches:
- Have present a living, growing vine, for example, a pot of ivy.

Let the children share what they know about the care of plants. Comment on how wonderful it is that a vine can grow so long, that even leaves far removed from the roots of the plant and the soil can draw their nourishment through the long main vine.

Pull a leaf off the vine and talk with the children about how the leaf will die now that it has been cut off from the source of its life.

- Extend the discussion by talking about grapevines. A grapevine has a big main vine and many smaller branches. It produces leaves, flowers and finally grapes. It is one of the most characteristic plants of Palestine and would have been very familiar to the people of Jesus's time. Show some pictures or slides of a large grapevine.
2. Relate the above discussion to the life of Jesus within us:
- Jesus liked to explain things by using images familiar to the people with whom he was speaking. In today's gospel Jesus is talking with his disciples. He uses the image of the vine and the branches to help them understand how they share his life.
- Summarize the ideas of Jn 15:5. In the verse, Jesus tells his disciples that he is the vine and they are the branches. Ask the children what they think Jesus meant by those words. Help them to realize that Jesus is saying that the disciples must live in him and share his life if they are to be his good disciples. Sketch a large vine and several branches while talking, write "Jesus" on the main vine and the names of some of the disciples on the branches. Finish the sketch by adding leaves and clusters of grapes.

- Extend the discussion by telling the children that Jesus meant his words for all his friends everywhere and always, including us, as well as for his disciples who were there when he said them. Add to the branches of the vine the names of several children and several adults whom all the children know.
3. Proclaim the gospel:
- Ask the children to stand and listen to the beautiful words of Jesus about his life in us.
- Acclaim the gospel with joyful alleluias. Have one child pick up the lectionary and carry it reverently to the leader during the singing.
- Proclaim enough of the gospel to impart its meaning and its mood, but not so much as to lose the attention of the children.

Relate the Good News to Our Lives

1. Ask the children to thank Jesus quietly for the wonderful privilege of sharing his life.
2. Then ask them how we can nourish the life of Jesus within us. As the children talk, include thoughts from our reading from the letter of John (not limited necessarily to the extremely brief simplification of the LMC): we know that Jesus remains in us if we keep his commandments to believe in him and to love one another. Help the children to be practical, particularly on the last point.
3. Make a poster to symbolize our desire to live in Jesus:
- Have ready a poster board with a large vine painted on it. Or paint the vine on a large grocery bag completely cut open. Give each child a paper leaf.
- Tell the children that we will glue the leaves onto the vine as a sign that we want to live in Jesus.
- Ask the children to think about specific ways they will try, during the next few days, to nourish the life of Jesus within themselves. Do not ask the children to speak their thoughts aloud, but only to reflect prayerfully.
- Collect the leaves and glue them to the vine. Write across the bottom of the poster the words of Jesus "I am the vine, you are the branches." Let the children carry their poster into the church when they rejoin the adult assembly and place it near the ambo.
- Provide appropriate, reflective background music as the children assemble their poster.
4. Tell the children of the words of Jesus in Jn 15:7. Discuss the wonderful promise of Jesus that he will give us what we ask if we live in him. Then lead the group in praying the general intercessions, confident that God hears our prayers and answers them.
5. Give the children pictures of a grape vine to take

home and color. Or have a calligrapher make a hand-out with Jesus's words "I am the vine, you are the branches." Let the children take home the papers and decorate them with vines and branches and fruit.

6. Conclude the liturgy of the word by teaching the children a song about Jesus's analogy of the vine and the branches.

Other Possibilities:

1. For older children, include the opening verses of the gospel which speak of God the Father as the vine-dresser who prunes the vines and trims them clean to increase their yield. Discuss how God might prune and trim us so that we will share more fully the life of Jesus within us.

2. Explain to older children that, as always for the last three Sundays of the Easter season, the gospel reading is from John's long discourse of Jesus to his disciples at the last supper. Although it might at first seem strange that we return during the Easter season to the night before the death of Jesus, it is not at all strange if we think of the death and resurrection of Jesus as one glorious event, as does the author of the fourth gospel. With the closest friends of Jesus we listen to his loving, intimate words of parting as he faces the hour of his glorification by the Father. It is a privilege, indeed, and one which we, unlike the disciples, experience with an Easter faith.

3. The reading today from the Acts of the Apostles focuses on the great apostle Paul. It would be good to remind the children of some of the exciting facts about the early life and the conversion of Paul. Then continue to speak of Paul as one who believed in Jesus and loved him with his whole being, one who really understood that his life derived its meaning from the life of Jesus within him.

4. It would appropriate for the Easter season and would also be excellent preparation of the children for today's liturgy of the word to study Paul in more detail than the time during our liturgy itself allows. The *Sadlier Scripture Series* filmstrip "Paul" offers a good summary of the life and work of Paul. Although it is too difficult for younger children, it contains good material for older children and for the leader.

5. Share with older children more of our reading from the first letter of John. Focus on John's injunction to love in deed and not just in word. Give examples of people who act upon their Christian faith in exemplary ways. Include people whom the children know or who are at least local people, and not just the very famous. If the leader cannot think of "ordinary" people who lead exemplary lives, he or she should think harder. There are wonderful Christians all around us and we all—adults as well as children—should learn to notice and to value and to emulate them.

Sixth Sunday of Easter

Lectionary for Masses with Children	Lectionary for Mass
*Acts 10:25-26,34-35,44-48	*Acts 10:25-26,34-35,44-48
Ps 98:1-2,3-4	Ps 98:1,2-3,3-4
**I Jn 4:7-10	**I Jn 4:7-10
**Jn 15:9-14	**Jn 15:9-17

Focus: "Love one another as I have loved you." We rejoice in the great love of Jesus and pray to obey his command to imitate that love.

Gather the Children

1. Gather the children in their worship space, still decorated in all Easter finery. Tell the children explicitly that we continue to celebrate Easter. Light the Easter candle and sing an Easter song.
2. Ask the children why we gather for our special liturgy of the word. Help them remind each other that we are here to listen to the word of God and to respond faithfully to that word with unselfish love.

Reflect on the Meaning of Love

1. Have a large felt or poster board heart.
• Ask the children what a picture of a heart makes people think of. Let them share their ideas about loving and being loved. As the children talk, lay on the heart felt or heavy paper letters spelling "love."
• Ask the children to think about what the world would be like if everyone were loving. Help them to realize that when people are loving, people are more likely to be happy.
2. To summarize the discussion and to help the children associate love and joy, place on the heart, surrounding the word "love," pictures of people with joyful faces.

Proclaim the Gospel

1. Set the scene:
• Tell the children that our gospel today, like last week's gospel and next week's gospel, tells us things Jesus said to his disciples at the last supper.
• Ask the children to imagine that they were at the last supper. Describe the mood of the meal. Focus on the great love that the members of the group had for each other and on their joy at being together. Quiet, reflective music would help recreate the mood of the meal.
• Remind the children that Jesus knew that he would soon die and rise to new life. The disciples, however, did not seem to understand what was about to happen. Ask the children what they think Jesus said to his friends as the time came for him to leave them and return to God. Tell the children that Jesus assured them of his love and told them once again that the way to live in his love was to love each other.
• Ask the children how they would feel if they were

with Jesus as he talked about leaving them. Ask them if the words of Jesus would make them stronger and less afraid. Help them to see that the words of Jesus, though spoken during hours of sadness and fear, filled his disciples with love and joy and a desire to prolong and to share that love and joy.
2. Ask the children to stand and listen carefully to some of the last words of Jesus to his disciples. Acclaim the gospel with a joyful alleluia. Have one child pick up the lectionary and carry it reverently during the singing to the leader. Then proclaim the gospel.
3. Ask the children to think quietly for a few moments about the great love of Jesus for us, about the love he wants us to have for each other, and about the joy he wants to share so fully with us. Then lead the children in a short prayer thanking God for all these things.

Profess with the Children That God Is Love

1. With older children it would be better for the leader to rearrange the presentation to maintain the traditional order of proclamation of the readings, and proclaim the first reading before the gospel. Younger children, however, will understand the readings more easily and more fully if the leader first proclaims the gospel and then expands upon Jesus's words about love with the ideas of the second reading.
2. Prepare the children to hear the second reading by presenting some background information:
• Refer to the above discussion about the meaning of love. Say to the children that another of our readings today tells us something very important about love. Remove the word and the pictures from the heart and lay on the heart three short horizontal lines in a row, two lines in a row below the first three, and four more lines in a row below the second two. Arouse the curiosity of the children by telling them that the spaces represent a message about love which we will hear when we read the reading.
• Explain that our reading is part of a letter that a Christian of the early years of the church wrote to some of his friends. We do not know for sure who wrote the letter, but we call him John. John wanted to tell his friends about the great love God had for them. The children will listen to the reading with more interest if the leader has printed the reading on a big piece of stationery and sealed it in a big envelope. Take the letter out of the envelope while asking the children if they would like to hear it.
3. Ask the children to listen carefully to the letter of

John for his beautiful words about love. Ask them further to see if they can discover what the sentence on the heart is. Then proclaim the reading.

4. With the help of scrambled felt or heavy paper letters spelling out "God is love," let the children identify the message on the heart. Give the children as much help as they need to do it quickly. Remove the horizontal lines and glue the words onto the heart.

5. Ask the children to profess their faith in our God who is love by responding in song "Amen! Alleluia!" to each of the following statements. The children might sing their response to the melody they used for their profession of faith on Easter Sunday.

> We believe in God who is love.
> We believe that God showed us that love by sending us Jesus.
> We believe that Jesus loves us.
> We believe that Jesus gave his life for us.
> We believe that Jesus wants us to share his joy.
> We believe that Jesus is our friend.
> We believe in the Holy Spirit, the Spirit of Jesus, who helps us love each other as Jesus loves us.
> We believe that we will live forever in the love of the Father, the Son and the Holy Spirit.

6. Let the children offer suggestions as to how we can love each other as Jesus loves us. Help them to be specific and practical. Then pray in the general intercessions that we and all of God's children everywhere will love each other as Jesus asks us, and so be his friends and share his joy.

7. Give each child a heart-shaped pendant with the message "God is love!" written on it. Make the pendants of red felt or red poster board and red ribbon, and write on them with white paint pen. Ask the children to wear their pendants all day to proclaim to others the wonderful truth that God is love.

Other Possibilities:

1. To deepen in the minds and hearts of older children the meaning of the statement that God is love:

● Ask the children why they think John wrote to his friends that God is love. Help them to see that it was God's action in their lives that led the early Christians to say that God is love. Bring into the discussion ideas from the gospel we have just heard. Then extend the discussion by including some of the ideas we have considered during the last several Sundays: the great love of God, who sent us Jesus; the love of Jesus, who lived and died for us, who wants to give us peace, who is our good shepherd, who wants to share his life with us as the vine and the branches share life. During the discussion show symbols of God's love which the children have used during recent liturgies of the word. Lay the symbols on the heart which proclaims that God is love. Tell the children that John must have had all these things in mind when he wrote to his friends.

● Ask the children how they would explain that God is love to someone who has never heard about Jesus. Strive to implant in the minds and hearts of the children that, just as Jesus revealed the love of God to the world in which he lived by the way he lived, so we also reveal the love of God to the world in which we live by the way we live.

2. Make a banner to proclaim that God is love by gluing the heart we have used throughout the liturgy onto a piece of heavy cloth, threading a rod into a casing sewn into the cloth, and attaching a cord to the rod. Decorate the banner with lace, ruffles or other sewing trim that pleases the children. Have ready a pole to hold and carry the banner. Let the children carry the banner into the church when they rejoin the adult assembly and place it near the ambo. In this way, the children will share with the assembly their symbolic expression of the simple, yet profound, profession of faith that God is love. After the liturgy hang the banner in the children's gathering space so that they may see it during future liturgies of the word.

3. There are several other profound and beautiful ideas in today's gospel, any one of which could be developed fruitfully with children—Christian joy, for example, or friendship or God's choice of us.

4. The story of Peter and Cornelius in Acts 10, of which our first reading is a part, would be an interesting one for the children to hear. Use it to show how Peter deepened his understanding of the meaning of God's love. The story also calls to our attention the work of the Holy Spirit in the church, an appropriate consideration as we prepare for the feast of Pentecost, the great celebration of the outpouring of the Spirit on the world.

5. There is good, reflective music to support our thought this day that God is love. Clarence Rivers' "God Is Love" (from *American Mass Program*) is simple and inspiring.

Feast of the Ascension

Lectionary for Masses with Children	Lectionary for Mass
**Acts 1:8-11	**Acts 1:1-11
*Ps 47:1-2,5-6,7-8	*Ps 47:2-3,6-7,8-9
*Eph 1:17-21	*Eph 1:17-23
Mk 16:15-20	**Mk 16:15-20

Focus: Be my witnesses to the ends of the earth.

Gather the Children

1. For today's feast of the Ascension decorate the children's gathering space with all the joy of Easter. In addition to a white gathering cloth, a large white candle, and other Easter decorations, have around the room large cardboard silhouettes of various familiar and unfamiliar countries, including the United States. We shall use the silhouettes as the liturgy progresses. As always display the lectionary prominently.

2. Welcome the children happily and thank them for their presence at our holyday liturgy. Remind the children that we continue today our rejoicing in the glorious Easter victory of Jesus over sin and death. Light the Easter candle and pray the traditional Easter verse:

Leader: Christ is risen, alleluia!
All: Christ is truly risen, alleluia!

3. Tell the children that our celebration today centers on the fact that after God raised Jesus from the dead, God took Jesus to heaven and made him king of the entire universe. Make frequent use of the word "ascension" so that the children become familiar with it. Teach the group a lively song which celebrates either the ascension of Jesus to God or his dominion over all. If the leader chooses a hymn the assembly will sing after the children return from their separate liturgy of the word, it will please the children as well as enhance the community celebration.

Proclaim the First Reading

1. Our first reading today presents the opening verses of the Acts of the Apostles. In the passage Luke describes the ascension of Jesus as the conclusion of a resurrection appearance of Jesus to his disciples. To introduce the story, draw upon our Easter gospel readings and remind the children of some of the times Jesus showed himself to his friends after he rose to new life. Remind the children also, calling upon the thoughts of our last two Sunday readings from the gospel of John, that Jesus was fully aware, even from before his death, that he was soon to return to God and leave his disciples without his physical presence. Show the children a great artist's picture of the resurrected Jesus with his disciples, and talk of the love that Jesus and his friends had for each other.

2. Remind the children, once again drawing upon our recent readings from John's gospel and also anticipating the celebration of Pentecost, that Jesus did not plan to leave his friends entirely on their own as they set about their mission of carrying out his work after his death. Jesus promised to send them the Holy Spirit as a helper, a teacher, a comforter.

3. Ask the children to listen carefully during the proclamation of the reading both for Luke's description of the ascension of Jesus and for Jesus's description of what was to be the mission of his disciples after his return to God. Then proclaim the reading.

4. Review quickly Luke's description of the ascension of Jesus, using a well-known work of art or, for younger children, simply the flannel board. Help the children to notice that the presence of the Holy Spirit was to help the apostles of Jesus be his witnesses throughout the world.

Proclaim the Gospel

1. Tell the children that our gospel reading today gives another account of the ascension of Jesus. The passage forms the (traditional) conclusion of the gospel of Mark. Tell the children that, because we always listen with special attention to the gospel, we will read the story of the ascension once again. Ask older children to listen for likenesses and differences between the gospel account of the ascension and Luke's account of the event in Acts.

2. Ask the children to stand. Acclaim the gospel suitably for Eastertide, ideally in song and procession, and then proclaim the reading.

Illustrate Our Witness to Jesus

1. Ask the children what Jesus wanted his disciples to do after his return to God. Help the group to repeat the injunction of Jesus which we read in Acts to be his witnesses "even to the ends of the earth" or his command in the gospel to "proclaim the good news to all creation." Explain the work of missionaries in spreading the gospel, speaking of their work both among people in remote parts of our world and among people in unevangelized parts of our own country.

2. Teach the children to sing Robert E. Kreutz's

Proclaim his marvelous deeds
to all the nations.

3. Then conduct the following simple ritual to illustrate the witness to himself that Jesus commands.

• Divide the children into small groups. Give one child in each group a cardboard silhouette of a familiar country, and, if necessary, help the children to identify the countries. Give another child in each group a paper cross as a symbol of the saving work of Jesus in the world.

• The leader should face the first group of children

and ask the question, "Does Jesus want us to be his witnesses to the country of . . .?" The children should answer "Yes!" The child who holds the silhouette should lay the silhouette on the gathering cloth, and the child who holds the cross should place the cross on the silhouette. The action should continue until each group has had its turn.

• When all the silhouettes are on the cloth, the entire group should sing Kreutz's verse several times.

Profess Our Faith in Jesus

1. Our readings today focus our attention on various articles of our faith, beliefs which we profess when we pray the familiar creeds, the Nicene Creed and the Apostles' Creed. Point out this fact to older children and pray a creed with them.

2. Younger children might profess their faith by repeating after the leader:

Jesus rose from the dead. Alleluia!
Jesus ascended into heaven. Alleluia!
Jesus is seated at the right hand of God. Alleluia!
Jesus will come again in glory to judge the living and the dead! Alleluia!
The kingdom of Jesus will have no end. Alleluia!

To sing the alleluia's would, as always, be ideal. If several children, chosen and prepared in advance of the liturgy, accompany the singing of the alleluia's with simple musical instruments, the profession of faith will be joyous and even more impressive.

Other Possibilities:

1. Guided by Luke's statement in today's reading from Acts that Jesus, after his death, showed himself to his disciples for forty days, the church commemorates the ascension of Jesus on the fortieth day of Easter. The fortieth day falls on the Thursday after the Sixth Sunday of Easter. It is likely, however, that Luke meant the number forty as a symbolic suggestion of completeness. Acts, the gospel of Luke and the "longer ending" of the gospel of Mark record the ascension as a resurrection appearance. Matthew does not describe the ascension directly, but stresses the continuing presence of Jesus with the church. John's great last supper discourse, from which we always read for the last three Sundays of Easter, clearly pictures as one great event the death of Jesus, his resurrection and his return to God. Today's feast, then, is not a historical commemoration, but a focusing on one aspect of the resurrection of Jesus: Jesus lives now in glory with God and shares his dominion over all. The readings ask us to consider our role in continuing the work of Jesus in the world. Ascension Thursday is a holyday of obligation for American Catholics.

2. Tell older children that our first reading (using the longer selection of the LM) serves as a bridge between the two great works of Luke, his gospel and the Acts of the Apostles. The passage presents a summary of the third gospel and a preview of the Acts of the Apostles, two volumes which their author quite likely conceived as a single work. What does Luke state was the subject matter of his "first account"? What is the power that Luke states the Holy Spirit would give the apostles? Tell the children that the book of Acts does really show the spread of the church from Jerusalem, the center of sacred history (especially for Luke), to surrounding Judea, to neighboring Samaria, and eventually to Rome, which easily fits Luke's first-century middle eastern description of "the ends of the earth." Draw upon our Easter readings from Acts to illustrate the spread of the gospel.

3. Give more thought to today's gospel:

• Ask older children to look in their bibles at Mk 16:9-20, the passage in which our gospel reading is embedded. Show them that the passage includes what seems to be a concise summary of resurrection appearances which other gospels, particularly Luke's and John's, record with greater length. For example, the passage gives a very short retelling of Luke's long Emmaus story. Point out the great commission of Jesus to his disciples. Only in Mark does Jesus promise them the power to perform "signs." It is a power which we see employed many times in Acts, especially by Peter, John and Paul. Point out the specific inclusion of the seating of Jesus at "God's right hand."

• Discuss further the meaning of the "signs" that Jesus promised would accompany those who believe the good news. Did Jesus mean his words literally? Surely such signs are attested in Acts. Are they historical fact? Does God really sometimes suspend the usual laws of nature? If the signs are not historical fact, what are they? What is their purpose? Do those who believe the good news today have the power to work "signs"?

• Tell the children that no one knows for sure how Mark ended his gospel. Some ancient manuscripts end with 16:8, but, because that ending is so abrupt and so strange, many scholars think that Mark's original ending has been lost. (Recall, however, Paul Achtemeier's thoughts on the ending of Mark, to which we referred in our discussion of Mk 16:1-8, our Easter gospel.) Verses 9-20, which the church has traditionally accepted as the conclusion of Mark's gospel, comprise the so-called "longer ending" of the gospel. The passage is very old, probably from the second century (JBC). Most scholars agree that the passage cannot be Mark's because it differs significantly from the rest of Mark's work in style and thought. The manuscript tradition preserves two other, shorter and also decidedly non-Markan, endings of the gospel. The "shorter ending" of the gospel seems to be a partial vindication of the disciples, whom Mark so often describes in less than favorable terms. The strange third ending, the "Freer Logion," is probably a fourth or fifth century gloss. St. Jerome knew of it. The passage is contained in a manuscript in the Freer Gallery of Art in Washington, DC.

4. Psalm 47 celebrates the glorious reign of the Lord over all the earth. The joyful prayer calls upon all people to clap their hands and shout for joy because the Lord is king. Verses 6-7 suggest that the psalm was recited during the coronation of the king of Israel or perhaps on the anniversary of his coronation. The use of the psalm in today's liturgy illustrates the ease with which the church applies to the Lord Jesus Old Testa-

ment concepts of God. Explain the psalm to the children and then pray it in song. Younger children would love to take the psalm literally and praise God by clapping, shouting, singing and horn-playing.

5. Present to older children our beautiful reading from the letter to the Ephesians:

• Read the children Eph 1:15-16. These verses introduce today's lectionary selection as a prayer for the readers of the letter, for whom, because of their faith in the Lord Jesus and their love for each other, the author of the letter gives abundant thanks.

• Explain that the reading is a petition that "the holy ones" and "believers" to whom the letter is addressed know God clearly and understand the work God has accomplished in Christ. After the children grasp the flow of the reading, proclaim the reading to them using the simplified version of the LMC so that the children might more easily understand the reading and appreciate its beauty. Then let the children compose their own prayers for the church today, basing their thoughts on the thoughts in the passage upon which they have just reflected.

• Reread the last lines of the passage and let the children comment on the aptness of the reading for today's feast of the dominion of Christ over the church, indeed, over the universe.

• It is an interesting fact that "the letter of Paul to the Ephesians" was probably not written by the apostle Paul, was quite likely not composed for the church at Ephesus, and even deviates in structure from the usual New Testament letter. If the children are interested, send them to a good New Testament commentary to find supporting evidence for the three assertions.

6. The lovely village of Tissington in Derbyshire, England, celebrates the feast of the Ascension with wonderful splendor. In thanksgiving for their water, the villagers "dress," that is, decorate, their five wells with biblical scenes that are made of bark, lichens, moss and hundreds of fresh flower blossoms. People come from far and wide to view the remarkable scenes. The villagers and many of their visitors celebrate an Ascension Day liturgy in the village church, then process to the wells for their blessing. Tradition has it that the custom of "well-dressing" on Ascension Day began in the little village in the mid-fourteenth century, when the villagers believed that their pure water preserved them from the ravages of the Black Death. Tell the children about the celebration and suggest that later at home they draw biblical scenes of their own using only pictures of flowers. Or arrange for an artist to draw a scene of flowers for the children to take home and color.

Seventh Sunday of Easter

Lectionary for Masses with Children	Lectionary for Mass
**Acts 1:15-17,20-26	**Acts 1:15-17,20-26
Ps 103:1-2,19-20	Ps 103:1-2,11-12,19-20
*I Jn 4:11-13	*I Jn 4:11-16
**Jn 17:11	**Jn 17:11-19

Focus: We await the coming of the Holy Spirit. While we wait we pray for the love, the joy, the peace which the Spirit gives.

Gather the Children

1. Once more have present all the Easter decorations. Sing an Easter song, light the Easter candle and tell the children that we are still celebrating Easter, the Great Sunday.
2. Pray with the children that we will listen well to the word of God and be faithful witnesses to that word with our lives.

Proclaim the Gospel

1. Set the scene:
• Tell the children that our gospel today, as for the last two Sundays, is part of John the Evangelist's account of the last supper and presents some of the things that Jesus said to his disciples at that supper on the night before he died. Because Jesus knew he was soon to leave his friends, he gave them a "good-bye talk" or, more technically, a "farewell discourse." Ask the children to think about the sadness of Jesus and his friends, of the great love they had for each other, and of the joy the disciples felt in the presence of Jesus. Give the children a few quiet moments to think. Play reflective music to help recreate the mood of the occasion.
• Tell the children that John concludes the last discourse of Jesus to his friends with a prayer. Ask the group to imagine Jesus and his friends standing up, with outstretched arms, open hands and eyes raised to heaven, the classic Jewish attitude of prayer. Ask the children to think of Jesus speaking to God while his friends listened.
• Tell the children that Jesus prayed first for himself, then for his disciples, and finally for all those who would ever believe in him, including us. Our gospel today is that part of Jesus's prayer in which he prays for his disciples. He asks God to protect them and to help them keep and share the word of God which he has given to them.
• Because the gospel is reflective and not at all active, the children will respond more eagerly to the presentation if they have something to look at. Show them a slide or a picture of the last supper by a great artist.
2. Proclaim the gospel:
• Ask the children to stand and assume the attitude of prayer of Jesus and his friends while we read the gospel.
• Acclaim the gospel with an appropriate alleluia, then proclaim the reading slowly and prayerfully, re-taining the majestic beauty and intimacy of the prayer. For older children the leader might like to proclaim more than the one verse selected by the LMC.
3. Ask the children to sit down quietly and to think about how much Jesus loved his friends. Remind them that Jesus loves us, too. Lead the children in quiet prayer for the love, the joy and the care of Jesus and the Father for us. The leader may pray as follows:

Father,
we love you.
Live in us with your love
and let us live in you.
Protect us,
as Jesus protected his friends.
Fill us with your word of love
and give us the joy of Jesus.
Make us one in love with each other,
even as you and Jesus are one.
We pray this through Jesus,
your Son and your word of love.
Amen.

Anticipate the Great Feast of Pentecost

1. Summarize Jesus's promise of the Holy Spirit and his ascension. Use the account given in Acts 1:1-11, the first reading from the feast of the Ascension, this past Thursday. (The leader should not assume that all the children went to church on Ascension Thursday.) Discuss the sadness and the fear the disciples must have experienced once Jesus had returned to God. Enhance the story with slides or pictures.
2. Tell the children that after Jesus returned to God, Mary, the mother of Jesus, and the friends of Jesus prayed constantly and waited for Jesus to keep his promise to send the Holy Spirit.
3. Summarize today's first reading and the choice of Matthias to replace Judas. Begin by reminding the children who Judas was, and tell them that one of the things the friends of Jesus did while they waited for the Holy Spirit was to choose someone to replace Judas as one of the twelve apostles. Point out the following:
• The disciples wanted someone who had personally witnessed the saving events and could effectively spread the good news. They wanted a person who had been with them from the baptism of Jesus until his ascension.
• The disciples prayed, placing the choice in the hands of God.
• Matthias was the person the disciples chose to join the twelve

4. Pray for the coming of the Holy Spirit:
- Help the children to look forward to Pentecost by discussing what the Spirit would do for the friends of Jesus: the Spirit would remind them of all Jesus had said and done and give them the power to be his witnesses to all the world.
- Tell the children that we celebrate the coming of the Spirit next Sunday on the great feast of Pentecost.
- Relate the gift of the Spirit to our own lives by praying in the general intercessions that the Spirit will come to us and fulfill the promises of Jesus. For example, pray:

Leader:	My brothers and sisters in God's family, let us pray for the coming of the Holy Spirit into the world today. Please respond, "Spirit of Jesus, come to us."
	That the Holy Spirit will live in the hearts of all of God's children and fill them with love and joy and peace, we pray,
All:	Spirit of Jesus, come to us.
Leader:	That the Holy Spirit will remind us of all that Jesus said and did, we pray,
All:	Spirit of Jesus, come to us.
Leader:	That the Holy Spirit will give us the courage to tell others about Jesus, we pray,
All:	Spirit of Jesus, come to us.
Leader:	That the Holy Spirit will make us one, just as Jesus and the Father are one, we pray,
All:	Spirit of Jesus, come to us.
Leader:	Loving God, send your Holy Spirit to fill the hearts of your children and to renew us in your love. May the Spirit fill our minds with light. May the Spirit keep us faithful to Jesus. May the Spirit comfort those who are sorrowful. May the Spirit give us joys that never end. We pray these things, as we pray all things, in the name of Jesus.
All:	Amen.

5. Teach the children to sing a prayer for the coming of the Holy Spirit.

6. Because children associate balloons with joy, it would be appropriate to give them balloons today as a reminder of the joy of the Spirit whose coming we await. After the liturgy, at the most-used entrance to the church, have bunches of red and yellow and orange balloons tied with ribbons on which "Come, Holy Spirit!" is written. Let the assembly enjoy the balloons as they leave the church, then give the balloons to the children to take home. Or use paper balloons with yarn strings. Fire-colored and wind-filled balloons will also help prepare the children and the adult assembly for Pentecost, when we will know the presence of the Spirit in wind and fire.

Other Possibilities:

1. Older children might be able to appreciate some of the magnificence of chapter 17 of John's gospel. The chapter has been called "the Johannine ascension" because Jesus seems already to be in the very presence of God. Jesus prays his intimate prayer aloud in the presence of the disciples and we, too, hear it. It is as if "the disciple and the reader are party to a heavenly family conversation" (AB, 29A, p. 747). It is a privilege, indeed, that we hear the prayer of Jesus revealing the union of Jesus and the Father which Jesus calls us to share. Older children might be interested in the parallels of Jn 17 to the petitions in the Lord's Prayer (which John does not record): "Father in heaven," "May your name be holy," "Your will be done," "Deliver us from the evil one." After reflecting on the meaning and the majesty of the gospel, it would be good to urge the children to recite the Lord's Prayer with special attention during today's liturgy of the eucharist.

2. Develop the theme of joy which Jesus wants us to have to the fullest, as he states in the gospel. The hallmark of the Christian is joy—not laughter in the midst of tears, but a deep abiding joy that comes from union with Jesus and the Father through union with each other. Draw upon the ideas of our beautiful reading from the letter of John. Challenge older children to be people of true Christian joy.

3. Older children might enjoy seeing pictures of the last supper by different great artists. There is a very interesting series of pictures of the last supper in The World of Leonardo from the Time-Life Library of Art. Show the pictures to the children. Include Salvador Dali's picture of the last supper from another source. Encourage the children to react uninhibitedly and then to discuss the ideas which must have been in the artists' minds as they interpreted the scene and created their paintings. Share the wonderful efforts of modern experts in the restoration of Leonardo's masterpiece, surely one of the most significant paintings of all times.

4. D. Clarence Rivers' "God Is Love" (from *American Mass Program*) is well-suited to today's readings. The song's refrain quotes the last line of the second reading, which the LMC omits.

5. The children would enjoy creating a poster depicting our wait for the Holy Spirit. Show a happy child reaching for a bunch of balloons with yarn strings. Write on the balloons gifts we ask of the Holy Spirit.

Lectionary for Masses with Children	Lectionary for Mass
**Acts 2:1-11	**Acts 2:1-11
Ps 104:1 and 24,30-31	Ps 104:1,24,29-30,31,34
*I Cor 12:4-7,12-13	*I Cor 12:3-7,12-13
*Jn 20:19-23	*Jn 20:19-23

Pentecost Sunday

Focus: Come, Holy Spirit, fill our hearts with your love!

Gather the Children

1. Assemble the children happily in their separate gathering space. The leader's constant joy in the presence of the children speaks most effectively to them of the loving care of the church for its young members. Continue to use the white Easter gathering cloth. Have present a cluster of red, orange and yellow candles, perhaps seven, the number of the traditional gifts of the Holy Spirit. As always display the lectionary prominently.

2. Remind the children why we come together for our special liturgy of the word. Ask for a volunteer child to lead the group in prayer that we will listen well to God's word today and always.

3. Tell the children that today is the last day of the Easter season. It is the great feast of Pentecost, the day on which we celebrate the coming of the Holy Spirit. Light the fire-colored candles in honor of the Holy Spirit.

4. Ask one child to hold the lectionary high while all sing to rejoice in the presence of God in word and assembled faithful. Sing any familiar Easter hymn or any hymn which celebrates the presence of God's Holy Spirit.

Proclaim the First Reading

1. Have the children sit down around the gathering cloth and ask them to listen carefully as we read from the bible the story of what happened on the first Pentecost. Proclaim the first part of Luke's account of the Pentecost experience, Acts 2:1-4a.

2. Explain the reading:
- Remind the children of the promise of Jesus before he died to send the Holy Spirit to his disciples. Ask the children what the Holy Spirit would do for the disciples. Help them to realize that the Holy Spirit would remind the friends of Jesus of all Jesus had said and done and give them the strength to tell others about it.
- Tell the children that today, on the feast of Pentecost, we celebrate the fulfillment of the promise of Jesus.
- Review the story of the first Pentecost, the story we just heard proclaimed in the words of Luke. Use pictures to enhance the presentation, perhaps a flannel board for younger children. Depict the believers, including Mary, fearful and gathered together. Ask the children to recall what the believers heard and saw. Then add symbols of driving wind and tongues of fire. Summarize the remaining part of the reading, Acts 2:4b-11, thus sharing with the children the immediate remarkable result of the Spirit's presence.

3. Respond to the reading, as the believers might have rejoiced in the Spirit, with Ps 104.

Rejoice in the Gift of the Holy Spirit

1. Talk with the children about the difference the Holy Spirit made in the lives of the disciples. Draw upon today's gospel as well as other liturgies we have celebrated this Easter season to illustrate the presence of the Spirit:
- The Spirit filled the disciples with peace when they had been so worried.
- The Spirit made the disciples strong and brave when they had been timid and afraid.
- The Spirit reminded the disciples of all Jesus had said and done.
- The Spirit inspired the disciples to go out to all the world and proclaim the good news of Jesus.

2. Talk with the children about how the Holy Spirit is present today, applying the above ideas to our own lives.

3. Pray the general intercessions, asking for the gifts of the Holy Spirit. Sing the response "Come, Holy Spirit":

Come Ho - ly Spir - it.

The leader and the children might pray as follows:

Leader: My brothers and sisters in God's family, let us pray for the presence of the Holy Spirit in our lives today. Please sing, in response to our petitions, "Come, Holy Spirit!"

For your love, which warms our hearts, we pray,

All: Come, Holy Spirit!

Leader: For your wisdom, which lights our minds, we pray,

All: Come, Holy Spirit!

Leader: For your strength, which bends our wills, we pray, we pray,

All: Come, Holy Spirit!

Leader: For your peace, which frees our souls, we pray,

All: Come, Holy Spirit!

Leader: For your comfort in our sorrow, we pray,

All: Come, Holy Spirit!

Leader: For your joy that never ends, we pray,

All: Come, Holy Spirit!

Leader: Loving God, send out your Spirit and renew the face of the earth. Fill the hearts of your faithful with your Spirit, and make the fire of the Spirit's love burn within them. We ask this in the name of Jesus the Lord.

All: Amen.

Share with Others the Good News of the Holy Spirit

1. Give the children a symbol of the Holy Spirit to wear as they rejoin the adult assembly:

• Have ready on a poster board a large flame composed of many smaller flames. Have the smaller flames made of contact paper of fire colors and laid on the poster board in the shape of a large flame.

• As a sign that we all share the gifts of the Spirit give the children each a paper flame. Tell then to remove the backing from the contact paper and attach their flames to their clothing.

2. Sing a song of joy in the spirit. Or sing "Spirit, Lift Me Up" to Honeytree's "Father, Lift Me Up" as an expression of our longing for union with the Spirit. If possible use a song which the entire assembly will sing today. Urge the children to sing the song again later with their families, perhaps as they pray at mealtime.

Other Possibilities:

1. Today's readings present two different accounts of the coming of the Holy Spirit. John, in our gospel, places it on Easter Sunday; while Luke, in our reading from the Acts of the Apostles, places it on the day of Pentecost, fifty days after Passover, originally a Jewish harvest festival and later a celebration of the giving of the law to Moses. The literal meaning of the word "Pentecost" is, in fact, (the) "fiftieth" (day). In the above outline, we have chosen to focus on the coming of the Holy Spirit as related by Luke because it is the more common understanding of the event.

Although it would only confuse younger children, older children might be able to understand how the two accounts do not contradict but, in fact, complement each other. John makes very clear that the Spirit is the gift of the risen Christ. He associates the gift of the Spirit with the commissioning of the disciples to reach out to all the world with the forgiveness of sin. It is this passage, in today's gospel, which Catholics have traditionally cited as the scriptural basis for the sacrament of reconciliation. Luke's account of the coming of the Holy Spirit marks the beginning of the church as a community wider than the Twelve, for Luke shows the immediate result of the presence of the Spirit to be the beginning of the apostolic preaching. Present the two accounts to the children, and then talk with them about how we attain a fuller understanding of the nature and action of the Holy Spirit because of the two accounts.

2. Pentecost has been called the birthday of the church. Some might think it appropriate for little children to have birthday cake and party favors, but such symbolism seems empty in comparison with the richness of the biblical symbolism of wind and fire. If the leader did not do so last Sunday, he or she might give little children fire-colored balloons to take home, as a sign of our joy in the Spirit, or small candles to burn at home.

3. With older children focus specifically on fire and wind as symbols of the Spirit:

• Ask the children why they think Luke uses fire as a symbol of the Holy Spirit. Bring out the capability of fire to warm, to light, to comfort, to purify. Ask why Luke uses wind to symbolize the Holy Spirit, and point out that wind is strong, invisible, life-giving. Then help the children relate the qualities of fire and wind to the Spirit.

• Instead of beginning with a completed poster and distributing the flames, consider constructing the poster. Give the children construction paper flames and let them write on the flames the gifts they ask of the Holy Spirit for the world today. Then collect the flames and glue them onto the poster in the shape of one big flame. Complete the poster by gluing on letters to spell out "Come, Holy Spirit!" Let the children carry their poster into the church when they rejoin the adult assembly and place it near the ambo.

• Or make a banner celebrating the presence of the Spirit: onto a long strip of heavy red cloth or red construction paper, glue a simple white dove and many yellow and orange flames. Carry the banner into the church and hang it so that all the assembly, including the children, can see it.

4. The second reading presents a chance to speak about the infinite worth of each individual. Each of us has different gifts and no one of us is better or worse than the next because of our gifts. The point is that each of us must use our gifts for the good of all. To stimulate children to think about such things is surely valuable in a world so filled with selfishness and jealously, in a world in which so many people measure their own worth in terms of how much better they are than others.

To familiarize the children with Paul's analogy of the Christian community and the human body (I Cor 12:12-26) would be good preparation for today's liturgy.

5. The seven gifts of the Holy Spirit, referred to in the sequence for Pentecost, are love-gifts of the Spirit which guide and strengthen the Christian to live ever more perfectly according to God's plan for personal sanctification. The prophet Isaiah names the gifts as qualities which the messiah will possess (Is 11:2, but to count seven, see, for example, the note in the Saint Joseph Edition of *The New American Bible*). Encourage older children to look up the gifts in their bibles and to learn about them. Urge the children to think about and pray for particular gifts of the Spirit on the seven days of the coming week:

for fear of the Lord,
    the foundation of all the gifts, which imparts a childlike fear of displeasing God;
for piety,
    which inclines us to look upon God as our parent and upon other people as our brothers and sisters in God's family;
for knowledge,
    which leads us from created things to revealed truths;

for fortitude,
> which gives us courage and perseverance in the face of moral difficulties;

for counsel,
> which enables us to do the best thing in a particular situation;

for understanding,
> which helps us to grasp the meaning and the importance of revealed truths;

for wisdom, the greatest of the gifts,
> which enables us to see all things with the eyes of God.

Suggest that the children draw symbols of the gifts of the Spirit, or, more simply, write the names of the gifts in careful, colorful lettering.

6. Give older children copies of the sequence for Pentecost Sunday. The translation which follows this outline, which seems quite suitable for children, is taken from *The Daily Missal of the Mystical Body*, edited by the Maryknoll Fathers (New York: P.J. Kenedy and Sons, 1961). The leader might also consider the translation of Peter Scagnelli along with the musical setting which appears in Worship III. Let the children read the sequence silently and think about its meaning, then ask them to read it aloud together. Talk with the group about the meaning of the prayer. Let the children take home their copies, decorate them, and pray the sequence every day during the coming week, the traditional octave of Pentecost.

Sequence For Pentecost

Holy Spirit, come and shine
On our souls with beams divine
Issuing from your radiance bright.

Come, O Father of the poor,
Ever generous of your store,
Come, our heart's unfailing light.

Come, Consoler, kindest, best,
Come, our soul's most dearest guest,
Sweet refreshment, sweet repose.

Rest in labor, coolness sweet,
Tempering the burning heat,
Truest comfort of our woes.

O divinest light, impart
Unto every human heart
Plenteous streams from love's bright flood.

But for your blest Deity,
Nothing pure in us could be;
Nothing harmless, nothing good.

Wash away each sinful stain;
Gently shed your gracious rain
On the dry and fruitless soul.

Heal each wound and bend each will,
Warm our hearts benumbed and chill,
All our wayward steps control.

Unto all your faithful just,
Who in you confide and trust,
Deign the sevenfold gift to send.

Grant us virtue's blest increase,
Grant a death of hope and peace,
Grant the joys that never end.
                    Amen. Alleluia!

Trinity Sunday

Lectionary for Masses with Children	Lectionary for Mass
*Dt 4:39-40 Ps 33:4-5,6 and 9,20 and 22 *Rom 8:14-17 *Mt 28:16-20	*Dt 4:32-34,39-40 Ps 33:4-5,6,9,18-19,20-22 *Rom 8:14-17 *Mt 28:16-20

Focus: Father, Son and Holy Spirit one in three!
All praise be yours, O Blessed Trinity!

Gather the Children

1. Welcome the children happily and gather them in a circle in their worship space. Have three candles present, but do not light them yet. Teach the children a song in praise of our triune God. Terrye Coelho's round "Father, I Adore You" would be a good choice, as would Honeytree's "Father, Lift Me Up" (continue with "Jesus," then "Spirit"). Accompany either song with simple gestures. Let one child enthrone the lectionary in its place of honor during the singing.
2. Remind the children why we gather for our special liturgy of the word, and then pray quietly that we will listen well to the word of God in the next few minutes and all our lives.
3. Review the words of the doxology the Glory Be to the Father. Add a few simple gestures. Then pray the prayer with the children.

Proclaim the First and Second Readings

1. Tell the children that today's readings call us to praise God because of all God has done. Ask the children to listen as we read about some of these wonderful things and to allow what we hear proclaimed to lead us to praise God. What follows is not an attempt to explain the readings to the children, but an attempt to call them to praise and thanksgiving. To understand and appreciate the readings requires much more intellectual sophistication than young children have.
2. Proclaim the Old Testament reading:
• Remind the children—some of them will never have heard about it—that long ago God rescued the people under the leadership of Moses from an unhappy life and led them to a new and happy land.
• Proclaim the first reading. The leader ought to include in the proclamation, especially to older children, some part of Dt 4:32-34, which the LMC omits entirely, thus recounting some of the wonderful works of God which stir God's people to the momentous conclusion of Dt 4:39-40 that there is no other god but the Lord God of Israel.
• Ask the children to imagine that they are the people of long ago for whom God did such wonderful things. Ask them to praise God and thank God for being their God. Sing again our opening song in praise of our triune God.

3. Proclaim the second reading:
• Remind the children—some may never have heard of him—that St. Paul was a brave and tireless apostle of the risen Christ. Paul was filled with the Holy Spirit and told many people about Jesus. Ask the children to listen to something Paul wrote to the people who lived in the city of Rome. Then proclaim the second reading, perhaps shortening it for very young children.
• Ask the children to imagine that they are the Christians of Rome and have just read Paul's letter telling them that they are children of God. Ask the children to praise and thank God for such a wonderful thing. Sing again our song in praise of the triune God.

Celebrate the Trinity

Note: The author is both acutely conscious of and uncomfortable with the emphasis on God as male which is part of our traditional conception of the Trinity (in fact, of God in general). It would seem unfair, however, to impose upon impressionable youngsters contemporary controversial reformulations of trinitarian theology.
1. The doctrine of the Trinity, that in God there are three persons who subsist in one nature, is not explicitly and formally a biblical belief and was not even formulated by the church until the fourth and fifth centuries (McKenzie, DOB). The biblical experience of God, both in the Old Testament and in the New Testament, is, however, most definitely threefold, and today's readings place before our eyes this threefold experience of God. We experience God as God is in himself, as God goes forth out of himself in revelation and redemptive action, and as God creates in the hearts of human creatures a believing response to that revelation and redemptive action. (See PNL, p. 383.) Phrasing this less precisely, though in terms that children might more easily understand, we experience God as love itself, God as creative and saving love and God as sanctifying love. The mysteries of our faith are not meant primarily to be analyzed and explained, but rather to be entered into and appreciated. Thus we celebrate today's feast of the Trinity not by burdening the children with facts and explanations, but by immersing them into our triadic biblical experience of the Trinity, particularly as depicted in the readings for today's liturgy of the word.
2. Using the flannel board, review the works of God, God the Father, the Son and the Holy Spirit, as we experience them in the scriptures:
• Spell out "Father" on the flannel board. God is our

Father, faithful and forgiving. God is love itself, as we read several weeks ago, in the first letter of John. Add to the flannel board a picture of a father and a child or something else to call to mind the love of a father. An imaginative leader might also work into the presentation maternal qualities which God embodies, striving, while not confusing the children, to draw their image of God away from the exclusively male. Sing the first verse of Coelho's or Honeytree's song.

• Spell out "Son" on the flannel board. Out of the abundance of God's love God created the world and created us. When humankind failed to love God in return, God promised us Jesus. Jesus, God's son, gift of the Father, shows us by his life and death who the Father is and shows us the way to the Father. Add to the flannel board pictures that remind us of Jesus, gift of the Father to us. An imaginative leader might refer occasionally to Jesus as God's child, and not exclusively to Jesus as God's son. God's earthly child, of course, had to be either male or female. Sing the second verse of Coelho's or Honeytree's song.

• Spell out "Holy Spirit" on the flannel board. With the help of the Holy Spirit we respond to the love of God and follow the way of Jesus to the Father. Add to the flannel board pictures of people showing love for others, thus calling to mind the Holy Spirit, gift of the Father and the Son, who enables us to respond to the love of God. Ask the children if they remember when very recently we celebrated the presence of the Holy Spirit among us. The leader might be interested to know that the Hebrew word which translates into English as "Spirit" is feminine. (The Greek word is neuter.) Sing the third verse of Coelho's or Honeytree's song.

3. Tell the children that we call the three persons of God together the Trinity. Spell out "Trinity" on the flannel board. We believe in one God in three persons, the Father, the Son and the Holy Spirit: we believe in one God who lives and tells us about himself and calls us to himself. Today, on Trinity Sunday, we praise God and celebrate all that God has done and continues to do for us. Light the three candles in honor of the three divine persons. Sing all three verses of Coelho's or Honeytree's song in praise of our triune God.

Proclaim the Gospel

1. Tell the children that in our gospel today, Jesus sends the disciples out into the world to call all people to be his friends, to baptize them in the name of the Father, the Son and the Holy Spirit, and to teach them all he has taught his earthly followers. Jesus promises his friends that he will be with them always.
2. Ask the children to stand to listen to the words of Jesus. Acclaim the gospel joyfully in song and then proclaim it.
3. Respond to the gospel by stating that we do indeed accept the message preached by the disciples. Do so by saying—better, singing—a profession of faith.

Make the Good News Our Own

1. Explain the traditional use of the shamrock as a symbol of the Trinity: one stalk but three leaves, as there is one God but three persons.

2. Make a poster to proclaim our faith in the Trinity:
• Put a large paper shamrock on a poster board. Glue onto its leaves the pictures used above which recall the works of the Father, the Son and the Holy Spirit.
• Write on the poster board, or have already nicely lettered, the acclamation which is our focus today.
3. Ask the children to pray quietly in praise and thanks to God, who is Father, Son and Holy Spirit, for all God is and does.
4. Give each child a small paper shamrock to take home. Have "Father," "Son" and "Holy Spirit" written on the leaves and "Trinity" on the stalk.
5. Dismiss the children with a trinitarian blessing. Ask the children to bow their heads and pray for God to bless us. Then pray, with arms extended over the children: "May the blessing of God, the Father, the Son and the Holy Spirit, come upon you and remain with you forever." The children should respond, "Amen." Even better, the leader may sing the blessing and the children sing their response. Show the children how to make the Sign of the Cross during a blessing.

Other Possibilities:

1. Older children might appreciate the dramatic quality of the first reading, in particular, the longer form of the LM:
• To establish the background of the reading, ask the children what they remember about Moses. Help them remember that Moses was a great leader of God's people long ago, so great that Jewish people to this day look upon God's action through Moses as the greatest sign of God's love and care for them.
• Tell the children that our reading is part of the traditional set of eloquent last speeches that Moses gave his people when he knew he was soon to die. He reminded them of the wonderful things that God had done for them and he urged them to be faithful to God in return. The children might liken the words of Moses to the parting words of a parent to children.
• Ask the children to listen to the reading, not only for its good advice, but also for its lively, engaging dramatic quality. Proclaim the reading, using the longer form of the LM, and then discuss its effect on the crowd of listeners. They would have been moved by the rhetorical questions to call out "No!" and to respond at the end with "Of course, we will! Hurray for God!"
• The children might enjoy rewriting the speech for modern times. Suppose they were great leaders who were about to die and wanted to impress upon those they were to leave behind the goodness of God and the importance of doing God's will. What would they say to their followers? This activity would be helpful preparation for the liturgy or good follow-up.
2. Ask older children if they remember any prayers in which we mention the Father, the Son and the Holy Spirit. Include the Sign of the Cross, the Glory Be to the Father, the Gloria and the Profession of Faith at mass, the Apostles' Creed, the Baptismal formula. Most prayers are addressed to the Father, and end with (approximately) "We pray in the name of your Son, Jesus, and with your Holy Spirit." Tell the children to listen carefully to the presiding priest's prayers during the lit-

urgy of the eucharist when they rejoin the assembly today.

3. With older children dwell more on the gospel message. What is the role of young Christians today in making disciples of all the nations? What does it mean to do everything Jesus has told us? Does it make a difference in our lives that Jesus is with us always? Why did the church choose this particular gospel for today's feast?

4. In place of using the flannel board, especially for older children, have slides of things that remind us of the three persons of the Trinity. Write "Father," "Son" and "Holy Spirit" on the leaves of a shamrock. Scramble letters to spell out "Trinity," let the children decipher the word, then write "Trinity" on the stalk.

5. Instead of a shamrock, use another symbol of the Trinity. There are many such symbols, for example, a triangle or a trillium. A more sophisticated symbol, which will interest older children, is a set of three interwoven circles, interwoven so that if any one circle is removed, the remaining two circles are entirely separated.

6. The Athanasian Creed is a profession of Christian faith, probably written in southern France in the fifth century. It is a beautiful, prayerful statement of faith in the Trinity and in the Incarnation. It was probably not written by St. Athanasius, an Egyptian saint and leader of the church who died in the fourth century. The Creed bears the saint's name, however, because it contains the truths which he firmly believed and courageously upheld against those who claimed that Christ was not equal to God, but inferior to God. (This mistaken belief, called the Arian heresy, flourished in the fourth century.) Say a shortened form of the beautiful creed with older children. A presentation of the first part of the creed, shortened, simplified and arranged in parts, follows.

A Profession Of Faith

A Reading of the First Part of the Athanasian Creed

All: We worship one God in Trinity,
and Trinity in unity,
neither confusing the Persons,
nor dividing the nature.

Group 1:   For there is one Person of the Father,

Group 2:   another of the Son,

Group 3:   and another of the Holy Spirit.

All: But the Godhead
of the Father, of the Son and of the Holy Spirit
is one,
the glory equal,
the majesty co-eternal.

Group 1:   Such as the Father is,

Group 2:   such is the Son,

Group 3:   such is the Holy Spirit.

All: The Father, the Son and the Holy Spirit are uncreated.
The Father, the Son and the Holy Spirit are infinite.
The Father, the Son and the Holy Spirit are eternal.
And yet
there are not three
eternals, uncreateds and infinites,
but only One.

Group 1:   So also the Father is almighty,

Group 2:   the Son almighty,

Group 3:   and the Holy Spirit almighty.

All: And yet there are not three almighties,
but one Almighty.

Group 1:   So the Father is God,

Group 2:   the Son is God,

Group 3:   and the Holy Spirit is God.

All: And yet there are not three Gods,
but one God.

Group 1:	So also the Father is Lord,
Group 2:	the Son is Lord,
Group 3:	and the Holy Spirit is Lord.
All:	And yet there are not three Lords, but one Lord. Our Christian faith calls us to believe in every Person by Himself to be God and Lord.
Group 1:	So there is one Father, not three Fathers;
Group 2:	one Son, not three Sons;
Group 3:	one Holy Spirit, not three Holy Spirits.
All:	And in this Trinity no Person is greater or less than another, but the three Persons are equal and eternal together. So that in all things the Unity in Trinity and the Trinity in Unity is to be worshipped. Amen.

Lectionary for Masses with Children	Lectionary for Mass

**Ex 24:3-8
  Ps 116:12-13,17-19
----- 	
**Mk 14:12-16,22-26
	**Ex 24:3-8
	  Ps 116:12-13,15-16,17-18
	  Heb 9:11-15
	**Mk 14:12-16,22-26

Corpus Christi

Focus: God has made a new and eternal covenant with us and sealed it with the blood of Jesus. Let us celebrate God's great love!

Gather the Children

1. As the children enter the room welcome them joyfully to their special celebration of God's word. In addition to the usual lectionary and candles, have present a cross, a goblet or other cup suitable for a festive meal and an unsliced loaf of bread.
2. Light the candles. While one child holds the lectionary high, lead all the children in song to acknowledge the presence of God in the word.
3. Remind the children why we gather as we do, and then invite them to pray quietly that God will fill our hearts and our lives with the word.

Focus on the Meaning of Covenant

Note: To the reader familiar with the Old Testament, there are two problems in the translation of today's readings. First, in the Old Testament reading, the Hebrew word which is usually translated with the English "covenant" is rendered "promises." The word "promises," however, suggests an extremely deficient theology of the Mosaic covenant, which was not a one-sided promise on God's part, but a mutual agreement between God and the people. Secondly, the gospel reading uses the word "agreement," an acceptable translation, for what we usually read as "covenant"; but then, the fact that the concept of covenant is common to both readings is obscured in the English. For older children, who deserve introduction to the traditional and important scriptural term "covenant," the leader should use "covenant" consistently in both readings, if necessary explaining a covenant as an agreement. A careful use of the word "promises" is acceptable for younger children, for which approach see the suggestion under "Other Possibilities" below.
1. Write "agreement" on a piece of newsprint and brainstorm the meaning of the word.
2. Help the children realize that our lives are filled with agreements:
• Let them discuss agreements in their own lives. As they talk, jot down on the newsprint the contracting parties. Some examples:

Parent-child: If you do your chores, I will give you your allowance. If you help rake all the leaves, we will go to a movie this afternoon. If you hit your sister again with that stick, I will send you to your room.

Teacher-student: If you do good work, I will give you a good report card. If you do the extra problem on your test correctly, I will give you extra points. If your behavior continues in that fashion, I will give you a demerit.

Friend-friend: Let the children suggest these.

• Extend the discussion to include such agreements as a job contract, a building contract, a marriage contract.
3. Tell the children that the bible contains numerous agreements, or contracts. Some of these were solemn agreements, usually spoken and not written, and made with much ceremony. Such a "solemn, ritual agreement" (McKenzie, DOB) is called a covenant. Write "covenant" in large letters on the newsprint.
4. Continue to probe the meaning of covenant by telling the children that in the Old Testament, covenants were made not only between persons and between nations, but also, and most importantly, between Yahweh and the people of Israel. Write "God-Israel" on the newsprint.

Proclaim the First Reading

1. To introduce the reading, ask the children if they know of any Old Testament covenants between God and the people of Israel.
• On a second sheet of newsprint, write "covenant" across the top, divide the remaining space into two columns, and write "Old Testament" at the top of the first column.
• Remind the children briefly of the covenant which God made with Noah and his sons and all their descendants. God promised never again to destroy the earth by water, and Noah and his sons and their descendants promised not to kill people and not to eat meat with blood still in it (because blood was regarded as the seat of life and therefore sacred). As a sign of the covenant between God and all living beings, God set the rainbow in the clouds. (See Gn 9:1-16.) Write "Noah" and draw a rainbow in the first column of the newsprint. Part of this passage was our first reading for the First Sunday of Lent. Perhaps some of the children will remember.
• Remind the children of the covenant which God made with Abraham. God promised to make Abraham the father of many nations, of even more people than there are stars in the sky, to give them land, to be their God; and God asked Abraham and his descendants that every male among them be circumcised. (See Gn 17:1-14.) Write "Abraham" and draw a starry sky on the newsprint. A related passage was our first reading for the Second Sunday of Lent. Perhaps some of the

children will remember the promise of God to Abraham.

• Finally, ask the children if they remember the most important covenant between God and the people of Israel. Remind them of the promise of God to Moses: "If you hearken to my voice and keep my covenant, you shall be my special possession, dearer to me than all other people, though all the earth is mine" (Ex 19:5). In return for the privilege of being God's chosen ones, the people of Israel agreed to abide by all the commandments of God. This covenant was called the Mosaic covenant or the Sinai covenant (because it was at the top of Mount Sinai that God spoke to Moses and gave him the commandments). Write "Moses" and draw the tablets of the commandments on the newsprint. Our first reading for the Third Sunday of Lent was a proclamation of the ten commandments. The children may remember.

2. Tell the children that our first reading today describes the acceptance by God and the Israelites of the covenant made through Moses. As a sign that God and the Israelites agreed to the terms of the covenant, Moses led them in a ceremony. The leader should read all of Ex 24, better yet, Ex 19-24, as background.

• Moses erected an altar and twelve pillars at the foot of Mount Sinai. The altar symbolized God; the twelve pillars symbolized the twelve tribes of Israel and thus all the people.

• Then a sacrifice was offered and the blood of the victims, which symbolized their lives, was collected. As the death of the victims was final, so also the covenant which it ratified was final.

• As a symbol that the covenant partners shared a common life, Moses splashed half the blood on the altar and sprinkled the other half on the people.

3. Proclaim the first reading:

• Have written on a piece of paper, in large letters so that the children can read the words easily, "We will do everything that the Lord has told us." Then ask the children to imagine that they are the Israelites participating in the sealing of the covenant. Ask them to answer, when prompted, with the sentence on the paper.

• Proclaim the reading from the book of Exodus dramatically, indicating to the children to read their sentence at the two points in the reading at which the people speak.

4. In thanksgiving to God for the covenant teach the children, or simply listen to, a song which sings of the covenant love of God.

Proclaim the Gospel

1. Focus the children's attention on the new covenant:

• Tell the children that "testament," as in Old Testament and New Testament, means "covenant." Write "New Testament" at the top of the second column on the newsprint. (The Greek word "diatheke," which in the bible signifies covenant, means either "agreement" or "last will." Unfortunately, when the bible was translated into Latin, the word "testamentum," which means "last will," was used for "diatheke.")

• Next, tell the children, that the covenant God made with the Israelites through Moses was so central to the Israelite religion that we Christians refer to the entire Hebrew scriptures (with a few additions) as our "old covenant" or "Old Testament."

• Ask the children what they think "New Testament" or "new covenant" means. Let them speculate briefly and then ask them to listen carefully to the proclamation of the gospel.

2. Acclaim the gospel in song and then proclaim Mk 14:22-26.

3. Help the children understand and appreciate the "new covenant":

• Christians consider themselves bound together and bound to Jesus in a new covenant relationship. Write "new covenant" on the newsprint.

• In today's gospel, indeed, in each of the four accounts we have of the institution of the eucharist, Jesus himself relates his blood to the new covenant, thus calling to mind the blood of the old covenant:

Just as the blood of animals sealed the old covenant, the blood of Jesus seals the new covenant.

Just as the sprinkling of blood on the altar and the people signified that God and the people shared a common life, so our sharing of the blood of the covenant signifies (and effects) our participation in the life of Jesus and of each other. Draw a cup on the newsprint under "new covenant."

Just as the death of the animal signified the finality and total commitment of the old covenant, so also the death of Jesus signifies the completeness of the new covenant on God's part, and the reception of the eucharistic cup signifies its completeness on the part of the Christian. Thus the eucharist and the cross are intimately related. Add a cross to the newsprint, near the cup.

• Unlike the terms of the old covenant, the terms of the new covenant are never spelled out specifically. Rather, the new covenant is "written upon the hearts" of God's people, binding them to each other in a relationship of love, whose demands, simple, yet profound, far surpass those of any written commandments.

Make the Good News Our Own

1. Make a banner depicting our acceptance of the new covenant and let the children carry it into the church and place it near the ambo as they rejoin the assembly for the liturgy of the eucharist:

• Give each child a simple figure with upraised arms, representing himself or herself. If there is time, let the children personalize their figures with names or faces or clothes. If the leader sees the children before the liturgy, they can prepare their figures then.

• In the center of the banner glue a large cup, representing the cup of the covenant.

• As a sign that the children personally accept the new covenant, collect the figures and glue them onto the banner around the cup.

• The response to our psalm, "I will take the cup of salvation," would be an appropriate explanatory phrase. Words on banners, however, should not be necessary, unless they are integral to the design.

2. As a symbol to take home, give each child a small figure holding a cup or, more simply, just a cup.

3. Remind the children before they return to their par-

ents that we are about to celebrate the liturgy of the eucharist. Ask them to listen closely to the words of the presider when he recites the institution narrative. The words are similar to the words of Jesus in our gospel today.

4. Conclude the liturgy of the word with a eucharistic hymn, ideally one which the entire assembly will sing during the liturgy of the eucharist.

Other Possibilities:

1. On Holy Thursday, of course, the church celebrates the institution of the eucharist as part of the great Easter triduum. The feast of Corpus Christi, set apart from our meditation on the passion and resurrection of Jesus, is a joyful feast celebrating the gift of the eucharist. The emphasis in our liturgy of the word today should be on celebrating the eucharist and not in attempting to explain it. Today's feast offers good opportunity to relate the liturgy of the word to the liturgy of the eucharist, and to prepare the children for the liturgy of the eucharist, which they will shortly celebrate with the entire assembly.

2. Younger children will neither understand nor appreciate the above discussion of covenant and the blood of the covenant. Focus on "promise" with them: God promised the Israelites through Moses that he would take care of them; through Jesus he promises us something even more, that we will share the very life of Jesus. The eucharist, which these little ones will one day receive, is the fulfillment of the promise. Proclaim the gospel for the little ones and make the banner, perhaps including on it a loaf of bread as well as a cup. Lead them to faith that when we share the eucharist we share, in a way that we cannot understand, the life of Jesus, and we receive strength to reach out to others in love. Teach the little ones a simple eucharistic hymn.

3. Pray the responsorial psalm as an acknowledgment of all the good things the Lord has done for us. Older children might enjoy reading it in parts.

4. In many countries of the world, processions, complete with banners and flowers, and often out of doors, are held on this day in honor of the eucharist. The leader might want to organize a simple procession with the children, perhaps even as part of the gift procession.

The children can make a banner as described above. Each child should have a flower—fresh flowers they have brought from home or paper flowers they have made previously or simply flowers supplied by the leader. Let one child carry the banner and lead the procession. The rest of the children should follow with their flowers. Display the banner in a place of honor in the church and let the children lay their flowers at the foot of the banner.

5. Enrich older children's experience of covenant by reminding them of the oath that Tom Sawyer and Huckleberry Finn swore to each other, promising never to tell anyone about the murder they witnessed of young Dr. Robinson by Injun Joe. The oath, written by moonlight on a pine shingle and signed in blood, stated:

> Huck Finn and Tom Sawyer swears they will keep mum about this and they wish they may drop down dead in their tracks if they ever tell and rot.

Have the oath written in a child's handwriting on a shingle-shaped piece of paper, with the initials "TS" and "HF" written in red poster paint. Whisper it to the children. Write "Tom-Huck" on the newsprint as a further example of an agreement.

6. It seems possible that the analogy of the vine and the branches in Jn 15, our gospel for the Fifth Sunday of Easter, has eucharistic overtones, perhaps prompted by the words "the fruit of the vine" in the institution narratives (AB, 29A, p.672-4). At any rate, the analogy of the vine and the branches seems a good one for describing the new covenant relationship. Use the analogy, drawing upon the children's familiarity with it, to help them understand the new covenant relationship that Christians have with Jesus and with each other.

7. Today is a good day to introduce older children to some of our traditional eucharistic prayers and hymns. For example, help them to read and understand "O Bread of Life" ("O Salutaris Hostia") or "Humbly Let Us Voice Our Homage" ("Tantum Ergo"). Or summarize some of the thoughts in the "Lauda Sion," which forms the sequence of today's liturgy. All three of these famous prayers were written by Thomas Aquinas in the thirteenth century.

Tenth Sunday of the Year

Lectionary for Masses with Children	Lectionary for Mass
**Gn 3:9-15	**Gn 3:9-15
*Ps 130:1-2,3-4,5 and 6-7	*Ps 130:1-2,3-4,5-6,7-8
II Cor 4:16-5:1	II Cor 4:13-5:1
**Mk 3:20-26,31-35 or Mk 3:20-21,31-35	**Mk 3:20-35

Focus: We rejoice in Jesus who saves us from the power of evil.

Gather the Children

Note: The leader must find out which is the proper Sunday of the Year to use on the Sunday after the feast of Corpus Christi. The particular Sunday we use varies with the year because it depends upon the date of Easter. A religious appointment calendar often contains the information we need.

1. Welcome the children joyfully to our celebration of God's word. Remind them why we and the adult assembly celebrate separate liturgies of the word. Be sure the children realize that they are participating fully in our Sunday assembly.

2. Today would be a good day to teach the children a new gospel acclamation. Sing the acclamation as a sign of our joy in God's word.

3. The great seasons of Lent and Easter are behind us now and our celebrations of Trinity Sunday and Corpus Christi, both solemnities of the Lord, are completed. Today we return to what the church calls "the season of the year" or "ordinary time" (though our Sunday celebration of the paschal mystery is hardly ordinary!), and we resume our systematic reading of the scriptures and our reflection upon how we can live our Christian lives ever more in accord with the word of God we hear. For older children, illustrate with a simple liturgical calendar, pointing out the Sundays of the Year between the Christmas feasts and Lent, and the Sundays of the Year from now until the end of the liturgical year.

Reflect Gratefully on God's Mercy

1. Guide the children in a simple examination of conscience:

• Have several stand-up figures of children and adults with happy faces. Let the children mention things which make people happy.

• Read the children a short description of something wrong a person might do. For example, read: "Brad has just come home from school. He has a lot of homework. His little sister runs up to him eagerly and asks him to play with her. Brad tells her to get lost because he has more important things to do than play with a baby. His sister goes away from him in tears." Write "Brad" on one of the figures. Ask the children how Brad would feel after he has hurt his sister. Help them to see that acts of unkindness make people unhappy. Turn Brad to face the wall.

• Continue with other descriptions until all but one of the figures have names and are facing the wall. Carefully adapt the descriptions to the age and experience of the particular group of children.

• Let the final figure represent the children in the group. Ask the children to think, without speaking, of times when they have done wrong. Then turn the final figure to face the wall.

2. Help the children express sorrow for their failings. Encourage them to share spontaneous prayer. Teach them a simple song of sorrow. Or sing the Kyrie:

Lord, have mer - cy. Christ, have mer - cy. Lord, have mer - cy.

Ky-ri - e e-le - i-son. Chri-ste e-le - i-son. Ky-ri - e e-le - i-son.

Assure the children of God's mercy and forgiveness of all our wrongdoing.

3. Help the children resolve to make up for their faults:

• Ask for a child willing to role play. Read the child the description of Brad's undesirable behavior. Then ask the child what Brad could do about his act of unkindness to his sister. Then let the child turn around the figure of Brad so that his happy face shows once again. Do the same with the other figures, except for the figure who represents the group.

• Finally let the children recall what they have done wrong and think of ways to correct the wrong. Turn the final figure around.

Proclaim the Reading from the Old Testament

1. Today the leader has the opportunity to share with the children one of our famous pre-historical Old Testament stories. He or she should certainly read all of Gn 3 to prepare to tell the story.

2. Ask the children if they know the names of the first man and woman. Let them share any details they remember about the creation stories. Then summarize the second creation story, Gn 2:4b-25, by telling the children that God made a man, put him in the wonderful garden of Eden, ordered him not to eat from one particular tree in the garden, then made a woman to be his companion.

3. Tell the children the story of the fall of the man and the woman, Gn 3:1-7. This story of the fall comes from the same tradition as the second creation story. Be dramatic, yet faithful to the scriptural account. Use large figures like the ones above to enhance the story.

4. Ask the children to listen carefully as we read from the bible the conversation between God and the man and the woman after God discovered that they had disobeyed. Proclaim the reading.

5. Summarize the punishment of the man and the woman: the woman would bear children in pain, the man would have to work hard for food, the two were banished from the garden of Eden.

6. Talk with the children about the tendency of all of us to sin against God, as Adam and Eve did. Ask them who it was who lived long after Adam and Eve and never disobeyed God. In this way help the children to realize in their own simple way that Jesus is the "new Adam," the representative of the human race who was completely obedient to God.

Proclaim the Gospel

1. Tell the gospel story:
• Remind the children of the activity of Jesus that we observed in the early part of Mark's gospel as we read almost continuously from it during the Sundays of the Year, in this lectionary Year B, before Lent began: Jesus taught with authority, healed the sick, and forgave sins. If the children made a poster to summarize the activity of Jesus, show it to them once again.
• Remind the children of the reaction of the people to the power of Jesus's words and deeds: some people thought he was wonderful, but others began to hate him and even plotted to kill him.
• Continue by describing the problem in today's gospel: some people thought Jesus had great power because the devil was at work in him. But Jesus told them how they could know that his was not the devil's power. Jesus told them to remember that he himself had driven evil spirits out of people. If Jesus were on the side of the evil spirits, he would not drive them away. The leader might illustrate Jesus's argument with characters from a popular movie or story.
• Tell the children that some of Jesus's relatives were also worried about him. Jesus's reply to their worries was that it was more important to do God's will than to be a relative of his.

2. Focus on the compliment that Jesus gives to those who do the will of God. We cannot all be Jesus's blood relatives, but we can all do God's will.

3. Acclaim the gospel joyfully and them proclaim it. For younger children, the leader might use only verses 31-35.

Make the Good News Our Own

1. Illustrate graphically our desire to do God's will:
• Quickly make a tree by cutting out a trunk and a cluster of green leaves. Have ready some paper apples.
• Ask the children to think of the forbidden fruit in the garden of Eden as that of an apple tree. (We don't know what kind of fruit it was.)
• Tell them that God has not forbidden us to eat apples, but that there are certain things that God does ask us to do or not to do. Let the children suggest some of

these things. Write their suggestions on the apples and place the apples in the tree.
• Give the children a few quiet moments to think, using the apples for ideas, of how they will try especially hard to obey God in the week to come.

2. Sing once again the song of sorrow which the children sang earlier in their time together.

3. Give the children long streamers with the sentence "Do the will of God!" The children can take their streamers home and decorate them. The assembly will also enjoy seeing the children rejoin their parents carrying their streamers.

Other Possibilities

1. Older children would surely enjoy considering more deeply the story of the fall of Adam and Eve. Ask them why the author of the story chose a serpent as the villain. Let them analyze briefly the clever tactics of the serpent. What might it mean to "know what is good and what is bad"? Point out how Adam and then Eve "passed the buck." What natural phenomena do the punishments of Adam and Eve explain? Or, to put the question in another way, how does the story help explain our human condition?

2. Psalm 130 is the one of the seven traditional penitential psalms. Pray it with the children as an expression of sorrow for our sin and an expression of confidence in God's forgiveness.

3. Today's gospel presents us with several provocative thoughts. The leader might share some of them with older children.
• The words of Mark about the family of Jesus are harsh ones. Apparently even they thought that Jesus was possessed by the devil. Since Mark follows this statement with an incident of such outright accusation of Jesus by the scribes, Mark may be foreshadowing the widespread rejection of Jesus that eventually led to his death. Notice that Jesus does not deny his natural relationship with his family, but rather subordinates it to a deeper relationship, that of total commitment to the will of God. The leader would do well to compare Mark's treatment of this incident with Luke's (Lk 8:19-21). Luke understands the words of Jesus as a compliment to his family.
• The Greek text allows that the "brothers" of Jesus may be only close relatives of Jesus and not other children of Mary. "However one interprets this passage about the 'brothers' of Jesus, it is to be noted that the doctrine of Mary's perpetual virginity is not based on Markan texts" (JBC).
• An unforgivable sin? "Yes!" says Jesus. It is to ascribe the words and works of Jesus to the devil and not to the saving power of God. (The LMC omits the verses of the gospel which refer to this unforgivable sin.)

4. Ask older children why they think the compilers of the lectionary chose to pair the ancient story of the fall of humankind with today's gospel.

Eleventh Sunday of the Year

Lectionary for Masses with Children	Lectionary for Mass
**Ez 17:22-24	**Ez 17:22-24
*Ps 92:1-2,12-13	*Ps 92:2-3,13-14,15-16
II Cor 5:6-10	II Cor 5:6-10
**Mk 4:30-34	**Mk 4:26-34

Focus: From small beginnings the kingdom of God will grow to glorious fullness.

Gather the Children

Note: The leader must find out which is the proper Sunday of the Year to use on the Sunday after the feast of Corpus Christi. The particular Sunday we use varies with the year because it depends upon the date of Easter. A religious appointment calendar often contains the information we need.

1. Welcome the children with great joy to their special liturgy of the word. Remind them that we come together to listen carefully to God's word and to discover its meaning for our lives.

2. If today is the first Sunday "of the Year" after Lent and Easter and the solemnities of Trinity Sunday and Corpus Christi, comment on this fact. The presider wears green today. The leader might use green candles in the children's gathering space and a green gathering cloth. The lectionary returns us to our systematic reading of the scriptures, which we put aside when Lent and its special readings required our attention. Today, in this lectionary year B, we resume, in particular, our study of Mark's gospel. Show the older children a simple liturgical calendar.

3. Teach the children a new gospel acclamation and sing it to acknowledge the presence of God in the word. Or sing a song whose theme is listening to God's word.

Reflect on the Teaching of Jesus

1. Describe the scene pictured in Mk 4:1-3: Jesus had begun to teach the people by the side of the lake. Such a huge crowd gathered to hear him that he decided to get into a boat and pull out a distance from the shore. From there he taught the people in story form, urging them to listen carefully to his teaching.

2. Focus on the interest of the crowd:
• Ask the children why people flocked to hear Jesus.
• Ask them what Jesus taught.
• Ask older children what made Jesus such a good teacher.

3. Point out Jesus's use of parables in his teaching:
• Write the word "parable" in large letters. Ask older children if they know what a parable is.
• Tell little ones that a parable is a story with a message for our lives. Everyone listens better if the teacher uses stories.
• Tell older children that a parable is a story with a twist. Parables are shockers. They force us to listen because they end so unexpectedly. Ask the children to recall some of Jesus's parables.

4. Relate the importance of the teaching of Jesus in his own day to our lives today. Tell the children that we will listen to the teaching of Jesus in our gospel reading and hear two parables that Jesus spoke to the crowd. He meant the parables for us also.

5. Pray with the children that we will always listen well to the teaching of Jesus.

Proclaim the Gospel

1. Help the children grasp the meaning of the parables of our gospel. The leader of a group of younger children might choose to present only the second parable, the only parable which LMC includes.
• Prepare the children for the first parable by drawing simple pictures showing the growth of a seed into a mature plant. Or show slides of the stages of the growth of a plant familiar to the children, perhaps a tomato plant. Remark on the mystery of growth. The farmer or the gardener really does remarkably little. Have some seeds and a basket of summer produce.
• Prepare the children for the second parable by asking them to think of acorns, then of oak trees. Help them to appreciate the enormous growth of the acorn. Then show them some mustard seeds (which are not really the smallest of seeds). Tell them that the mustard seed grows into a surprisingly large bush. The mustard tree is common in Palestine, the land where Jesus lived.

2. Tell the children that Jesus was a sensitive teacher. He talked to the crowds about things that were familiar to them from their everyday lives. In the parables which we read today in our gospel, Jesus wanted to teach the people about the kingdom (or reign) of God. He talked about seeds and their growth to do so.

3. Ask the children to stand to listen to the gospel. Acclaim the gospel joyfully in song and then proclaim it. The leader who wishes to include both gospel parables should not limit the proclamation to the verses in the LMC.

Make the Good News Our Own

1. Relate the parables to the work of Jesus to spread the kingdom of God:
• Tell the children that Jesus, in the parables we read today, was teaching people about the kingdom of God on earth. The message of Jesus was that from very small beginnings God's kingdom would grow phenomenally.
• On the bottom of a large sheet of paper draw a seed. Tell the children that the seed represents Jesus, one special person who lived on earth to teach about God's concern for people. Write "Jesus" near the seed. Begin

to draw a tree growing from the seed. Talk about the little band of disciples that Jesus gathered to help him in his work. Write the names of some of the disciples near the base of the tree. Draw the rest of the tree. In its leafy branches write the names of some of the many people today who follow the way of Jesus. Include the names of some of the children and the names of some adults whom the children know. Stress that the Christian church is very large today, much larger than anyone could have imagined in its early years. Give older children specific facts about the size of the church today and about the variety of its members.

2. From the parables of growth, draw some encouragement for own work for the kingdom:

• Ask the children what we can do to help spread the kingdom of God on earth. Encourage the children in little things. The little things are often all we can do, and today's gospel assures us that great things can come even from little things.

• Involve older children in a discussion of quality and quantity.

3. Sing with joy to celebrate the growth of the kingdom of God in our midst.

4. It is early summer. Give the children flower seeds to take home. Give them flower pots on which is written "God's kingdom grows!" Tell the children to plant their seeds and watch them grow. The growing plants can remind them of the wonderful growth of God's kingdom. The plants can remind the children also that even they can take part in helping God's kingdom to grow.

Other Possibilities:

1. Proclaim the first reading to older children:

• Ezekiel was one of the Israelites deported to Babylon in 597 BCE. It is there that he received his call to speak the word of God to Israel. Ezekiel's call is thrilling and thrillingly imaginative. Read it in chapters 1-3 of his book. Our reading today comes from the set of prophecies Ezekiel uttered before Nebuchadnezzar's destruction of Jerusalem in 587 BCE.

• The reading is part of "the allegory of the cedar and the eagles." The leader should read all of Ez 17 to place the passage in its immediate context. Verses 1-21 relate events of contemporary history in an allegory followed by an explanation. The remainder of the chapter, our reading, continues the allegory and speaks of messianic restoration. The "great eagle" is Nebuchadnezzar, king of Babylon. The "topmost branch" of the "crest of the cedar" is Jehoiachin of the house of David, whom Nebuchadnezzar defeated. The "seed of the land" is Zedekiah, whom Nebuchadnezzar placed on the throne of Judah. The second "great eagle" is the Pharaoh of Egypt. Thus the allegory tells of Zedekiah's revolt against Babylon at the instigation of Egypt. Ezekiel, and also Jeremiah, viewed Zedekiah's spurning of his oath to Nebuchadnezzar as a repudiation of the plan of God and worthy of divine punishment. The chapter ends, with our reading, on a note of hope: God will restore Israel in happiness under a new Davidic king.

• Share some of these facts with older children and then proclaim the beautiful promise of Ezekiel.

• Ask the children why they think the compilers of the lectionary paired the reading with today's gospel.

2. Draw upon the symbolism of the cedar of Lebanon, tended by God, to help the children appreciate the description in Ps 92 of the happiness of the just person. Then pray today's selection from Ps 92 in praise of the Lord who blesses good people (or, in better biblical idiom, "the just").

3. It is clear from even a brief survey of his gospel that Mark thought of teaching as a characteristic activity of Jesus. (For specifics, see chapter 7 in Achtemeier's Mark.) But Mark reports surprisingly little of the content of that teaching. In fact it is only in his chapter 4 that Mark gives us the content of a lengthy teaching session of Jesus. Chapter 4 contains three parables of Jesus and some of his sayings. The first parable is the parable of the seed, which Matthew and Luke also record. The second two parables are the ones which make up today's gospel. Only Mark's Jesus tells us the parable of the seed growing of itself. All three synoptists give us the parable of the mustard seed. The three parables of Mk 4, as well as the sayings in Mk 4:21-25, all speak of the contrast between small beginnings and great endings. As Mark states they each tell us something about the reign of God. Their message centers on Jesus, and it is this: What Jesus has begun, insignificant though it may seem to be, will inevitably result in the triumph of the glorious rule of God. Tell the older children briefly of the content of Mk 4:1-34 and then proclaim the whole of today's gospel. Explain the two parables. Challenge the children with specific action based on the gospel. Center their thoughts both on the growth of the kingdom and God's end-time harvest of the crop.

Twelfth Sunday of the Year

Lectionary for Masses with Children	Lectionary for Mass
**Jb 38:1,8-11 *Ps 107:23-24,25 and 28,29-30 II Cor 5:14-17 **Mk 4:35-41	**Jb 30:1,8-11 *Ps 107:23-24,25-26,28-29,30-31 II Cor 5:14-17 **Mk 4:35-41

Focus: We rejoice in Jesus whom even the wind and the sea obey!

Gather the Children

Note: The leader must find out which is the proper Sunday of the Year to use on the Sunday after the feast of Corpus Christi. The proper Sunday to use varies yearly because the Sunday depends upon the date of Easter. A religious appointment calendar often contains the information we need.

1. Welcome the children and remind them why we gather for our special liturgy of the word. Ask them to pray quietly for a moment that God will fill our minds and our hearts with the word.

2. To acknowledge the presence of God in the word proclaimed, have one child hold high the lectionary while all sing joyfully. Enthrone the lectionary and light candles near it.

3. If this is the appropriate Sunday, tell the children that today, after the seasons of Lent and Easter and the solemnities of Trinity Sunday and Corpus Christi, we return to "the season of the year" (or "ordinary time"). Show older children a simple liturgical calendar to illustrate the flow of the liturgical year. We resume our systematic reading of the scriptures and our reflection upon how we can live our lives as faithful, creative Christians. In this lectionary year B, Mark's gospel dominates our attention during the Sundays "of the year."

Proclaim the Gospel

1. Prepare the children for the gospel by reflecting on the nature of storms:

• Have a large painted lake. Ask the children if they have ever been to a lake or to the seashore. Help them describe the water on a sunny, peaceful day.

• Have a painted boat and place it on the lake. Ask the children if they have ever been in a boat. Encourage them to share their memories.

• Add storm clouds and large waves to the scene. Ask the children to imagine that they are out in the lake and that a storm has suddenly come upon them. Let them express their surprise, their disappointment, their fear.

2. Tell the children the gospel story, helping them to experience in their imaginations the terror, the relief and finally the wonder of the disciples. Include the interesting information in Mk 4:1 because it explains why Jesus was in the boat.

3. Proclaim the gospel:

• Ask the children to stand and listen to the story the way Mark recorded it in his gospel.

• Acclaim the gospel in song and then proclaim it.

4. Ask the children the question the disciples asked each other about Jesus, "Who is this? Even the wind and the sea obey him!" Help the children to grasp the astonishing fact that Jesus, by his actions, was proclaiming to his friends that through him God was present in the world.

5. In response to the gospel, acknowledge the wonders, the love and the care of God in song. Enhance the singing with simple gestures. Little children always like gestures.

Make the Good News Our Own

1. Focusing on a less literal interpretation of the gospel story, help the children to see that Jesus is with us in the storms of our lives:

• Ask the children if they have ever been afraid. Lead them away from fear of storms at sea, and help them to think of fears which arise from rough behavior and thoughtlessness, from selfishness and greed, from arguing and fighting. Sometimes children are the cause of these fears among themselves. Sometimes parents cause children to fear. Sometimes fear arises from a situation entirely beyond immediate human control. The leader must be gentle in talking to children about fear. We never wish to increase the fear of children, but we must recognize their fears so that we can assure them effectively of God's loving care.

• Ask the children if Jesus has a message for us in today's gospel, some thought to help us in times of fear. Help them to realize that when Jesus calmed the storm and stilled the fears of the disciples, he was telling us, too, to remember that he is with us in times of fear and danger, to make us unafraid and faith-filled, happy and free.

• Ask the children to pray quietly, each child in his or her own heart, that we will never forget that Jesus is always with us and cares about us, even when we are sad and afraid.

2. Help the children assimilate the gospel message of faith and hope in the presence and loving care of Jesus:

• Have a painted figure representing Jesus and place it lying down in the boat.

• Add other painted figures, representing ourselves, frightened by the storms of our lives.

• Stand up the figure of Jesus. Remove the storm clouds and wild waves, showing the original calm sea. Add a setting sun.

3. Pray the general intercessions, asking for confidence

in the presence of Jesus at all times in our lives, but especially in times of fear and danger.

4. As a reminder of our liturgy today and, more importantly, as a reminder that Jesus wants to calm our fears and make us happy, give each child a small boat on a gentle sea to take home.

5. Conclude the liturgy with a song that reminds us prayerfully of the constant presence and care of God through Jesus.

Other Possibilities:

1. There are a number of books which the leader might use to enhance the children's understanding of the fear and wonder associated with the calming of a storm. Within the story *Ride the Cold Wind*, by Anico Surany, is a wonderful description of two children out on Lake Titicaca in Peru when a storm comes upon them suddenly. Charlotte Zolotow and Margaret Bloy Graham's *The Storm Book* contains a vivid description and picture of a fisherman pushing his small boat to safety in the fury of a summer thunderstorm; the story ends by describing the calm, clean, glistening feeling everywhere after the storm subsides.

2. Show slides of the sea, of fishing boats, of a storm on the sea.

3. Older children would be interested in some facts about Lake Galilee. It is a small lake, nearly 700 feet below sea level, and almost entirely shut in by surrounding hills. Particularly in the evening, as warm air rises from the surface of the lake and the colder air from the mountains rushes down to take its place, violent winds can develop, turning the normally quiet waters into a sea of wild, high waves which could easily endanger a small fishing boat.

4. For older children, rather than using drawings of the sea to illustrate the gospel story, show a picture of a stormy sea only when discussing the storms in our lives, and write on the back of the picture some of the experiences we encounter that cause fear to disfigure our lives. Let the children compose a short prayer to remember the presence and the loving care of Jesus in our times of fear, and write the prayer on the back of a picture of a calm sea.

5. *Jesus and the Storm*, from the Augsburg Publishing House *What the Bible Tells Us Series*, presents our gospel story of the calming of the storm in very simple language, faithful to the biblical account, and with beautiful pictures. Read the story to younger children. Show the lovely pictures.

6. Older children would surely enjoy the first reading. Introduce the reading by telling them about Job. Job was a wealthy man and a good man, and Yahweh bragged about him to Satan. Satan protested to Yahweh that Job was good only because Yahweh had blessed him so much. To settle the argument Yahweh allowed Satan to take away all Job's wealth, his family, and finally his health. Job tried desperately to understand what had happened to him. In the end Yahweh spoke to Job "out of the storm" and told him that no one should presume to understand the ways of God. In our reading today, part of Yahweh's magnificent speech to Job, Yahweh asks Job if he is master of the sea. The sea is pictured as a baby, needing care and discipline. Explain the reading to the children, then proclaim it to them. Follow the proclamation with the responsorial psalm. Finally lead the children to appreciate the choice of the reading from Job and the verses from Ps 107 to accompany today's gospel.

7. Find a song which praises God who is Lord even of the storm. Older children might enjoy singing Thomas Dorsey's "Precious Lord, Take My Hand." Or invite several cantors to sing the song for the group.

Thirteenth Sunday of the Year

Lectionary for Masses with Children	Lectionary for Mass
*Wis 1:13-15;2:23-24	*Wis 1:13-15;2:23-24
*Ps 30:4-5,10-11-12	*Ps 30:2,4,5-6,11,12,13
*II Cor 8:7,9,13-14	*II Cor 8:7,9,13-15
**Mk 5:21-24,35-43	**Mk 5:21-43 or 5:21-24,35-43

Focus: We believe in Jesus who has power even over death.

Gather the Children

1. Welcome the children happily and remind them why we gather for our special liturgy of the word.
2. Greet the Lord present in the word by having one child hold high the lectionary while all sing a joyful song of praise to God. Place the lectionary where all the children can see it. Light candles near it.

Proclaim the Gospel

1. Prepare the children to hear the gospel:
- Ask the children to speak of times when they were sick. Since many of the children will want to describe in detail their experience of sickness, the leader must be prepared to end the discussion tactfully.
- Focus on the worry of their parents, particularly if their child was very sick. They talked to the doctor, visited the doctor, did all that the doctor advised, perhaps even took the child to the hospital. They did many special things to make the child happy. To maintain the interest of the children have a thermometer, an empty medicine container, a blanket, a quiet game.
- Ask the children to imagine that a friend is very sick, and that nothing the child's parents or doctor can do seems to make the child any better. Ask them to imagine that the parents are beginning to think that the child might even die. Help the children to understand, in some small way, the fear, the sorrow, the desperation of the parents when they realize that the life of their child may be near its end. Suggest also that the parents would pray to God, asking God with all their hearts to heal their child.
2. Relate the above discussion to the (short form of) the gospel:
- Help the children to appreciate the worry of Jairus, the child's father.
- Recall last week's gospel story of the calming of the storm, and tell the children that today's story takes place after Jesus has returned in the boat to the side of the lake on which he lived.
- Remind the children of Jesus's growing fame because of his teaching and his healings, and tell them that Jairus must surely have heard of Jesus because Jairus was one of the religious leaders of the people. Ask the children if they can think of anything that Jairus might do to help his child. Supply enough hints so that the children think that Jairus should go to Jesus.
3. Tell the children the story, and then discuss the rejoicing of Jairus's family.

4. Acclaim the gospel in song, then proclaim it.

Respond to the Gospel

1. Inspire the children to pray by helping them enter into the life of the little girl as she lay dying:
- Discuss the feelings of the child as she lay so sick, perhaps even knowing that she was dying.
- Suggest that the child was a child of prayer, as we might expect since her father was an official of the synagogue.
- Ask the children to pray as the child might have prayed. Say—better, sing—a prayer of trust in God's love and care.
2. Inspire the children to praise God by helping them rejoice with the child after she was healed:
- Ask the children to imagine the feelings of the child as new life transformed her wasted body.
- Ask the children to help make up a prayer of praise that the child might have spoken to God as she looked at Jesus and realized what had happened to her. Record the thoughts of the children and shape them into a prayer. Pray the prayer with the children. Perhaps the adult assembly would like to hear the children's prayer of praise as a communion meditation.
3. Pray the general intercessions, extending the concern of the children from the little girl to the many people who are sick and suffering today.

Make the Good News Our Own

1. Let the children pantomime the gospel story:.
- Choose children to take the parts of the child, her parents, Jesus, several messengers. Let the remaining children be friends and relatives of the child.
- Supply a few props and costumes: a blanket to cover the sick child, a cloth to wipe her face, simple robes for Jesus, the parents, and the messengers, something for the child to eat. Children usually are less self-consciou about their acting if they use even very simple props or costumes.
- The leader should tell the story, beginning with the care and concern of the parents, proceeding with the gospel story, and ending with the children's prayer of praise for the wonderful thing that happened.
2. As a reminder of our liturgy today and to help the children's parents, who worry so much about so many things, give each child the following activity paper to take home. Have written on the paper in large letters the words of Jesus "Don't worry. Just have faith." Instruct the children to take the papers home, to color the letters and decorate the papers, and then to give them to their parents as a reminder not to worry so much, but rather to remember the words of Jesus which we

heard today. Or trace the hand of a child and cut out copies to give to the children to take home. Tell the children that the hand represents our hands. Ask them to let the hand remind them that Jesus takes our hands in many ways today and cares for us, just as he took the hand of the little sick girl and gave her life.

3. If there is time, say a profession of faith.

Other Possibilities:

1. *Jesus and the Little Girl,* from the Augsburg Publishing House *What the Bible Tells Us Series,* gives a simple, sensitive rendition of the story of the cure of the child. The book is beautifully illustrated.

2. Before the liturgy have children draw pictures of the cure of the child. Use the pictures to illustrate the story.

3. For older children tell the story of the cure of the child, and then expand the story to include the cure of the woman with a hemorrhage (which the LMC omits entirely). The delay in the journey of Jesus not only heightens our concern for the sick child, but at the same time emphasizes for us that it is faith in Jesus and not some mysterious magical power that enables him to heal and to save. After the proclamation of the gospel, it would be good for the children to profess their own faith.

4. Point out to older children that in just five chapters of Mark's gospel we have already read that Jesus healed many people. Ask the children to look in their bibles during the coming week and count the cures of Jesus in the first five chapters of Mark. To review the great works of Jesus will prepare the children for the rejection of Jesus by those who had known him for years, the account of which is next week's gospel.

5. The two gospel stories which the LM presents to us today add fascinating detail to the life story of Jesus. They depict Jesus pushed about by the admiring and curious crowd. Jesus reacts with genuine emotion: he reacts with surprise and confusion to his cure of the woman; he reacts with sympathy toward Jairus and his wife; he reacts with exasperation, even pain, at the crowd of noisy, ridiculing mourners at Jairus's house; he reacts with tenderness toward the child; he reacts with good common sense when he instructs the child's family to give her something to eat. Details such as these, so liberally supplied by Mark, bring the human person of Jesus vividly to life in the mind of the reader. Use today's gospel to give older children a sense of Mark's lively portrait of Jesus.

6. Discuss with older children the effect on the child of her cure by Jesus. What were her thoughts? How did she tell her friends the story of her cure? Was her life changed by the remarkable thing that happened to her when she was twelve years old? Did she become a devoted follower of Jesus? How did she finally face death?

7. Discuss death with older children. How can a dying person believe in the power of Jesus to give life? Is there anything we can do to spread the good news of the power of Jesus over death to those who face imminent death?

8. Share the first reading with older children. All, obviously, must die physically; the author refers to spiritual death. Discuss the symbolism of physical death as the sign of our separation from God. Then discuss the significance of the raising of Jairus's child from death: it is a sign of the power of Jesus to call us to life after sin has separated us from God. Pray the responsorial psalm in thanksgiving for the gift of life. Or pray in song for a happy death.

9. Use the second reading as an encouragement to the children to be generous.

Fourteenth Sunday of the Year

Lectionary for Masses with Children	Lectionary for Mass
Ez 2:2-5	Ez 2:2-5
Ps 86:5-6,15-16	Ps 123:1-2,2,3-4
*II Cor 12:7-10	*II Cor 12:7-10
**Mk 6:1-6	**Mk 6:1-6

Focus: We pray to believe in Jesus and to follow him even when it's hard.

Gather the Children

1. Greet the Lord, present in the word, by singing a lively song of praise. Accompany the singing with simple gestures to involve little children more fully.

2. Ask the children to share their ideas about why we have our special liturgy of the word. Be sure the children realize that we and the adult assembly are both listening to God's word and thinking about its meaning for our lives.

3. Reverently open the lectionary and place it in the center of the children's gathering space. Then light candles near the lectionary as a further reminder of the presence of the Lord in our midst.

Proclaim the Gospel

1. Prepare the children for the proclamation of the gospel:

• Remind the children of the amazing works of Jesus:

Ask if anyone remembers the astonishing act of Jesus that we heard about last week. Let the children tell what they remember about how Jesus raised to life the dead daughter of Jairus.

Ask the children if they remember any other wonderful things Jesus did. Encourage them to speak of his wonderful teaching and his many healings, so much of which we have heard proclaimed on Sundays in this lectionary year B.

Ask the children what they think people were saying about Jesus, as they heard more and more about the things he said and did.

• Tell the children of the rejection of Jesus by the people of Nazareth:

Tell the children that, even though we might expect everyone to believe in Jesus and to love him because of what he said and did, there were some people who wouldn't accept him.

Ask the children if they remember where Jesus grew up. Tell them that the story we are about to hear happened in Nazareth, the hometown of Jesus.

Tell the group that Jesus made a visit to Nazareth. Speculate about his thoughts: he was anxious to see his mother, his relatives and his friends; he would miss Joseph, Mary's husband and his foster father, who was probably dead by now; it would be good to visit his home, to see all the familiar faces and places and things; he had lots to talk about, lots to ask about, lots to catch up with.

Tell the children what finally happened at Nazareth. The sabbath is the holy day of the Jewish people. On the sabbath they gather together in their synagogues to pray and to learn, just as we do in church on Sunday. On the sabbath Jesus went into the synagogue in Nazareth and began to teach. The people who heard him were amazed at his wisdom and they remembered his marvelous actions. But as they thought about who he was—a person who had grown up with them and whom they thought they knew all about, a person just like themselves—they became annoyed. They wouldn't listen to him or believe in him. Jesus must have been disappointed and hurt. Because the people wouldn't believe in him, he did very few miracles in Nazareth, but spent his time visiting nearby villages and teaching.

2. Ask the children to stand and listen carefully while we read the story from the bible. Sing a joyful gospel acclamation and then proclaim the gospel.

3. Respond to the gospel in prayer:

• Give the children a few moments to pray silently that we will never lose our faith in Jesus, that we will always believe in his love and his kindness and in his power to heal and to help us.

• Lead the children in a profession of faith, asking them to respond, perhaps in song, "I do believe!" to each of the following questions:

> Do you believe in God who made heaven and earth and who made us, too?
> Do you believe in Jesus who lived on earth to show us that God loves us and cares for us?
> Do you believe that Jesus teaches us about God?
> Do you believe that Jesus has the power to heal?
> Do you believe that Jesus shows us how to live?
> Do you believe in the Holy Spirit, the Spirit of Jesus, who is with us today to help us follow Jesus to God?
> Do you believe that after we die we will live with God forever?

4. Ask the children if they would like to have something to remind all the people in the assembly, including their parents, to be strong in their belief in Jesus. Pin on each child a piece of bright fabric on which is printed, "I believe in Jesus! Do you?"

Make the Good News Our Own

1. Today's gospel not only reminds us to have faith in Jesus, but also encourages us to be strong and faithful

in doing what Jesus wants of us, even though at times it is difficult. Although few of the youngest children understand ridicule and rejection, we use this opportunity to encourage the children to follow the way of Jesus.

● Talk with the children about the difficulties we sometimes face in trying to be good. Help them to be positive; the discussion should not degenerate into a session of blaming others, for example, their siblings, for their failings.

● Summarize for the children, or, if there is time, read or tell the children *Pepito's Story*, by Eugene Fern. It is the story of a little boy who loves to dance, but whose friends make fun of his dancing. In spite of his embarrassment and his loneliness, Pepito uses his gift of dancing to help a little girl who is sick. Discuss how brave and faithful Pepito was to do what he knew was the kind thing, even though he was afraid that the other children would laugh at him.

● Ask the children if they remember a time when people laughed at Jesus when he came to help someone who was sick. Remind the children thus that people laughed at Jesus when he came to the dead little daughter of Jairus and said she was only sleeping.

2. Ask the children to bow their heads and to pray that they, like Pepito and, especially, like Jesus, will always be thoughtful and kind, even when it's hard. Ask the younger ones to repeat this prayer:

> God, our Father,
> Thank you for Jesus
> who loves us so much.
> Help us always
> to follow his example,
> to be kind and thoughtful
> even when it's hard.
> Amen.

3. Sing a profession of our love for Jesus.

Other Possibilities:

1. For a shorter story than *Pepito's Story*, use *Apt. #3*, by Ezra Jack Keats. The author tells the story of two boys and a blind man. At first afraid of the man and reluctant to go near him, the children eventually discover something wonderful about him. Or, especially for older children, use Taro Yashima's *Crow Boy*. It is the story of a child who is misunderstood and rejected by his classmates, but befriended by a teacher who discovers the boy's remarkable talent. Each of these stories encourages the reader not to reject someone who seems strange, but rather to be open to the good in others. If the leader has difficulty finding the stories, he or she might ask the public librarian for additional suggestions. There are many suitable stories.

2. There are often news stories of people who have strong beliefs and who act on their beliefs or express themselves in ways that arouse irritation, rejection, even hatred, in others. The issues abound: nuclear weapons, disarmament, draft resistance, aid to the poor, capital punishment, abortion, the gay community, street children, etc. Introduce older children to people who are actively involved in some genuinely Christian but controversial issue. Use this opportunity to influence the children gently to be open to those whose opinions differ from their own.

3. Older children may themselves have faced ridicule and rejection by their friends for what they are or for what they believe. Smart children are sometimes rejected by their classmates, so also those who refuse to follow the crowd in undesirable behavior, so also those whose parents are involved in controversial issues. Children frequently reflect the prejudices of their parents. With acceptance and gentle sensitivity, encourage the children to share their experiences. Listen to their ideas, but do not "preach." End the discussion by praying with the children for open minds and generous hearts.

4. Share with older children Paul's thoughts in our passage from the apostle's second letter to the Corinthians. We do not know what Paul's "thorn in the flesh" was (as various translations from the Greek phrase it). Some think it was a speech impediment or other physical ailment. Whatever it was, Paul at first prayed for release from the problem, but finally became content to bear it knowing that the Lord was with him in his weakness. Proclaim the reading to the children and then invite them to comment upon Paul's willingness to suffer for the sake of Christ, indeed Paul's boasting of his weakness. What reason does Paul give for his joy in his suffering? Are we as accepting of our handicaps as Paul was?

Fifteenth Sunday of the Year

Lectionary for Masses with Children	Lectionary for Mass
*Am 7:10-15 Ps 85:8-9,10-11,12-13 Eph 3:1-10 **Mk 6:7-13	*Am 7:12-15 Ps 85:9-10,11-12,13-14 Eph 1:3-14 or 3:1-10 **Mk 6:7-13

Focus: The Twelve carried on the mission of Jesus. We pray to carry on the mission of Jesus in the world today.

Gather the Children

1. Welcome the children eagerly, taking care to see that the children know our joy in their presence. Pay special attention to those children who are with the group today for the first time, including those who are visiting. The leader should be aware that children are often uncomfortable doing new things.
2. Remind the children why we gather for our special liturgy of the word. Stress that we want not only to hear the word of God, but to reflect upon how that word can touch and change our lives.
3. Invite a child to hold the lectionary high while all sing to acknowledge the presence of God in the word. Enthrone the lectionary where all the children can see it and light candles near it.

Proclaim the Gospel

1. Prepare the children for the gospel:
- Talk with the children about preparing for a trip. Let them mention things they and their parents do to get ready: they plan where to go, how to go, where to stay; they make reservations for transportation and accommodations; they arrange for cash or credit; they choose clothes and games and books and pack all their things; sometimes they prepare food to take along. Have items presents, such as a suitcase, a bathing suit, a game, a plane ticket, some money, a jar of peanut butter, to help hold the interest of younger children. Tell the children that our gospel story today is about a trip, but not a vacation trip.
- Turn the attention of the children to Jesus and the Twelve by reminding them of Jesus's choice of twelve companions to help him in his mission to preach the good news. (See Mk 3:13-19 for Mark's account. The evangelists do not agree on the names of the Twelve.) Ask the children which of the Twelve they remember by name. Have thirteen figures, stiff ones that will stand up, to represent Jesus and the Twelve.
- Tell the children the gospel story: Jesus gathered the Twelve together and sent them out, two by two, to do work like his among the people. As the leader talks, he or she should move the figures in pairs. But Jesus told the Twelve to travel "light"—not to take food or money or a suitcase or even a change of clothes. The leader should remove the traveling supplies and contrast the traveling condition of the Twelve with our usual burdened traveling condition. Suggest that Jesus did not want the Twelve to spend time worrying about looking after their things. He was urging them to concentrate on the meaning of their mission.
- Review the work of the Twelve: they proclaimed the message of Jesus, they urged people to change their lives, they healed the sick. (The translation chosen by the LMC renders the venerable "anoint with oil" by "putting olive oil on them.") Give one figure a placard stating "God loves you!" and another a placard stating "Be good now!" Give another figure a bandage and a pair of crutches. Tell the children that during their travels, the Twelve stayed in the homes of people they met. The leader might have several simple houses and place them near the figures.
2. Acclaim the gospel in song and then proclaim it.

Make the Good News Our Own

1. Talk with the children of the great responsibility of the Twelve to assist Jesus in his mission. Suggest that some people whom they met were receptive and responsive, others disinterested, even rude; but the Twelve surely kept on with their work, even when there were problems. Next week we will hear about what happened when the Twelve returned to Jesus.
2. Ask the children who helps Jesus today to reach people with the good news of God's love.
- Talk of people in the local community—parents, teachers, priests.
- Introduce them to mission work. The leader might look in Maryknoll or another mission magazine for pictures and specifics.
- Finally, remind the children that we all, even children, must help spread the good news by how we live. Let the children share their ideas about how we can do this, and then pray that we will do it faithfully.
3. Let the children symbolize their resolve to try to help in the mission of Jesus and the Twelve:
- Give each child a small figure, similar to the larger figures representing the Twelve. Have written on the figures the words "Go and tell!" Ask the children to personalize their figures in some way.
- Then ask the children to stand and hold up their figures as a sign that they wish to help continue the mission work of the Twelve. If the number of children does not prohibit it, ask each child, "Will you go and tell others about Jesus?" The child should answer, "Yes!"
4. Teach the children a song whose theme is our reaching out to others with the good news of Jesus.
5. Conclude with the general intercessions, focusing both on the needs of those who have not heard the gospel and on the needs of those who proclaim the gospel.

Other Possibilities:

1. There are various other aspects of today's gospel which might interest older children:

• Does the instruction of Jesus to the Twelve to travel unencumbered suggest an urgency in spreading his message? Might this have been a reaction to the rejection of Jesus in Nazareth, last week's gospel passage and, in fact, the passage in Mark which immediately precedes our gospel today?

• Is it really possible to travel with so little? Would we dare to travel with so little today? What does it say about the faith of the Twelve?

• The specific instruction of Jesus to take no food points the way to Jesus's miraculous feeding of the crowd, which, after the Twelve return to Jesus next week, will occupy our attention for several Sundays. Without "spoiling the story" for the children, be sure that they notice and remember Jesus's charge to take no bread.

2. Talk to older children about the lively, courageous prophet Amos whom we meet in today's first reading. Amos was the earliest of the prophets whose writings have come to us. He was active in the eighth century BCE, during the reign of Jeroboam, a time of peace and prosperity in Israel. Amos bravely and dramatically denounced the immorality and empty rituals of the people and their leaders, calling them back to the high moral and religious demands of Yahweh. At least some of his prophecies were delivered at the great cult center of Bethel, from which, as we read today, Amos was finally expelled by Amaziah, the priest in charge of the sanctuary. Read to the children today's passage from the book of Amos. (The LMC, unlike the LM, sensitively begins the pericope with its initial explanatory verses.) Discuss the difference between Amos, who bravely denounced the government for its injustices and inhuman policies, and Amaziah, for whom religion existed to promote loyalty to the status quo (Fuller, PNL). Relate the message of Amos to the needs of the world today. Pray for prophets who are courageous enough to proclaim the word of God when no one wants to hear it "like it is."

3. Help the children compose a letter of thanks to some person they know or know about who helps to spread the good news of Jesus in the world today—a religion teacher, for example, or a foreign missioner.

4. Suggest to older children that they become involved in the life of the parish and so help to make known the love and care of God, as Jesus did. They can assist their parents in various parish activities; they can be altar servers; they can be school of religion assistants; they can work in the nursery. Older children are capable of many things, but need encouragement and imaginative leadership.

5. Read or tell the children *The Poppy Seeds*, by Robert Clyde Bulla, the story of a little boy who spreads happiness in his village in a simple way. Encourage the children to follow the example of Jesus and the little boy and find ways to make others happy.

Sixteenth Sunday of the Year

Lectionary for Masses with Children	Lectionary for Mass
*Jer 23:3-6	*Jer 23:1-6
**Ps 23:1-3,3-4,6	**Ps 23:1-3,3-4,5,6
-----	Eph 2:13-18
**Mk 6:30-34	**Mk 6:30-34

Focus: We rejoice in Jesus, who cares for us as a shepherd cares for sheep. We pray that we will show the same love and concern for others.

Gather the Children

1. Welcome the children with joy and remind them why we gather each Sunday for our special liturgy of the word.
2. Place the lectionary reverently in its place of honor and light candles near it. Then ask the children to pray quietly for a moment that the word of God will always fill our minds and our hearts with thoughts of God's love and care. J.S. Bach's "Sheep May Safely Graze" would be lovely background music as the children and the leader reflect on God's love.

Rejoice in the Lord Our Shepherd

1. Talk about sheep and their shepherd:
• Ask the children what they know about sheep and shepherds. Bring out that sheep are affectionate, docile, unaggressive animals, relatively defenseless and in constant need of care and supervision. They need their shepherd to lead them to grassy pastures for food and to water. They need their shepherd for protection from wild beasts, such as lions and bears, for protection from theft, to lead them to shelter in bad weather.
• Tell the children that sheep have always been very important to the people of Palestine. They furnish wool for clothing. They give milk, cheese, butter and meat. Flocks are large and everywhere, their presence and habits familiar to all the people.
• Have pictures of sheep and shepherds. Slides would be excellent. Or use simple sketches.
2. Help the children to appreciate the biblical image of the Lord as our shepherd:
• Tell the children that in the bible there are more than five hundred references to sheep!
• Talk about the qualities of the shepherd that are like the qualities of God, and so help the children understand why the people of Israel thought of God as their shepherd and themselves as the shepherd's sheep.
3. Rejoice in the Lord, our shepherd:
• Pray Ps 23. Have slides illustrating the phrases of the psalm, for example, of a green pasture, of a peaceful pond, of a path, of an adult leading a child. If slides are not available, use pictures, even pictures drawn by children. Let the young artists hold up their pictures at the appropriate times during the praying of the psalm.
• Teach the children to sing a simple song which speaks about God as our shepherd.

Proclaim the Gospel

1. Tell the children that in our gospel today Jesus thinks of the crowds of people who followed him as sheep without a shepherd.
2. Summarize the gospel story:
• Ask the children if they remember what the Twelve did in last week's gospel story. Help them to recall that Jesus sent them out to preach and to cure the sick, and so to carry on his work. Today we will hear about what happened when the apostles returned to Jesus.
• Picture the invitation of Jesus to his friends as a delightful invitation to be together to rest and to picnic, to talk about their experiences, to enjoy each other's company. Describe the disappointment that must have been theirs when it became apparent that they could not be alone together. Finally, highlight Jesus's heartfelt care and compassion for the crowd that caused him to put their needs ahead of his own.
3. Acclaim the gospel in song, and then proclaim.

Respond to the Good News

1. Ask the children how Jesus showed in the story that he was like a good shepherd to the people. Lead into a discussion about the constant love and care of Jesus for all the people he met. Ask the children why the image of Jesus as a good shepherd is a helpful one. Ask them if they remember the time that Jesus spoke specifically of himself as the good shepherd; in this way remind them of our liturgy on Good Shepherd Sunday, the Fourth Sunday of Easter.
2. Pray silently with the children in thanksgiving for Jesus who loves and cares about others so very much. Then invite any willing child to share his or her prayer with the group.
3. Suggest that we all try to imitate Jesus in the concern and the care we show to others. Let the children offer ideas of how we can do so. Help them to be practical.
4. Pray in the general intercessions that Jesus will continue to show love and care for all people. Pray that we all will show the same love and concern for others that Jesus did.
5. Give each child a paper with the outline of a large sheep. Ask the children to take their papers home and to draw within the outline pictures of themselves doing things to show love and concern for others.

Other Possibilities:

1. With older children, enrich the presentation of the Lord as our shepherd by focusing more deeply on the biblical analogy of leaders and shepherds:
• Talk about leaders: What do leaders do? Do good

leaders care about those who follow them? How do they show their care? Focus on a good leader's willingness to help his or her followers even when it's hard.

• Then discuss why a good leader might be likened to a good shepherd.

2. Proclaim the Old Testament reading to older children:

• Tell the children about the remarkable man and prophet Jeremiah. Jeremiah loved his people deeply and he gave his life to his mission of calling them back to Yahweh. "Jeremiah realized that the word of Yahweh had the double aspect of judgment and renewal, doom and promise" (Anderson, UOT, p.349). Jeremiah's efforts to reform the social, religious and political life of his people were largely in vain, and he lived to see the destruction of Jerusalem and the deportation of most of her people to Babylon. In his work, which was probably collected and edited by his "secretary" Baruch, Jeremiah reveals his inner thoughts and feelings profoundly and beautifully. He shows himself a man of sensitivity and loyalty, of courage and gentleness.

• In today's LM reading Yahweh, through the prophet Jeremiah, utters an indictment against the unfaithful leaders of Israel, whom he compares with uncaring shepherds; and he himself promises to gather the scattered flock and return it to the meadow, then to appoint good shepherds to care for the sheep and to protect them. The LMC picks up the reading with the Lord's promise of restoration. Proclaim the reading to the children, in either its longer or its shorter form, and then pray silently with them in thanksgiving for the love and care of Yahweh.

• The reader will notice that the translation chosen by the LMC replaces the imagery of "flock" and "shepherds" with the terms "people" and "leaders." While it is true that the new vocabulary carries the technical meaning of the verses, the traditional vocabulary invests the surface meaning of the verses with the commanding power of ancient and rich tradition. Rather than altering the time-honored biblical imagery, it would be better to retain it (but see immediately below), thus stimulating the poetic imagination of the children, explaining the psalm response, and anticipating the gospel imagery. (The latter imagery is, no doubt, the reason for the choice of the Jeremiah reading anyway: see, for example, the "Introduction" of the LM, section 3-c.)

3. The biblical image of God as our shepherd is beautiful and profound; but to the children of today, who rarely, if ever, see sheep and shepherds, the image unfortunately does not speak unaided.

• Challenge older children to think of additional images of God and the people that might speak to today's young people.

• As an example of a modern-day good shepherd, introduce the children to the work of a missioner. The July 1982 issue of *Maryknoll* magazine has, beginning on p.13, an informative and moving short article on the work and martyrdom of Brother James Miller in Central America. A picture of "Brother Santiago" carrying a lamb in his arms accompanies the story!

4. Pray all of Ps 23 with older children, thus including verse 5, the single verse of the psalm which the LMC omits. Send home copies of the psalm, perhaps with a picture to color. Arrange the psalm in parts for parents and children and suggest that the children pray Ps 23 with their families as part of their mealtime prayer.

The Lord Is My Shepherd

A Reading of Psalm 23

Children:	The LORD is my shepherd; I shall not want.
Parents:	In green pastures the LORD gives me rest.
Children:	Beside restful waters the LORD leads me.
Parents:	The LORD refreshes my soul.
Children:	The LORD guides me in right paths for his name's sake.
Parents:	Even though I walk in the dark valley I fear no evil.
Children:	For you are at my side with your rod and your staff that give me courage.
Parents:	You spread the table before me in the sight of my foes.
Children:	You anoint my head with oil.
Parents:	My cup overflows.
Children:	Only goodness and kindness follow me all the days of my life.
Parents:	And I shall dwell in the house of the LORD for years to come.

Lectionary for Masses with Children	Lectionary for Mass
*II Kgs 4:42-44	*II Kgs 4:42-44
*Ps 145:10-11,15-16	*Ps 145:10-11,15-16,17-18
Eph 4:1-6	Eph 4:1-6
**Jn 6:1-15	**Jn 6:1-15

Seventeenth Sunday of the Year

Focus: Let us praise the Lord who feeds us, who answers all our needs.

Gather the Children

1. In addition to the usual lectionary and candles, have a picnic basket filled with small loaves of bread, enough loaves for each child to have one. Hide the loaves under a picnic cloth. On top of the cloth, so that they are visible to the children, have five loaves of bread and two fat, perhaps paper-stuffed, fish.

2. Greet the Lord, present in the word, in song. During the singing have one child carry the lectionary to its place of honor in the children's gathering space. Light the candles.

3. Remind the children why we gather for our special liturgy of the word. Then pray quietly with the group that our minds be filled with God's word and our lives with God's good things.

Proclaim the Gospel

1. Prepare the children for the proclamation of the gospel:
• Ask the children to think of a time when they were on a picnic. Let them share their experiences, which, most likely, have been happy ones. End the discussion by suggesting that it would be nice if we could have a picnic together this very afternoon.
• Ask the children what they remember about last week's gospel story, Mk 6:30-34. Give them enough hints to recall that Jesus, though he wanted to rest and be alone with the Twelve, turned generously to the large crowd of people who had followed him and began to teach them.
• Suggest, basing the narrative on Mk 6:34-44 as well as on today's gospel, that Jesus spoke to the people until it was quite late, thus time to think about eating.
• Continue the story as it is told in today's gospel. Tell the story vividly, yet faithfully. Include Philip's consternation at the thought of buying bread for more than five thousand people, the boy's few loaves and fish, the actions of Jesus, the pleasant springtime (Passover was near, see also Mark's charming 6:39-40) outdoor setting of the picnic-like meal, the abundance of food, the reaction of the people and Jesus's sudden withdrawal to the mountain alone. Stress, not something "magical" about the meal, but the generous hospitality of Jesus in whose presence there is joy and plenty.

2. Tell the children that we will listen to the story of the feeding of the hungry crowd as John wrote it in his gospel. Ask the children to stand. Acclaim the gospel joyfully in song and then proclaim it.

Make the Good News Our Own

1. Retell the gospel story quickly with the help of the children, using the contents of the picnic basket. At the appropriate time, uncover the small loaves of bread and give them to the children. Do not let the children eat the bread, but rather suggest that they take it home and share it later with their families.

2. Lead the children to gratitude for the generosity of Jesus:
• Ask the children to imagine that they were present when Jesus fed the hungry crowd, that they shared the bread and the fish Jesus provided. Ask them what they would have done after the meal. In this way draw from the children expressions of their gratitude to Jesus for his gifts.
• With the children's help compose a thank-you note to Jesus, something that a child in the crowd might have written to Jesus the day after the wonderful meal.
• Teach the children to sing, "We praise you, we bless you, we thank you!"

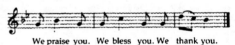

We praise you. We bless you. We thank you.

The acclamation is one of the acclamations of Eucharistic Prayer for Children II. Read prayerfully the thank-you note composed by the children, singing the acclamation several times before and after the prayer.

3. Pray the general intercessions, asking God that we, like Jesus, will notice and respond to the needs of other people. For example, pray:

Leader:	My brothers and sisters in God's family, let us pray that God will answer the needs of all people. Please respond: "Bless your children, Lord."
	Many people all over the world are hungry. For them we pray:
All:	Bless your children, Lord.
Leader:	Many people do not have enough clothes to wear. For them we pray:
All:	Bless your children, Lord.
Leader:	Many people do not have proper homes. For them we pray:
All:	Bless your children, Lord.
Leader:	Many children cannot go to school. For them we pray:
All:	Bless your children, Lord.
Leader:	Many people are sick. For them we pray:
All:	Bless your children, Lord.
Leader:	Many people are lonely. For them we pray:
All:	Bless your children, Lord.

Leader:	Many people do not have peace and joy. For them we pray:
All:	Bless your children, Lord.
Leader:	Loving God, we know that you are near to all who call upon you. Feed us, feed all your children, with your life and your love. Help us to follow the example of Jesus, who was always ready to help people. We pray in the name of Jesus and with your Holy Spirit.
All:	Amen.

4. In thanksgiving to Jesus for the gift of food and, indeed, for his many gifts, teach the children a simple eucharist-related hymn. Because we will spend the next several Sundays reading additional passages in the sixth chapter of John's gospel, a eucharist-related hymn seems a particularly good choice for today. The children should continue to sing the same hymn for the next few weeks.

Other Possibilities:

1. Because Mark's gospel is short, the church inserts into the middle of "ordinary time" in lectionary year B five Sundays whose gospel readings come from the gospel of John. The first of these insertions, today's gospel, tells the story of the feeding of the hungry crowd, which in Mark's gospel immediately follows the return of the apostles to Jesus after their missionary adventures, which we read in last Sunday's gospel. For the next four Sundays we will read from the remainder of John's chapter 6, thus interpreting the miracle in Mark as a foreshadowing of the eucharist. On the following Sunday, we will resume our systematic study of Mark's gospel. To the interested reader of the Sunday gospels it is as if a spotlight has been thrown upon the story of the feeding of the hungry crowd. In light of the centrality of the eucharist in our Catholic tradition, the leader should consider sharing these observations with older children, though perhaps next Sunday would be a better time to do so.

2. The story of the feeding of the hungry crowd is the only miracle of Jesus recounted in all four gospels. Discuss with older children the importance of this miracle as a sign of the abundance of God's love and care for us.

3. Continue the discussion of the gospel by focusing on the immense problem of hunger in the world today. Wealthy nations in general and many wealthy—and not so wealthy—people in particular are blind to the plight of the poor and to the needs of the future. They fatten themselves, while others starve; they ir-responsibly consume and waste the world's resources, thus jeopardizing the future of the entire world. Children, of course, are not responsible for global problems and cannot solve them; and adults must be careful not to instill in them a sense of guilt. But today's readings call all of us, even children, out of our shortsightedness and self-centeredness and urge us to examine our own habits and attitudes to see if we, who are the hands of God in the world today, are intensifying the world's problems or are preparing ourselves to feed the poor and answer their needs. Discuss all this with older children and stimulate them to be imaginative and creative, yet practical, in responding to the needs of the poor.

4. Proclaim today's Old Testament to older children. It may come as a surprise to them that Jesus was not the only one in scripture to feed a crowd with just a little food. Elisha was a vigorous figure, an ecstatic "madman" (II Kings 9:11, see Anderson, UOT, p.224), who exhibited considerable political influence. He was admired, it seems, more as a wonder worker than as a man of God, and the stories about him show "a childish love of the marvelous, which is not always edifying" (McKenzie, DOB). Remark to the children that God always provides for people, as the story of Elisha illustrates; but how marvelously God provides for us through Jesus!

5. Focus on the providence of God by praying the responsorial psalm. Teach the children to sing the response, and then sing (or read) the verses, singing the response between them. Add a few simple gestures to help make the response a prayer arising from our whole being. Or simply have the children read the psalm in parts. Give them copies to take home to share with their families, perhaps as a prayer before meals.

6. To illustrate graphically the abundance of God's gifts, conduct the following simple activity. The leader should trace his or her hand, held with fingers together. Cut out two hands and staple them together, leaving unstapled the thumb side. Ask the children to think of some of the good things that God gives us. As the children suggest the gifts of God, write them on small slips of paper and insert them into the pair of hands, as if they are gifts held in the hands of God. Print on the hands the words of the psalm response

> You open your hand to feed us, LORD;
>   you answer all our needs.

7. In view of the eucharistic overtones of today's gospel and the unity expressed in the reading from Ephesians, sing with the children John Foley's "One Bread, One Body."

Eighteenth Sunday of the Year

Lectionary for Masses with Children	Lectionary for Mass
**Ex 16:2-4,12-15	**Ex 16:2-4,12-15
*Ps 78:3-4,23-24,25,54	*Ps 78:3-4,23-24,25,54
-----	Eph 4:17,20-24
**Jn 6:24-29	**Jn 6:24-29

Focus: We believe in Jesus who is the bread that gives life everlasting.

Gather the Children

1. Welcome the children with joy and sing in praise of God who is with us when we gather in God's name. As a sign of God's presence light candles near the lectionary.
2. Ask the children why we come together for our special liturgy of the word. Remind them that we and the adult assembly will both listen to God's word and think about its meaning for our lives.
3. In addition to candles and the lectionary have visible to the children today a loaf of bread and the thank-you note to Jesus that the children composed last week.

Proclaim the Gospel

1. Prepare the children for the gospel:
● Remind the children of last week's gospel story, Jn 6:1-15:

Point out the loaf of bread. Use it to encourage the children to talk about Jesus's feeding of the hungry crowd.

Ask why Jesus fed the crowd, and thus lead into reflection on the loving concern of Jesus for all people.

Ask the children if, following the example of Jesus, they tried during the past week to be caring, as Jesus always was.

● Read the thank-you note to Jesus which the children composed as part of our liturgy last Sunday, and focus briefly on the gratitude that the people whom Jesus fed should have felt.

● Lead into the action of today's gospel story by asking the children what they would have talked about with their friends the next day if they had been in the crowd which Jesus fed. Ask them if they would have been hungry again. In the course of the discussion, help the children to see that the people whom Jesus fed had the perfectly human desire to return to Jesus, to be with him in case he should do something else wonderful.

2. Summarize the action in today's gospel. After the feeding of the crowd the people were excited, so excited that Jesus was afraid they would want to make him their king. So he left them quickly and fled to the hills alone. The next day, however, the crowd sought him and found him. Jesus knew they had come to him because they wanted to see other wonderful things. He told them that he would give them something more wonderful than the food they had eaten the day before and which had left them hungry again a few hours lat-

er. He told them that he was thinking of a new food that would give them life forever. The people were confused. They wondered how Jesus could possibly give them something that good, but they wanted it. Then Jesus explained that he himself was that special food, the bread of life, and that whoever would come to him and believe in him would never be hungry or thirsty again.

3. There is disagreement among scholars as to whether, when Jesus speaks of himself as the bread of life in Jn 6:35 (the LMC omits the magnificent verse, only part of which is repeated in next Sunday's gospel), he is referring to himself as the revelation of the Father and calling for faith in who he is and what he says, or he is referring to himself as eucharistic bread, which thought becomes explicit in Jn 6:51-59. Because the concepts involved are abstract and difficult, because we are dealing with little children and because the eucharist is central to our Catholic tradition, let us assume that "bread of life" here means eucharistic bread. Ask the children if they have any idea what Jesus meant when he said that he himself is the bread of life. Lead them to realize that Jesus was promising himself to us in the eucharist, bread for us to eat so that we can live forever in union with Jesus and with each other.

4. Proclaim the gospel:
● Ask the children to stand and listen prayerfully to the beautiful promise of Jesus to give himself to us as the bread of life.
● Acclaim the gospel in song, and then proclaim it. The leader may well wish to supplement the selection of the LMC with more of the reading of the LM, particularly its final verses 34-35.

Make the Good News Our Own

1. Give each child a small simple paper figure. Distribute crayons and let the children mark their figures quickly with something personal—draw their faces, write their names, color their clothes.
2. Glue onto a poster board a figure representing Jesus with arms outstretched as if offering something to someone.
3. Ask the children what Jesus promises us today. After they respond, glue bread into the hands of Jesus, thus reminding us both of the bread with which he fed the hungry crowd and the bread of life which he promises us today.
4. Ask the children, some of whom may not yet have received the eucharist, if they want to share this special bread. After they respond, collect the figures which they have personalized and glue them onto the poster board as if they are about to receive the bread which Jesus offers.

Respond in Prayer to the Gospel

1. Profess our faith in the eucharist by asking the children to respond,

> Our loving God gives us all good things.
> The greatest gift of God to us is Jesus.
> Jesus is the bread of life.
> No one who goes to Jesus shall be hungry.
> No one who believes in Jesus shall thirst.
> The eucharist is a sign that we live forever with God and with each other.

2. Ask the children to thank God for the gift of Jesus in the eucharist and to pray in joyful anticipation of the day when we will all share the eucharist.

3. Lead the children in an appropriate eucharist-related hymn. The leader should consider using again the hymn the children learned last Sunday.

4. Pray in the general intercessions that all God's children will have enough bread to live well both physically and spiritually.

5. As a reminder of our liturgy of the word today, give each child a paper loaf of bread on which is printed "I am the bread of life" and "Jn 6:35."

6. Remind the children that when we rejoin the adult assembly we will celebrate the liturgy of the eucharist. Most of the assembly once again will share the bread of life, which is Jesus. Ask the younger children to pray again during the distribution of the eucharist, as we have prayed here together, that they, too, will soon share the eucharist with joy.

Other Possibilities:

1. Suggest to the parish liturgy planners that today the presider use one of the eucharistic prayers for children. Enlist the help of the parish minister of music to teach the children—and, in fact, to teach the entire assembly—to sing the responses.

2. Proclaim the Old Testament reading:

- Ask the children what they remember about the escape of the Israelites from Egypt. Sketch their crossing of the Red Sea and remind the group briefly of that great love-act of God. Some of the children may not know the story.

- Tell the children that the Israelites soon found themselves traveling in the desert. Ask what the children know about a desert. Sketch a desert and include details supplied by the children.

- Focus on the difficulty of finding food and water in the desert. The leader should read Ex 15:22-27 and all of Ex 16 in preparation for this liturgy of the word, and tell the children, dramatically yet faithfully, the story.

- Ask the children to listen carefully as we read the story from the bible. Proclaim the reading.

- Respond to the reading by praying the responsorial psalm, part of Ps 78. Teach the children to sing the refrain. The leader might consider letting older children read the verses in groups.

- Tell the children that when Jesus promised to give the people bread from heaven, as we read in our gospel reading today, some people thought immediately of what their great leader Moses had done in the desert so many years before. In preparation for the next few Sunday gospels, tell the older children that some of the people showed signs of becoming upset with Jesus because they thought he was claiming to be greater even than Moses.

3. With older children relate last week's gospel and today's gospel to the world situation. If last week's feeding of the hungry crowd prompted us to consider what we might do to alleviate poverty and waste in the world at large, then today's gospel might lead us to consider our responsibility to spread the word of God, who is Jesus, to the world (Fuller, PNL). The leader might enrich these consideration by informing the children of the ambiguity of Jn 6:35, to which we have already alluded: When Jesus identified himself as the bread of life, was he referring to himself as the word of God or as eucharistic bread?

4. Sing John Foley's "One Bread, One Body." The song is a prayer for unity through the eucharist, appropriate particularly if today we seriously consider our responsibility to share our bread—bread for physical life and bread for spiritual life.

5. Remind the children of the petition in the Lord's Prayer "Give us this day our daily bread." Ask the children to pray the Lord's Prayer with special attention during today's liturgy of the eucharist.

Nineteenth Sunday of the Year

Lectionary for Masses with Children	Lectionary for Mass
**I Kgs 19:4-8	**I Kgs 19:4-8
*Ps 34:1-2,3-4,7-8	*Ps 34:2-3,4-5,6-7,8-9
Eph 4:31-5:2	Eph 4:30-5:2
**Jn 6:48-51	**Jn 6:41-51

Focus: We thank God for the gift of believing in Jesus. We pray that God will draw us ever closer to Jesus, the living bread from heaven.

Gather the Children

1. Gather the children in a circle and lead them in song to greet the Lord, present in the word.
2. Remind the children why we gather for our special liturgy of the word. Pray with them that we will open our minds and our hearts to God's word.
3. Lay the lectionary reverently in its place of honor in the children's gathering space. Light candles near the book. Have present objects related to our last two liturgies of the word—a loaf of bread, for example, to remind us of the feeding of the crowd, and the poster which the children made, to remind us our desire to have the special bread promised by Jesus.

Proclaim the Gospel

1. Prepare the children for the proclamation of the gospel:
- Remind the group briefly of the events in the life of Jesus which have occupied our attention for the past two Sundays: the feeding of the hungry crowd (Jn 6:1-15) and Jesus's promise of the bread of life (Jn 6:24-35). Today's gospel continues the long discourse of Jesus which makes up most of the sixth chapter of John's gospel.
- With very young children, the leader may wish to dwell only on the excerpt from today's LM gospel which the LMC retains. Following the longer LM reading, the leader might lead older children to realize that the crowd around Jesus was becoming angry and was beginning to reject him because of his words.
- Review the gospel story thus far and continue it with today's reading. Younger children might enjoy a flannel board or stand-up figure presentation. Have figures of Jesus, the Twelve and the crowd, drawn in groups; also have bread and the baskets for leftovers. Let Jesus mingle with the crowd during the meal, then go off alone to the hills. Let the crowd disperse. Then let Jesus rejoin the disciples. Have the crowd search and finally find Jesus. Let Jesus speak to the crowd about the bread of life and, if the leader wishes to use the longer reading, let the people draw back in protest.
2. Proclaim the gospel:
- Suggest that the children imagine that they were there in the crowd, listening carefully to Jesus's words.
- Ask the children to stand to hear the words of Jesus. Acclaim the gospel in song, and then proclaim it, reading the words of Jesus slowly and thoughtfully. Even if the leader has chosen to dwell on the shorter reading of the LMC, he or she might consider including in the proclamation verses 44 and 47 because of their emphasis on faith.

Respond in Faith to the Words of Jesus

1. Remind the children that Jesus said that we can believe in him only if God makes it possible, that is, only if God gives us the faith to believe in him. We do believe in Jesus, and we must thank God always for our gift of faith. Ask the children to repeat the following prayer, line by line, in gratitude for the gift of faith:

Loving God,
thank you for calling us
to be your children.
Thank you for drawing to Jesus.
We believe in Jesus.
We believe that Jesus is your child.
We believe that Jesus is the bread of life.
We believe that we shall live forever.
Thank you for all your gifts to us.
Amen.

2. Ask the children if they remember from last week what wonderful gift to us Jesus had in mind when he said, "I am the bread of life." In this way remind them that Jesus was promising to give us the eucharist.

Make the Good News Our Own

1. As a reminder of our liturgy today, and especially as a reminder of the promise of Jesus to give himself to us as our bread of life, give each child a white paper plate. Tell the children to let the plate be a reminder of how Jesus fed the crowd of people outside, picnic-style, and then of how he promised them a better food, one to give them life forever. Ask the children to draw on their plates, after they go home, a picture of Jesus promising the people himself as the bread of life.
2. Remind the children to watch and listen carefully, after they rejoin the assembly for the liturgy of the eucharist, for the words and actions of the presider: like Jesus, the presider take bread, praises God and offers the bread to the (older) members of the assembly as their bread of life. Suggest to younger children that they pray, especially during the communion rite, that Jesus will come soon to them, too, as living bread.
3. Conclude the liturgy of the word with a simple eucharist-related hymn, ideally one which the children have sung for the past two Sundays.

Other Possibilities:

1. Suggest to the parish liturgy team that the presider use today one of the eucharistic prayers for children. Better still, arrange for the presider and the assembly to sing the prayer.

2. Older children might understand the difficulties the crowd encountered in believing what Jesus said:

• Remind the children that Jesus had promised to give a better bread than Moses had supplied in the desert. The people were confused at this because Moses was so important in their history. If Jesus was claiming that he could do something better than Moses, them he must be claiming that he was greater than Moses. This angered the crowd.

• Remind the children that Jesus told the crowd that he himself was this special bread from heaven. This also angered the people because they thought they knew all about Jesus, since they knew his parents.

• Help the children to realize that Jesus was asking the people to believe in him first, and then to accept what he said. He was not asking for an understanding of all that he said, but for a response in faith to who he was.

• Ask the children if they think the response of wonder and doubt of many people was irresponsible. Ask them if they have ever worried that they might have been among those who did not believe. In this way lead them to appreciate that faith is a gift from God, or, in the words of Jesus, that God must draw us to Jesus. Then pray with the children that we, who have the gift of faith, will be open to growth in our life of faith.

3. Suggest to older children that during the week to come they give some thought to the meaning of "eternal life." What does Jesus mean when he says that one who believes "has eternal life"? What does he mean when he says that one who eats the living bread "shall live forever"? We will return to thoughts of eternal life next week when we come at last to the explicitly eucharistic segment of the Johannine discourse in Jn 6.

4. Sing M. Suzanne Toolan's "I Am the Bread of Life," especially verse 1.

5. Share something of the life and work of the great and colorful prophet Elijah, champion of the "unique divinity of Yahweh" (McKenzie, DOB, p.232) and brave bearer of a strong social message.

• As background for today's first reading, tell the children of how Elijah, prophet of Yahweh, challenged "the four hundred and fifty prophets of Baal and the four hundred prophets of Asherah" to a contest which Yahweh dramatically and incontestably won for Elijah. Having thus infuriated the wicked queen Jezebel by defeating the prophets of her Phoenician religion, Elijah fled in terror, fearing for his very life. Our reading today picks up the story at this point.

• Proclaim the reading to the children. Discuss the miracle related there as a sign to Elijah that even "in his darkest hour Yahweh did not desert him, but mercifully supplied him with strength for a long journey that would lead to a new and keener sense of the sovereignty of God" (Anderson, UOT, p. 217).

• Entice older children to read "all about Elijah" in I Kgs 17-19 and 21. They will enjoy it. The leader will also enjoy it.

• Ask older children why they think the church chose today's reading about Elijah to accompany today's gospel. Is it a comment on the importance of the eucharist as food in our journey to God? Is it to provoke thought about the feelings of Jesus when he, like Elijah, was rejected because he did the will of God?

6. Pray the responsorial psalm as a prayer of longing for the good things of God, especially the eucharist.

Twentieth Sunday of the Year

Lectionary for Masses with Children	Lectionary for Mass
**Prv 9:1-6	**Prv 9:1-6
Ps 34:1-2,9-10	Ps 34:2-3,10-11,12-13,14-15
*Eph 5:15-20	*Eph 5:15-20
**Jn 6:51-58	**Jn 6:51-58

Focus: We long to share the life of Jesus!

Gather the Children:

1. In addition to the usual candles and lectionary, have on the children's gathering cloth a loaf of bread and a goblet.

2. Welcome the children joyfully as they enter the room. Remind them that we are here to celebrate God's presence among us and to listen to God's word. Light the candles near the lectionary as a sign of God's presence.

3. Ask the children to listen carefully to some words that an early Christian wrote to the people of the city of Ephesus. The leader should proclaim with sincerity the latter part of the reading, Eph 5:18c-20. It might interest older children that the writer of the letter to the Ephesians was probably not Paul himself, but a second generation Paulinist steeped in his master's thought.

4. To impress upon the hearts and minds of the children the words we have just heard, bring out two long, thin banners which say "Praise the Lord!" and "Give thanks to God!" Make the banners before the liturgy, if possible with the help of the children, by taping sheets of construction paper together, gluing on letters, outlining the letters with magic marker or paint pen, attaching the banners to cardboard tubes from hangers and inserting yarn strings. Hang the banners in the children's gathering space.

5. Ask the children where and when we can give heed to the words of the writer to the Ephesians to praise the Lord and give thanks to God. Help the children realize that we can do these things anywhere and anytime. Then join the children in a lively song of praise and thanks to God.

Proclaim the Gospel

1. Today marks the fourth of five consecutive Sundays on which we read from the sixth chapter of John's gospel. Today's gospel is deeply theological, but we do not wish to bore little children with theological intricacies. We use the gospel to instill in the children a longing for the eucharist.

2. Review quickly the actions and words of Jesus which we have contemplated for the last three Sundays. Jesus fed the hungry crowd. When the crown asked him to be their king, he promised something far better than the unending bodily food for which they were hoping: he promised them himself as the bread of life.

3. Use the flannel board or figures that will stand up to depict Jesus, his disciples and the crowd, and summar-ize today's gospel story. Jesus told the people that the living bread they must eat was himself, his own flesh and blood, a sharing in his very life. Some people in the crowd trusted Jesus. They believed in him even though they didn't understand how he could give them his body and blood as food. But others became upset at the words of Jesus. They began to argue about how Jesus could do what he said. So Jesus repeated his words in even clearer, stronger language.

4. Ask the children to stand and listen to the words which Jesus spoke to the crowd. Acclaim the gospel joyfully in song while one child carries the lectionary reverently to the leader; then proclaim the gospel.

Foster the Children's Love for the Eucharist

1. Ask the children when Jesus kept his promise to give himself to his friends as their food and drink. Then, using the above figures of Jesus and his disciples, remind the children of the words and actions of Jesus at the last supper.

2. Ask the children when in our own lives someone repeats the words and actions of Jesus at the last supper. Use the figures again, identifying the presider and the assembly with Jesus and the disciples. In this way help the children relate both the promise of Jesus in our gospel and the words and actions of Jesus at the last supper to our own liturgy of the eucharist. Encourage the children when they rejoin the adult assembly to watch and to listen for the words and actions of the presider when he repeats the words and actions of Jesus.

3. Among the little children present there will surely be some who have not yet received the eucharist. Talk to them about the joy that will be theirs when finally they will share fully in the eucharistic banquet. Let the children speak of their memories of the first eucharist of siblings or friends. If the children of the parish use a particular eucharistic preparation book, show the book to the children.

4. Lead the children in prayer to increase their longing for the eucharist:

• Teach them to sing "We praise you, we bless you, we thank you!" This is one of the acclamations of Eucharistic Prayer for Children II.

• Ask the children to sing the acclamation after each of the following statements:

Leader:	Jesus is the bread of life.
All:	We praise you ...
Leader:	If we go to Jesus we shall never be hungry.
All:	We praise you ...

Leader:	If we believe in Jesus we shall never thirst.
All:	We praise you ...
Leader:	Jesus feeds us with his own flesh and blood. He shares his life with us.
All:	We praise you ...
Leader:	Jesus gives us life forever.
All:	We praise you ...

• Allow the children a few moments of quiet to speak to God individually about God's gift to us of the eucharist.

5. Help the children make small banners to take home as reminders of our liturgy today:

• Give each child a piece of bright poster board on which have been written in light letters the words: "Eat ... Drink ... Eternal life is ours!" Have yarn strings, for hanging the banners, already threaded through holes punched on the top sides of the banners.

• Then give each child a loaf and a cup cut from gaily-patterned gift-wrapping paper. Direct the children to glue their cups and loaves onto their banners.

• If there is time, or after the children return home, they should color the letters on their banners.

Other Possibilities

1. Once again suggest to the liturgy planning team than the presider use today one of the eucharistic prayers for children. Better still, arrange, with the help of the parish minister of music, for the presider and the assembly to sing the prayer.

2. Read or tell the children the story *Suho and the White Horse* by Otsuka. The story tells of young Suho who loves his white horse. The horse is fatally wounded, but just before he dies he directs Suho, in his dream, to make a musical instrument from the bones, the hide and the hair of his body. Ever after when Suho hears the sound of the instrument he knows the presence of his beloved white horse. Use the story to help make the children comfortable with the gift Jesus gives us of his body. Do not spoil the story by "preaching" about it.

3. Older children might enjoy making one big banner instead of individual ones. Make the banner of burlap, make the loaf and the cup of gaily-patterned cloth, add words or symbols to indicate praise and thanks to God for the gift of the eucharist. Hang the banner where the children will see it easily and keep it there for several weeks.

4. Give the children copies of a simple recipe for "quick" bread. Suggest that they make the bread at home, with the help of their parents, and share it at dinner as a reminder that Jesus wants to share his life with us in the eucharist.

5. Verses 35-50 and verses 51-58 form thought units in Jn 6 that direct our attention to the eucharist. The two units contain remarkable similarities, but the eucharistic theme, present in both units, "comes to the fore" in the second unit "and becomes the exclusive theme" (R. Brown, AB 29, p.284). Verses 35-50 tell us that eternal life is the result of believing in Jesus. Verses 51-58 tell us that eternal life is the result of feeding on the flesh of Jesus and drinking his blood. Raymond Brown proposes the interesting hypothesis that verses 51-58 with their explicitly eucharistic language have their origin in a Johannine last supper scene. It is quite possible that a later editor of John's gospel added verses 51-58 to the gospel as he found it, thus using the second discourse to elaborate upon the eucharistic theme already present, though implicit, in chapter 6. (See Brown, op cit, 284-291.)

• Remind older children that John does not report the institution of the eucharist at the last supper. Let them comment, however, on how today's gospel reminds us of the words of Jesus at the last supper.

• Help older children to see a similarity between the full eucharistic liturgy of word and sacrament as we celebrate it today and the words of Jesus as the final editor of John's gospel reported them in verses 35-58, our gospels for the last several Sundays.

• It would be irresponsible of the leader to deny the fact that to eat flesh and to drink blood are repulsive thoughts to the modern mind. To the Semitic mind, however, "flesh and blood" is an idiom designating the whole person, thus, in our context, the very life of Jesus. Even so John's language was harsh to his contemporary readers, as the reaction of the people proves. Is John emphasizing by his language the realism of the flesh and blood of Jesus in the eucharist?

6. Extend to the children the invitation of wisdom recorded in our first reading:

• The book of Proverbs forms part of the wisdom literature of the Old Testament. Chapters 10 through 31 consist almost entirely of what we usually call "proverbs"—pithy observations and suggestions meant to guide individuals to earthly success and happiness. Chapters 1 through 9 form the prologue of the book. These opening chapters state the purpose of the book, which is to impart wisdom, and then describe and praise the virtue of wisdom. Scholars suppose that the prologue was composed by a person who assembled and edited the whole book in the late fifth century BCE.

• Wisdom 9 presents Wisdom and Folly personified as women. The two invite passers-by to partake of their banquets. Wisdom promises food and drink that give life and understanding. Fickle and senseless Folly promises stolen water and forbidden bread, signs of deceit and vice which lead to death. Our reading today is the invitation of Wisdom to her banquet. Arrange the reading so that older children may proclaim it to each other. The children might read the first part of the passage alternately in two groups and an individual reader read the words of Wisdom herself.

• Guide older children in a discussion of wisdom and its attractions. Do they see the invitation of Wisdom in our reading as potentially effective to their peers? Why? Challenge the children to think of other ways to present wisdom as attractive.

• Why did the compilers of the lectionary choose the invitation of Wisdom to her banquet to complement John's eucharistic discourse?

Twenty-First Sunday of the Year

Lectionary for Masses with Children	Lectionary for Mass
**Jos 24:1-2,15-17,18	**Jos 24:1-2,15-17,18
Ps 34:1-2,17-18,19-20	Ps 34:2-3,16-17,18-19,20-21,22-23
*Eph 6:1-4	Eph 5:21-32
**Jn 6:60-69	**Jn 6:60-69

Focus: With Peter we profess our faith in Jesus.

Gather the Children

1. Welcome the children with joy and remind them that we gather to listen carefully and prayerfully to the word of God and to let that word touch and transform our lives.

2. Sing a lively song of praise to God. Ask a child to raise high the lectionary during the singing, and then to lay the book reverently in its place of honor. Light candles near the book as a sign of God's presence.

Proclaim the Gospel

1. Beginning on the Seventeenth Sunday of the Year and continuing through today the church asks us to immerse ourselves in the sixth chapter of John's gospel and to meditate on the presence of Jesus among us both in his word and in the eucharist. In both these forms Jesus is our bread of life. In our liturgies of the word for our children, we have chosen to highlight the sacramental presence of Jesus in the eucharist. We conclude our reflection on Jn 6 today by joining Peter in his profession of faith in Jesus.

2. Using whatever aids the leader has chosen during the last few weeks, review the liturgies of the word of the past Sundays: Jesus fed the hungry crowd; the next day he promised a better food, one which is not perishable but gives life forever; the crowd grumbled; Jesus stated that the special food is his very flesh and blood.

3. Continue by relating the events of today's gospel: by this point even many of the disciples would not believe Jesus and left him. Jesus turned to the Twelve and asked if they too would leave him. Peter answered with a beautiful profession of faith.

4. Acclaim the gospel joyfully and then proclaim it.

Respond to the Gospel by Professing Our Faith in Jesus

1. Ask the children how they think the words of Peter affected Jesus. Bring out what must have been Jesus's human happiness at the trust and loyalty of his friends.

2. With the children profess our belief in Jesus:
- Teach the children to sing "Glory to God in the highest!"
- Have the children respond with their expression of praise to the following statements about Jesus:

Leader: Jesus is the bread of life.
All: Glory to God...
Leader: We will eat the living bread from heaven.
All: Glory to God...
Leader: We will have life forever.
All: Glory to God...
Leader: Jesus has the words of eternal life.
All: Glory to God...
Leader: We believe in Jesus.
All: Glory to God...

Make the Good News Our Own

1. Review the story of Peter's profession of faith in Jesus by letting the children retell it. Have large figures representing Jesus and the Twelve and use them to illustrate the story.

2. Encourage the children to resolve never to turn away from Jesus:
- Give the children each a large figure and crayons. Let the children personalize their figures quickly in some simple way.
- As a sign that they wish to stay with Jesus and not to leave him as some of the disciples did, let the children place their figures near Jesus with Peter and the rest.
- After the liturgy of the word give the children their figures to take home.

3. Conclude the liturgy of the word with a hymn which expresses our resolve to be faithful to Jesus.

Other Possibilities:

1. Once again suggest to the parish liturgy team that the presider today use one of the eucharistic prayers for children. Better still, plan, with the assistance of the parish minister of music, for the presider and the assembly to sing the prayer.

2. Proclaim the first reading:
- As background for today's reading from the book of Joshua, the leader should read Jos 23-24.
- Tell the children about Joshua. Successor of Moses and hero of the book that bears his name, Joshua led the Israelites to possession of the promised land by bloody military defeat of its inhabitants. Our reading today shows Joshua "old and advanced in years" (23:2) and about to go "the way of all men" (23:14). Joshua pleads with his people to choose Yahweh and to turn away from the gods worshipped in the land the Israelites had conquered. Joshua reminds the people of the faithfulness of Yahweh and of Yahweh's care for them through the years. He urges them, in stirring words, to fear and serve the Lord, and he announces that he and his family will do just that. The people respond by promising that they too "will serve the Lord and obey the Lord's voice" (24: 24), thus renewing the Mosaic covenant.
- Proclaim the reading to the children, striving to impart to them the significance of the occasion.

• Relate the reading to today's gospel: Just as Joshua called his people to "choose this day whom you will serve," Jesus called the Twelve to choose to stay with him or to leave him; and just as the Israelites chose to serve the Lord, so the disciples through Peter responded to Jesus, "Lord, to whom shall we go? You have the words of eternal life."

• Relate the first reading and the gospel reading to our lives today. What difficult and significant choices do we face? Whom do we choose to serve?

3. With older children explore the reasons so many of the disciples turned against Jesus. "To eat a person's flesh" was a Hebrew expression meaning to slander or to backbite. To drink blood violated the Mosaic law because blood symbolized life, over which God alone has dominion, and was thus regarded as sacred. So it was not unreasonable for those who sought surface meaning only to become angry and hostile. But "flesh and blood" was the common Semitic way of referring to the whole person. To those who, drawn by God, believed in Jesus, "flesh and blood" meant the life of Jesus; and to "eat his flesh and drink his blood" meant to share in his life. (See Vawter I, p. 259.)

4. Discuss with older children how people can refuse to accept Jesus in the eucharist today. Do they turn away from his words? Do they turn away from the eucharist as a constant reminder of the death of Jesus which we must share if we would share his life? Do we also turn away from the words of Jesus? Do we also turn away from participating in his death? With the children, resolve to eat the flesh of the Jesus and to drink his blood with greater understanding of its demands upon our lives.

5. Let older children compose a profession of faith in Jesus and the eucharist. Write their ideas on cut-outs of a large loaf of bread and a large cup. Then read their statements as a prayer. Read them to the assembly as a meditation after communion.

6. The leader should observe that the LMC has replaced, in today's reading from the letter to the Ephesians, the instructions to husbands and wives with the following verses of instructions to and about children, a sensitive and sensible change in a lectionary for children. If there is time, proclaim the reading to the children and discuss it. The theme of the reading, however, as is so often the case with the second lectionary reading, is not related to the theme of today's first and third readings.

6. Introduce to older children the ancient and lovely eucharistic prayer of the Didache. The *Didache*, or *Teaching of the Twelve Apostles*, dates from the early centuries of the Christian church, perhaps even the later first century. It is a compilation of writings dealing with morals and ethics, church practice and the second coming of Christ. The eucharistic prayer of the *Didache* "can be considered the golden link connecting Jewish prayer with the Christian eucharist" (Lucien Deiss, *Springtime of the Liturgy*, p. 74). An adapted reading of a portion of the eucharistic prayer of the *Didache* follows. The group might read the acclamations together, and the girls and the boys alternate reading the intervening verses.

A Eucharistic Prayer

Adapted from the Eucharistic Prayer of the *Didache*

Glory be yours through all ages!
First, for the cup,
we thank you, our Father.

Glory be yours through all ages!

Then for the bread broken,
we thank you, our Father.

Glory be yours through all ages!

The bread broken
was first scattered on the hills,
then was gathered and became one.

So let your Church be gathered
from the ends of the earth
into your kingdom.

Yours is glory and power through all ages!

We thank you, holy Father,
for your holy name
which you have made to dwell in our hearts.

We thank you, holy Father,
for the knowledge and faith and life eternal
which you have revealed to us through Jesus.

Glory be yours through all ages!

You have given food and drink
to your children
for their enjoyment
so that they may thank you.

To us you have also graciously given
a spiritual food and drink
that lead to eternal life.

Glory be yours through all ages!
Amen!

Twenty-Second Sunday of the Year

Lectionary for Masses with Children	Lectionary for Mass
*Dt 4:1-2,6-8	*Dt 4:1-2,6-8
Ps 15:2-3,3 and 5	Ps 15:2-3,3-4,4-5
**Jas 1:17-18,21-22	**Jas 1:17-18,21-22,27
*Mk 7:1-5,14-15,21-23	*Mk 7:1-8,14-15,21-23

Focus: We pray to listen well to the word of God and to do it.

Gather the Children

1. Welcome the children eagerly and talk with them about why we gather for our special liturgy of the word. Stress our desire as committed Christians to hear God's word, to live it and to spread it.

2. Because today's readings focus our attention on listening well to God's word, it is a good day to teach the children a new gospel acclamation. Add simple gestures to accompany the words. Then sing the acclamation with joy while one child holds high the lectionary. At the conclusion of the singing the child should lay the lectionary in its place of honor. Light candles near the book as a reminder that God is in our midst.

Talk about Listening and Doing

1. Talk with the children about the things we learn by listening. Lead into a short discussion of the importance of listening.

2. Focus on listening and then acting upon what we hear:

• Share with the children Hilaire Belloc's humorous poem "Matilda: Who Told Lies, and was Burned to Death." Read the poem dramatically and with obvious amusement.

• Discuss Matilda's refusal to do as she had been told. (We will assume that Matilda's Aunt spoke with her Niece about her Dreadful Lies.) Did Matilda listen to her Aunt? Did Matilda act on what she heard? Did Matilda get in trouble for not "listening" to her Aunt?

• Help the children to extract the point: do something about what you hear, and don't just listen to the words.

Talk about God's Word

1. Ask the children:

• Whose word do we gather every Sunday to hear and to celebrate? About whose word do we sing in the gospel acclamation?

• When do we listen to God's word? When does someone read it to us or tell us about it? Mention other times when we should listen to God's word; but stress that right now, during our liturgy of the word, is a particularly good time for us to listen to God's word.

• Where do we find God's word written down? In the newspaper? Show the children a newspaper. When the children suggest that we look in the bible for God's written word, show them an attractive bible. Show

them the lectionary. Tell the children that the lectionary contains stories and other readings from the bible arranged in the order in which we read them on Sundays.

2. Focus on our response to God's word:

• Why do we want to hear God's word? What does it tell us? How does it help us? Why do you think we call (part of) God's word "the good news"?

• After we've heard God's word, what should we do about it? Go home and forget it?

• How can we tell others about God's word? Stress that our kind and caring actions, even more than our words, tell others the good news.

3. Sing the new gospel acclamation once again as a song-prayer that we really will listen well to God's word and let it change our lives.

Proclaim God's Word

1. Share the reading from the letter of James:

• Ask the children to listen carefully as we read from the bible a part of a letter to some early Christians. The letter contains good advice about listening to God's word. Proclaim the reading.

• Help the children to understand the advice of the letter. Make use of the bad example of Matilda, who did not take to heart the words of her Aunt. Dwell on the beautiful thought of the letter "Welcome the word that has taken root in you" or, using the phrasing of the LMC, "Accept the message that is planted in you." 2. Proclaim the gospel:

• The leader should read all of Mk 7:1-23 to understand more fully today's gospel, which is difficult to present to little children. Tell the children that in the gospel we hear Jesus encourage the people to listen carefully to God's word and to try very hard to live its full meaning.

• Acclaim the gospel with the new acclamation, and then proclaim it. Focus especially on the words of Jesus: "Pay attention and try to understand what I mean."

3. Respond to God's word:

• Discuss how we can do God's word. Ask the children to recall some of the things Jesus tells us to do, and then elicit their ideas about how we can do them. Help the children to be practical.

• Pray with the children that we will all be good listeners and faithful doers of God's word.

Make the Good News Our Own

1. Make a poster to remind us of today's readings in the weeks to come:

- Before the liturgy prepare a piece of brightly-colored poster board by gluing on letters to spell out the advice of James "Welcome the word!" The leader may use the wording of the LMC, but it is less poetic than that of the LM.
- Talk about the growth of God's word in our hearts and in our lives. Talk about the growth of a flower, and then ask the children to think of a growing flower as a symbol of the growth of God's word.
- As the children watch, glue three felt flowers onto the poster, one a closed bud, one a bud beginning to open, one a flower in full bloom.
- Let the children explain to each other the meaning of the completed poster, thus reinforcing its thought and also helping those children who do not read.
- Let the children carry the poster into the church when they rejoin the adult assembly and place it near the ambo where the entire assembly will see it. After the liturgy hang the poster in a prominent position in the children's gathering space, and then refer to it during future liturgies of the word.

2. Give the children small "bibles" to take home. Make the "bible" by folding in half a piece of construction paper, writing "Holy Bible" on the cover and writing "Welcome the word!" on the inside page.

3. Show the children a good children's bible. Urge the children to ask their parents for bibles of their own.

Other Possibilities:

1. Since we will read from the letter of James for the next five Sundays, the older children might benefit from some background information about the letter. Traditionally, though probably inaccurately, the letter is attributed to James "the brother of the Lord," who was head of the Christian community of Jerusalem during the early years of its existence. The letter of James is one of the "catholic epistles," so called because they are addressed to Christians in general and not to particular churches or people. The letter is predominantly moralistic. It insists that profession of faith cannot take the place of good actions. The letter is short, and the leader would do well to read the entire letter, particularly chapter one, before preparing the liturgy. Draw on some of the images and examples of the author in chapter one to help the children realize that the advice of the letter, given nearly two thousand years ago, is pertinent even today.

2. Older children can understand much more of the gospel reading than we suggest in the above presentation for use with younger children. Help older children to see that external observance of the law is not what constitutes acting acceptably on God's word. Encourage the children to look into their own hearts to see where they fail to act as responsible and creative hearers of the word. Draw upon the first reading, part of the traditional farewell address of Moses to his people, to focus the attention of the children on the goodness of the law, which, when properly understood and observed, gives life.

3. To stimulate older children to be practical about the message in today's readings to live the word of God that we hear:

- Write on small cards several verses from the bible that suggest ways of acting. Use some of the advice of the letter of James.
- Ask a volunteer to draw a card, read the verse to the group and then suggest a practical way that children might do something about what they hear.
- If there is time let each member of the group have a turn. In any case, have enough cards so that each child can take one home and live its message during the following week.

4. As encouragement to older children and their parents to read the bible, and as encouragement also to parents and older children to read the bible to younger children, send home with the children a list suggesting bibles that the family might purchase and use at home. Include a good adult bible (such as the *New American Bible* or *The Jerusalem Bible* or the *New Revised Standard Version*), a simplified unabridged bible (such as *Today's English Version* or the New Testament *Good News For Modern Man*), as well as several bibles suitable for children of various ages (such as *The Taizé Picture Bible*, published by Fortress Press, *A Child's Bible* [two volumes], published by Paulist Press, Children's Bible, published by The Liturgical Press, *My Good Shepherd Bible Story Book*, published by Concordia). The leader might also recommend the two American Bible Society's 1991 publications upon which the LMC is based, *Contemporary English Version* and *Contemporary English Version: Bible for Today's Family* (New Testament).

Matilda: Who Told Lies, and Was Burned to Death
by Hilaire Belloc

Matilda told such Dreadful Lies,
It made one Gasp and Stretch one's Eyes;
Her Aunt, who, from her Earliest Youth,
Had kept a Strict Regard for Truth,
Attempted to Believe Matilda:
The effort very nearly killed her,
And would have done so, had not She
Discovered this Infirmity.
For once, towards the Close of Day,
Matilda, growing tired of play,
And finding she was left alone,
Went tiptoe to the Telephone
And summoned the Immediate Aid
Of London's Noble Fire-Brigade.
Within an hour the Gallant Band
Were pouring in on every hand,
From Putney, Hackney Downs, and Bow
With Courage high and Hearts a-glow
They galloped, roaring through the Town
'Matilda's House is Burning Down!'
Inspired by British Cheers and Loud
Proceeding from the Frenzied Crowd,
They ran their ladders through a score
Of windows on the Ball Room Floor;
And took Peculiar Pains to Souse
The Pictures up and down the House,
Until Matilda's Aunt succeeded
In showing them they were not needed;

And even then she had to pay
To get the Men to go away!

It happened that a few Weeks later
Her Aunt was off to the Theatre
To see that Interesting Play
'The Second Mrs. Tanqueray.'
She had refused to take her Niece
To hear this Entertaining Piece:
A Deprivation Just and Wise
To Punish her for Telling Lies.
That Night a Fire DID break out—

You should have heard Matilda Shout!
You should have heard her Scream and Bawl,
And throw the window up and call
To People passing in the Street—
(The rapidly increasing Heat
Encouraging her to obtain
Their confidence)—but all in vain!
For every time She shouted 'Fire!'
They only answered 'Little liar'!
And therefore when her Aunt returned,
Matilda, and the House, were Burned.

Twenty-Third Sunday of the Year

Lectionary for Masses with Children	Lectionary for Mass
**Is 35:4-7	**Is 35:47-7
*Ps 146:6-7,8-9,9-10	*Ps 146:7,8-9,9-10
*Jas 2:1-5	*Jas 2:1-5
**Mk 7:31-37	**Mk 7:31-37

Focus: Let us give praise for God's presence and action in our lives!

Gather the Children

1. Welcome the children joyfully and remind them why we gather for our special liturgy of the word. Be sure the children know that both we and the adult assembly are celebrating the same liturgy of the word.
2. Sing in praise of God who is always with us. During the singing have one child hold high the lectionary, then lay it in its place of honor. Light candles near the book as a sign of God's presence.

Proclaim the First Reading

1. By way of background, tell the children that the prophet and author of our first reading lived many years before Jesus. He lived at a time when his people were captives in a land far from their home, but were soon to return home. The prophet spoke to his people to give them hope. His words describe, in beautiful images, what it would be like as they traveled home.
2. Discuss the meaning of blind, deaf, lame, dumb. Have pictures of or sketch an eye, an ear, a leg, a tongue.
3. Ask the children to listen carefully to the reading and to remember the joyful things the prophet says will happen as the people return home. Then proclaim the reading.
4. To help the children understand the meaning of the prophecy and appreciate its beauty, ask them to recall specific joyful things the reading promises. As the children speak, show pictures or slides of, for example, a flower, a bird chirping, a child jumping, a choir to illustrate the new powers of the blind, the deaf, the lame and the dumb. Ask the children to describe what must have been the reaction of the people of Israel to the words of the poem.
5. Rejoice in the promise and the goodness of God by singing a song of praise to God. Add expressive gestures to enhance the participation of younger children.

Proclaim the Gospel

1. Ask the children to think of things Jesus did that might have reminded his people of the prophecy we just heard proclaimed. Encourage the children to recall the miracles of Jesus, enough so that they begin to realize that in Jesus the words of the prophecy were fulfilled.
2. Ask the children to stand and listen carefully to a story about Jesus, and to notice which of the prophecies he fulfills in the story.

3. Acclaim the gospel eagerly in song, and then proclaim it.
4. Ask the children what of Isaiah's prophecy Jesus did in our gospel story. Help the children to appreciate the wonderful gift of Jesus to the man by asking them what might have been the first sounds the man heard, the first words he spoke.

Respond to the Good News

1. Rejoice with the man who received from Jesus the gift of hearing and speaking:
• Remind the children that the psalms are song-prayers of the people of Israel. Suggest that the man Jesus cured, after thanking Jesus, might have praised God by praying one of the psalms.
• Psalm 146 is a hymn of praise to God. It lists the wonderful things Yahweh does for those who trust. Unfortunately it does not mention healing the deaf and dumb, but let us consider that implied (Fuller, PNL). The psalm is thus a fitting response both to the reading from the book of Isaiah and to the gospel. Pray the psalm with the children:

Teach the children to sing the psalm refrain, "Praise the Lord, my soul!" In the Pueblo Publishing Company's *Lectionary for Children's Mass*, the leader will find a simple melody. Or the leader may compose a simple melody.

Several prepared young singers might sing the verses of the psalm. The whole group should sing the refrain after each verse.

2. Relate the psalm and the healing of the deaf-mute to our lives:
• Discuss how God works among us today. Tell the children that, even though the work of God was most clearly manifest in the life of Jesus, God is every bit as present and active today as during the earthly life of Jesus. We must look more carefully, however, to recognize God's presence. God is with us in our joys and in our sorrows. God speaks to through people who love us. God guides us and keeps us from harm through people who care for us. God calls us throughout our lives, and one day God will welcome us into the kingdom to live there forever.
• Ask the children if there are some special things we would like to ask the Lord to do for people today. Include things mentioned in the readings and the psalm, and then encourage the children to add their own ideas. We would like God to help the sick, the old, the lonely. We would like God to stop war and give us peace. We would like God to protect those in danger. We would like God to bring unity and happiness to

families. The leader might bring along the newspaper for additional ideas. Use the thoughts of the children to formulate today's general intercessions.

3. Make a poster to give praise for God's presence and action in our lives:

- Have ready a large poster board with the responsorial psalm refrain "Praise the Lord, my soul!" painted or printed in the center.
- Give each child a figure with arms upraised in praise.
- Lead the children in a simple profession of faith in the presence and action of God today.
- Let the children glue their figures on the poster as a sign of their praise for all God does for us.

4. Give the children small figures, like the ones above, to take home. Suggest that each child draw a picture of something that reminds him or her of God's presence and then glue the praising figure onto the picture.

Other Possibilities:

1. To older children present more of the beautiful reading from the book of Isaiah:

- In preparing the liturgy the leader should read Is 35:1-10, the complete poem from which our reading is taken. Although it appears in the first part of the book of Isaiah, whose author we designate Isaiah of Jerusalem, it is similar in thought and language to the poems of Second Isaiah, whose work we thus suspect it to be (Brown, AB 20, p. 12).
- Acquaint the children with the historical situation of Second Isaiah. Israel had been conquered by the mighty Babylonians and its leading citizens deported to Mesopotamia. At the time of the writing of Second Isaiah, Cyrus the Great of Persia had arisen as a threat to Babylon, and the people of Israel living in exile recognized him as one who might liberate them.
- Proclaim the entire reading to the children, and then discuss its magnificent imagery and its profound expression of hope.
- If there is time, the older children can read and discuss the complete poem. Arrange the poem for them so that they may read it in groups. The children will enjoy the participation.

- Help the children to realize that by his curing of the blind, the deaf, the lame and the dumb, Jesus was calling his people to see his work as the work of God, just as the Israelites of old had seen the return from exile as the work of God.
- As a quiet meditation on the prophecy, play Dan Schutte's "A Time Will Come For Singing" (from *Gentle Night*).

2. Psalm 146 offers us a partial catalog of the works of God, seen through the eyes of the people of God of long ago. Older children might enjoy rewriting the psalm using images and events that are pertinent to their young lives. It would be good to share their work with the assembly as a meditation after communion or as a closing prayer. Or give the children large praising figures, like the ones above, and ask them to write on the figures verses of praise to God. Tape the figures in a cluster on the wall or let the children take them home.

3. The story of the man who came to hear and to speak in the presence of Jesus reminds us of the opportunity we have each Sunday to hear the word of God and speak it in our lives. Discuss with older children how the gospel is thus a symbol of what should happen at our liturgy. Dan Schutte's "You Are My Own," inspired by the call of the great prophet Jeremiah, prayerfully expresses our own call by God to speak God's words. The lines of the song

The Lord reached out his hand
and touched my tongue.
"I give my words to you
to speak my love"

clearly bring the gospel to mind.

4. The reading from the letter of James challenges us to examine our consciences with respect to how we show favoritism among people we meet. Pre-adolescent children (and certainly adults) are sometimes guilty of "discriminating in their hearts," to use the words of the letter, and today would be a good day to give some thought to overcoming our failures in this respect. Who are the people we look down upon? Are they the poor? the plain? the uneducated? What positive action can we take to treat all people as of infinite value? Jack Miffleton's "Rainbow Children" (from *Make a Wonderful Noise*) celebrates the differences among God's children in a way that younger children enjoy.

Twenty-Fourth Sunday of the Year

Lectionary for Masses with Children	Lectionary for Mass

**Is 50:4-8
  Ps 116:1-2,5-6,8-9
  *Jas 2:14-18
**Mk 8:31-35
	**Is 50:4-9
	  Ps 116:1-2,3-4,5-6,8-9
	  *Jas 2:14-18
	**Mk 8:27-35

Focus: We resolve to follow Jesus, even when it's hard.

Gather the Children

1. Welcome the children with joy and remind them why we gather for our special liturgy of the word. Sing praise for God's presence in the word. Then thank God in quiet prayer for calling us to listen now to that word.
2. In addition to the lectionary and candles, have on the gathering cloth a large crucifix. Invite the children to sit in a circle around the cloth. Light the candles and tell the children once again that candles remind us that God is in our midst.

Proclaim the First Reading

1. The leader might consider retaining the imagery of the first line of the LM reading, which the translation of the LMC omits in its simplification: show the children a picture of an ear and discuss the importance of our ears; then ask what "to open your ears" might mean.
2. Tell the children that our first reading was written by a person who lived more than five hundred years before Jesus. Ask the children to listen carefully to the reading because the writer will speak about listening.
3. Reading from the lectionary, proclaim the last sentence of Is 50:4 and Is 50:5, the opening lines of the reading.
4. Help the children respond to the reading "Thanks be to God." If necessary, have the children repeat the response once or twice. A celebration of God's word is not the place to "drill" the children, but it is important that children know and use our simple responses and so more easily both enter the liturgy personally and recognize their liturgy as one with the full adult liturgy.
5. Tell the children that the writer of our reading is speaking for a person whom God loved greatly. Because God loved the person so much, God asked him to do difficult things. It was not easy for him to accept God's plans, but he tells us that he listened carefully and obeyed.
6. Ask the children when God speaks to us. Help them to suggest people and events who communicate to us God's word. God speaks through our parents and our teachers, through our priests and other church leaders. He speaks to us through each other and through people who inspire us by their good lives and generous actions. God speaks to us when we read the bible and when we listen to the word proclaimed during our liturgy of the word.
7. Let the children voice spontaneous prayers that we will always try hard to listen carefully when God speaks to us.

Proclaim the Gospel

Note: In view of the constant liturgical importance of our profession of faith (not to mention the importance of the verses 8:27-30 in the structure of Mark's gospel), the leader might choose today to use the longer LM gospel, rather than the shorter version of the LMC.
1. Remind the children what "gospel" means. Our English word "gospel" comes from the Anglo-Saxon "godspell," which translates the Greek for "good tidings" and "to announce the good tidings" (McKenzie, DOB). The gospels are four accounts of the life of Jesus written by persons who lived during, or at least very close to, the time of Jesus. They had come to know Jesus well and to love him, and they wanted to share their knowledge and their love of Jesus with other people, including people like us who would live long after them.
2. By way of introduction to today's gospel passage and Peter's great profession of faith in Jesus, let the children recall some of the ways Jesus showed his great love and care for the people he met. Remind them of Jesus's cure of the deaf and dumb man which we read about in last week's gospel, of his feeding of the hungry crowd which we read about for several Sundays, of his raising of the dead child to life which we read about in early summer. Remind them of some of Jesus's other healings, so many of which we have heard proclaimed as we have read from Mark's gospel during this lectionary year B. Tell the children that Peter had witnessed many of Jesus's healings, including the cure of his sick mother-in-law, and had come to know that Jesus was a special person. To represent the actions of Jesus visually, record some of the children's recollections on brightly colored paper, cut into attractive shapes.
3. Proclaim the gospel:
• Tell the children that in today's gospel Jesus asks his disciples who they think he is, and that Peter answers. Ask the group to listen to how Mark tells us about it in his story of Jesus.
• Acclaim the gospel in song, if necessary helping the children to say the responses correctly, and then proclaim the gospel.
4. Ask the children to respond quietly to the gospel in their hearts, asking God that we, like Peter, will accept Jesus as the one sent from God and that we will follow Jesus wherever he goes.
5. Ask the children if they remember what Jesus did that most showed how much he loves us. Point out the large crucifix on the cloth. Then to impress upon the

children that Jesus's greatest act of love for us was his death on the cross, lay the cross on top of the shapes on which we recorded the wonderful actions of Jesus. Talk with the children about the importance of following Jesus in his loving concern for all people.

6. Respond to the gospel by professing our faith in Jesus:

• Ask younger children to repeat, line by line, the following profession of faith:

We believe in God.
God made heaven and earth.
We believe in Jesus Christ.
He lived for us.
He died for us.
He lives now with new life.
We believe in the Holy Spirit.
The Holy Spirit is the spirit of love.
We believe that we will live with God forever.

• Give older children copies of the profession of faith and let them read it together. Or let them formulate their own profession of faith by mentioning things they believe about Jesus. The leader should write down their ideas and then read them to the group as a creed.

Relate the Gospel to Our Lives

1. Help the children to think of practical ways in which we can follow Jesus, even at cost to ourselves. Suggest that Jesus is urging that we always try to make others happy. Then pass out pictures of happy people and let the children suggest kind things others might have done to make the people happy. Encourage the children to extend the discussion to include specific things they themselves can do to make people happy.

2. Give each child a paper pennant that says "I want to follow Jesus." Then let the children draw "happy faces" on their pennants or glue on small pictures of happy people. Let the children take home their pennants as a reminder to themselves and to their parents of the message of today's liturgy of the word.

3. Conclude the liturgy with a song about discipleship.

Other Possibilities:

1. There are many good short stories about children and adults who do kind and courageous things for others. The "picture book" section of the children's department of a good library will have such stories. It would be appropriate today, if there is time, to read or summarize such a story.

2. In the above outline we have omitted much of the gospel, parts of which are difficult for children, even for adults, to understand. For older children the leader might want to proclaim and discuss more of the gospel. The following points might interest the children:

• What might have prompted Jesus to inquire of the disciples who people thought he was?

• Why did Jesus order his disciples "not to tell anyone about him"?

• Why did Mark immediately follow Peter's confession of faith in Jesus, a climax in Mark's gospel, with Jesus's words about his suffering, death and resurrection?

• How strange Jesus's harsh words to Peter! Why did he say them?

• After the children have thought about the difficulties of the gospel passage, increase their understanding of both the person and mission of Jesus and the skill of Mark the Evangelist by sharing with them the conclusions of some of our scripture scholars. Mark, writing his life-story of Jesus, was concerned that people see Jesus not as a wonder-worker, not as a political savior, but as one sent from God to show us that the way to life is through suffering and death. Jesus might well have ordered secrecy about his work so that people would not claim him as messiah until they understood the meaning of his messiahship.

• It is interesting to think about what Jesus had in mind when, before his death on the cross, he asked those who would be his followers to "take up their crosses." Fuller informs us that the Greek word "stauros" for cross probably originally referred to the sign of ownership with which cattle were branded (PNL, 426). So to take up our crosses and to follow Jesus means to surrender ourselves completely to God and God's will for us, which is precisely what Jesus says in the last lines of our gospel. After the death of Jesus on the cross, the cross took on new and deeper meaning for Christians, but it had deep meaning earlier even for those who did not know how Jesus was to die.

• To help older children grasp the meaning of the words of Jesus to take up their crosses and follow him, give them small crosses and ask them to write on their crosses things they plan to do for others at cost to themselves. Collect the crosses and lay them around the large cross.

3. The second reading of these Sundays of the Year, unlike the first reading, is not chosen to correspond to the gospel, but is simply a semi-continuous reading of the New Testament letters. Today, quite by chance and quite fortunately, the reading from the letter of James offers practical commentary on the gospel. Help the children to understand the reading, and then ask them to rewrite the advice of James in the form of a modern letter so that it offers good practical advice to young people like themselves. Do this as a group project and share the resulting letter with the parents of the children or even with the entire assembly. We have read from the letter of James for three Sundays now and will continue to do so for the next two. Perhaps the children would like to start this project today and continue it during the next two weeks.

4. The reading from the book of Isaiah is the third of the "Suffering Servant Songs" appearing in Isaiah 40-55. Who this suffering servant of Yahweh is has been a great problem through the years to scholars, and there is as yet no universally accepted solution. In our reading today, the servant is the speaker. He describes his obedient acceptance of God's word and of all that God sends him, and he states his confidence that God will ultimately vindicate him. It seems likely that Jesus understood his own mission in terms of the suffering servant of the book of Isaiah, which fact explains the choice of the reading to complement today's gospel. Share these thoughts with older children. Then let them proclaim the reading to each other, perhaps arranged so that all the children can take part in the reading. Let each child take home a copy of the poem and illustrate it.

Twenty-Fifth Sunday of the Year

Lectionary for Masses with Children	Lectionary for Mass
- - - -	
*Jas 3:17-18	**Wis 2:12,17-20
Ps 122:1-2,8-9	Ps 54:3-4,5,6-8
**Mk 9:33-37	*Jas 3:16-4:3
	**Mk 9:30-37

Focus: If we want to be important in the eyes of God, we must serve others.

Gather the Children

1. Welcome the children with joy, and ask a child to remind the group why we come together for our special liturgy of the word. Then pray silently with the children that God will fill our hearts and our lives with the word.

2. Light candles as a sign of the presence of God and then greet the Lord, present among us, by singing joyfully. To accompany singing with simple gestures usually pleases little children.

3. If the children have not just celebrated the penitential rite with the assembly, then, in preparation for our readings, celebrate the rite now. The leader might lead the children in prayer as follows:

Leader: My brothers and sisters in God's family, we often fail to love others as we know we should, yet God always forgives us. Let us give praise for God's mercy and God's love.

You forgive us when we think we are better than our friends: Lord, have mercy.

All: Lord, have mercy.

Leader: You love us even when we do not love others: Christ, have mercy.

All: Christ, have mercy.

Leader: You forgive us when we do not serve others: Lord, have mercy.

All: Lord, have mercy.

Leader: May God remind us often who we are and who we are called to be. May God help us to follow the example of Jesus in loving and serving others. May God forgive us our sins and give us life forever.

All: Amen.

Proclaim the Gospel

1. Prepare the children for the gospel proclamation:

• Ask the children what it means to be important (or, using the wording of the LMC, to be "the greatest"). Accept their answers without criticism.

• Describe several "important" people, for example:

A rich person: have a pile of play money talk about the advantages of being rich.

A king or a queen: have a crown and talk about the wealth and glamour of royal life.

The president of the United States: have a picture of the presidential seal and talk about the president's privileges and responsibilities.

A movie star: use some "dress-ups" and discuss how some people virtually idolize movie stars.

A successful business person: have an airline ticket and talk about the travels of the president of a large company. Have a clock and talk about the person's busy schedule.

• Have all the props present on the gathering cloth so that the children can see them easily. Encourage the children to make suggestions about other "important" people and talk briefly about how so many people, especially adults, want to be like the people we have mentioned.

• Tell the children that Jesus knew people like these—rich people, successful people, people who were community leaders, beautiful women and handsome men. He knew that people wanted to be like that. But he also knew that there was a much better way to be important, and that was to be important in the eyes of God.

2. Proclaim the gospel:

• Ask the children to stand and listen carefully to the gospel because in it Jesus tells us—children and adults—how to be important in the eyes of God.

• Acclaim the gospel in song, helping the children to say the responses correctly, and then proclaim the gospel.

3. Help the children to assimilate the message of the gospel:

• Refer to the props on the gathering cloth and ask the children if any of the them represents Jesus's idea of importance. Produce a large sign that says "No!" and place it on top of the props.

• Make sure the children understand what it means to "serve others." Ask them if they remember any of the ways Jesus served others. Then help the children think of practical ways in which we can serve others. Some examples:

Don't think we're better than some people and leave them out of our play.

Don't always insist on having our own way.

Have time to help at home—set the table, clean up your things, help clean up someone else's things, be pleasant when corrected.

Be a good example to parents and other adults. Adults often think they are better than certain other people.

• Since our hands are frequently the means by which we serve others, have two large paper hands. Write on them "Serve" and "others!" and place the hands on top of the "No!"

Respond to the Gospel

1. Admit to the children and secure their agreement that we often fail to think of others before ourselves. But we know that our loving God will always forgive us if we are sorry. Remind the children that when we celebrate the penitential rite at the beginning of our liturgy, we give praise and thank for God's forgiving love. Recall the specific invocations we used today when we said the prayer because they were based on our gospel.

2. Teach the children a hymn whose theme is love and service.

3. As a reminder of our intention to serve others, give each child a paper hand to take home. Have written on the hands suggestions for small jobs that the children can do during the week to serve others: "I will serve others by . . ." Tell children who cannot read to ask their parents' help in reading the message, and in so doing to remind their parents that they too should serve others.

Other Possibilities:

1. There are many good stories about children and adults who find happiness in serving others. *Tico and the Golden Wings*, by Lio Lionni, is a short and very simple one. Read it to the children.

2. Once again it would be impossible to proclaim the entire gospel to little children and expect them to understand it. Older children, however, might profit from a careful presentation of more of the gospel than we have included above. Perhaps the following approach would help them apply today's gospel message to their lives:

• Give each child a piece of paper. Ask the children to write across the tops of their papers "Important People," and then to divide their papers into two columns. In the first column each child should write "An important person is . . ." and complete the sentence by describing briefly some "important" person, real or otherwise. Encourage some sharing of their descriptions.

• Tell the children that in today's gospel Jesus gives us his idea of what it is to be important.

• Proclaim the gospel, including Jesus's prediction of his death and resurrection (which the LMC omits) and his words about little children. Then provoke discussion, focusing on such questions as:

Does Jesus's description of an important person agree with yours? Does it surprise you? Is it hard to accept? Why?

What did Jesus mean by his words about little children? What qualities of little children was Jesus asking us to imitate? The leader must be sensitive to the fact that most of these older children do not look upon younger children—for example, their younger brothers and sisters—as ideal citizens of the kingdom of God!

• Why did Mark immediately follow Jesus's prediction of his passion and resurrection with his account of the argument among the disciples? What does it say about the difficulty of accepting a suffering savior? Refer to last Sunday's gospel and Peter's reaction to Jesus's prediction of his death.

• Allow some quiet time for personal thought and prayer about how we might better serve others. Encourage the children to share their reflections, but do not insist that they do so.

• Ask the children to complete the sentence "Jesus says that an important person is . . ." in the remaining column on their papers. Then ask the children to write across the bottoms of their papers this sentence: "This week I will try to serve . . . by . . .," thus focusing on a specific person and a specific action. Tell them to take their papers home and keep them in a place where they will see them occasionally, but where no one else will see them.

3. As was the case last Sunday, the reading today from the letter of James quite by chance and quite fortunately offers pertinent comment on today's gospel.

• Read the passage to older children, relate it to the gospel and elicit the reaction of the children.

• The children might benefit from a discussion of how we as a church community succeed or fail in practicing our faith by engaging in good works, as the author of the letter of James insists that we must do. Today would be a good day to introduce the children to some of the parish social ministry activities. Find out some things that children can do to help and present them to the group as opportunities to practice, and so to give life to, our faith. Children are unlikely to act unaided on their good intentions, so the leader should be prepared to offer practical help. Perhaps a group project would appeal to the children.

4. Proclaim to older children the Old Testament reading, which the LMC omits:

• The first reading today is taken from the book of Wisdom, part of the wisdom literature of the Old Testament. Written in Greek probably during the early part of the first century BCE, the book of Wisdom was the last of the Old Testament books to be written. Its author was a learned and devoted Jew who lived in Alexandria. His Jewish community existed in a time of faith crisis caused by, to mention a few things, constant contact with the pagan society which surrounded it, challenging scientific discoveries, disturbing new religious and philosophical systems. The author of the book of Wisdom immersed himself in the Jewish scriptures and sought to "draw divine guidance from the entire sacred literature of his people to give hope and consolation to his contemporaries" (JBC, p.557). Our passage today gives an explanation of why the just suffer at the hands of the wicked. The passage is part of a speech placed on the lips of the wicked, who claim that since death is final they might as well enjoy the good things of life. Today's reading describes their attitude toward the just, which follows naturally from their attitude toward life in general.

• Explain the reading to older children and then read it to them. Let them discuss its meaning. Help them to see why the church applies the reading to the sufferings of Jesus. Use the reading sensitively to console and to encourage children who sometimes themselves suffer at the hands of jealous others.

• A lively group might enjoy rewriting the reading in terms of their own lives.

Twenty-Sixth Sunday of the Year

Lectionary for Masses with Children	Lectionary for Mass
*Nm 11:25-29	*Nm 11:25-29
*Ps 66:1-3,4-5,16 and 20	**Ps 19:8,10,12-13,14
*Jas 5:1-6	*Jas 5:1-6
**Mk 9:38-41	**Mk 9:38-41

Focus: God remembers all our good deeds, no matter how small. We give praise for God's kindness to us.

Gather the Children

1. Welcome the children happily and remind them why we gather for our special liturgy of the word.
2. Sing joyfully to praise God who calls us together to hear the word.
3. Because the readings today, especially the words of James, ask us to reflect upon our failings, give special attention to the penitential rite. If the children have not already celebrated the rite with the adult assembly, the leader might lead them in prayer now as follows:

Leader: My brothers and sisters in God's family, God calls us through the word to be loving and kind to all people. Before we listen to God's word, let us praise God for forgiving us when we do not act as God wants.

You ask us to share what we have. You forgive us when we do not do it: God, we praise you.
All: God, we praise you.
Leader: You ask us to notice when other people need us and to help them. You forgive us when we do not do it: Jesus, we thank you.
All: Jesus, we thank you.
Leader: You ask us to use our hands, our feet, our eyes, our whole bodies for you. You forgive us when we do not do it: Spirit, we ask your mercy.
All: Spirit, we ask your mercy.
Leader: May God help us to listen well to the word and to love each other as we should. May God have mercy on us and forgive us when we fail to do so. May God give us life forever in happiness.
All: Amen.

Proclaim the Gospel:

1. Introduce the gospel by telling the children that today Jesus gives us good advice about how we can gain a reward in heaven. Ask the children to listen carefully to the proclamation. We focus upon the promise of Jesus that small kindnesses will not go without their reward.
2. Acclaim the gospel joyfully in song. Ask the children to say their responses carefully. Then proclaim the gospel, perhaps using only Mk 9:41 for younger children, and stating it positively.

Reflect upon the Kindness of Martin of Tours

1. In a world in which so many people see God as a divine bookkeeper tallying our offenses, it is indeed good news that God keeps careful count of even our small kindnesses. "Even a cup of cold water is big business and goes down on the credit side" (*The Interpreter's Bible*). Let us not limit the focus of the words of Jesus to the Twelve, but rather let us interpret his words as encouraging kindness toward any person at all.
2. As an example of someone who helped the needy, tell the children the story of St. Martin of Tours. Martin was born in the early fourth century in what is today Hungary. Although his parents were pagan, Martin became a Christian at the age of ten. His father forced him to enter the Roman army, and so Martin joined the cavalry. When Martin was stationed in France near Amiens, he came one cold winter day upon a poor beggar dressed in rags and suffering from exposure. In an act of charity that has become legendary Martin divided his cloak in two with his sword and gave half of it to the beggar. That night Jesus appeared to Martin wearing the beggar's half of the cloak and told him, "What you have done for the poor beggar you have done for me." Later in his life Martin served as bishop of Tours for thirty years. Even during his lifetime Martin was credited with many miracles. He was one of the first persons to be canonized who was not a martyr. His feast day is November 11. Martin is the patron saint of France.
3. Enrich the children's appreciation of Martin by showing them a picture of El Greco's magnificent and famous painting "Saint Martin and the Beggar."
4. In praise of God who gave us Martin, choose two children to pantomime the story of Martin and the beggar. Simple costumes and props will help the children act more freely: Martin can wear a cloak made of a paper bag tied on with yarn, and carry a silver poster board sword; the beggar can wear an old, frayed shirt and carry a cup. Martin, of course, should rip his cloak in half, an action which will impress the children. At the end of the pantomime, when Martin is looking at Jesus, ask the two children to hold very still. Then, while the rest of the children are looking at the tableau, ask a third child to pray to God that we will follow the example of Martin by acting kindly ourselves. If there is time, repeat the pantomime and the prayer with other children who would like to participate.

Respond to the Gospel in Our Lives

1. Encourage the children to earn money for the poor by doing small jobs at home. Give specific practical examples of ways they can help their mothers, fathers, grandparents, etc. Obtain or make a poor box for the children and show it to them. Tell them that they may bring to our gathering the money they make and put it in our poor box. Suggest various charities and let the children choose which one they wish to help. Point out the poor box in the church. Find out how its money is distributed and tell the children about it.

2. Praise God who rewards those who help others:
- God rewarded Martin who is now a saint and happy forever with God. Be sure the children know what a saint is. Thank God for people like Martin.
- God promises to reward us too, if we are kind, as we heard about in our gospel. Pray that we will always try to be kind to others.
- Sing again in praise of God who helps the poor and remembers the kind. To sing the selection of the LMC from Ps 66 would be appropriate.

3. Pray in the general intercessions for the poor and for those who help the poor.

4. As a reminder of the story of Martin and of our resolution to help the poor, give each child a small paper or inexpensive cloth cloak to take home. Suggest to the children that they use the cloak to create a picture of the story of Martin and the beggar. Or give each child a box in which to save money for the poor. If the leader chooses to do this, he or she should send home a note to the parents of the children explaining the box. It is not hard to draw a pattern for such a box so that the children can decorate the box and then, with the help of their parents, cut out and assemble the box. Or write to an appropriate museum and purchase post cards of El Greco's painting to give to the children to take home.

Other Possibilities:

1. The leader might illustrate the gospel message by using a children's story in place of the story of Martin. There are many good children's books whose theme is reaching out with love. The Seventh Mandarin, by Jane Yolen, tells of a mighty emperor and his seven mandarins. The men never even notice the poor beyond the palace walls, until one day a horrible accident occurs that changes their whole way of life to one of sensitivity to others' needs.

2. St. Vincent de Paul (1581-1654) is another popular saint with an interesting life appropriate for today's liturgy of the word. Vincent was known for his work with the poor, with prisoners, with children. He is usually pictured with a child and a loaf of bread, a tradition which surely brings to mind today's gospel. F. J. Sheed's *Saints Are Not Sad* has a good chapter on Vincent.

3. The reading from the letter of James contains many vivid images describing the fate of the rich. Let older children contrast the behavior of these rich with the behavior encouraged by the gospel. *The Seventh Mandarin* might provoke some interesting discussion on the subject. Or the leader might initiate discussion on some related topic in the news today and, with the children, decide on some positive, practical action that the parish, children included, might take.

4. In both the first reading from the book of Numbers and in the gospel, the theme of inclusion emerges. Discuss with the children the jealousy which some people, indeed, many people, have of their gifts and talents. Encourage the children to rejoice in each other and in the wonderful gifts we all possess. Pray in thanksgiving for each other and for the things that each of us can do well.

5. The latter part of today's LM selection from Ps 19 is a confession of our failings and a prayer to God to overcome them, things which every child and adult should do every day. Pray the appropriate parts of the psalm with older children, rephrasing the verses so that the children can understand the thoughts of the psalm and identify themselves with the psalmist. Talk with the children about how important it is that, each night, we quickly think over the day. Encourage the children to make up their own prayers of confession to God and to say their prayers as part of their daily prayer. Encourage the children also to use their prayers when they celebrate the sacrament of reconciliation.

Twenty-Seventh Sunday of the Year

Lectionary for Masses with Children	Lectionary for Mass
**Gn 2:18-24 Ps 128:1-2,3,4-5 ----- *Mk 10:13-16	**Gn 2:18-24 Ps 128:1-2,3,4-5,6 **Heb 2:9-11 **Mk 10:2-16 or 10:2-12

Focus: Jesus calls us to faithful love.

Gather the Children

1. Welcome the children happily and remind them that we gather to listen to God's word and to let it change our lives.

2. Ask the children to join hands and pray quietly that God will help us listen carefully to the word today and always. Light candles near the lectionary as a sign of God's presence.

3. Teach the children a lively song that expresses our joy in the Lord.

Pray to Acknowledge Our Imperfect Love and God's Loving Forgiveness

Note: The LMC risks a significant shift in focus today by omitting the principal common theme of the paired Old Testament-Gospel readings. Because of the distressing erosion in contemporary society of the ideal pictured in the readings, the author thinks it unwise to make the shift of focus, except possibly for the very youngest children. The following liturgy outline, therefore, keeps in mind the longer gospel reading of the LM.

1. Our gospel reading today, enhanced by the reading from the book of Genesis, speaks of lasting love in marriage. We shall try during this liturgy of the word to foster in the children the ideal of ever-faithful married love, an ideal which contemporary society seems rapidly to be abandoning. To accomplish this end, we shall encourage the children to be loving and caring in all their words and actions, especially within their families.

2. Join the children for a few moments of personal reflection on our failure to love as we should. Help little children to do so with a few specific questions concerning common childhood acts of selfishness. Then assure the children of God's merciful and loving forgiveness.

3. If the children have not already celebrated the penitential rite with the assembly, then pray with them now as follows:

Leader: My brothers and sisters in God's family, let us praise God who calls us to reach out to each other with love and care, and who forgives us when we do not do it.

Sometimes we think too much about ourselves and forget to show love for others. Still you love us: Lord, have mercy.

All: Lord, have mercy.

Leader: Sometimes we do not take the time to help others. Still you care for us: Christ, have mercy.

All: Christ, have mercy.

Leader: Sometimes we fail to share the joys and the sorrows of others. You always forgive us: Lord, have mercy.

All: Lord, have mercy.

Leader: We praise God for sending us Jesus to show us how to love each other. We praise God for sending us the Holy Spirit to remind us of what Jesus said and did. We praise God for forgiving us when we think too much about ourselves and too little about others. We praise God for calling us to life everlasting. We know that we will live forever with the Father, the Son and the Holy Spirit.

All: Amen.

Proclaim the Old Testament Reading

1. To prepare for proclaiming the reading from the book of Genesis, the leader should read all of the second creation account, Gn 2:4b-25.

2. Tell the children the story:

● Ask the children what they know about the biblical story of the creation of the world. Do not be concerned with biblical or scientific details, but simply strive to help the children realize that all creation comes ultimately from God.

● Ask the children if they remember the name of the first person whom God created. Have a large figure of a person, if possible a figure made by children before the liturgy. Have a child write "Adam" on the figure.

● Ask the children to imagine that they are Adam, just after he has been created by God. Ask them to imagine that, as they watched and marveled, God made a beautiful garden for their home. God made growing trees, beautiful to look at and good for food. God made water. God made the animals and the birds. The leader might have pictures of these things and show them as the story progresses. Then ask the children how Adam might have felt in the presence of all these gifts of God. Lead the children to realize that Adam, though very thankful to God, would like to have another person with him, to share his joy and complete his happiness.

● Ask the children if they know the name of the woman God made to be Adam's companion. Have a second large figure and let a child write "Eve" on the figure.

3. Ask the children to listen carefully as we read from the bible the story of the creation of Eve to be Adam's companion. Proclaim the reading.

4. Respond to the reading:

• Let the children offer prayers of praise and thanks for the wonderful gifts God gives us, especially for the gift of each other. Pray also with the children that in our families we will always rejoice in each other, as did Adam and Eve whose life together was the first family.

• Sing a hymn of praise and thanks to God. The leader might like to choose a particularly simple hymn and let the children make up additional verses. Suggest that the children sing their song at home as part of their daily prayer.

Proclaim the Gospel

1. In preparation for the gospel proclamation, discuss:

• How children feel when their parents are too busy to do things for them or with them;

• How parents feel when their children are too busy to do things for them;

• How children feel when their parents do take the time to be with them, to play with them, to read to them, to help them.

2. Help the children realize that Jesus was a very busy person. Help them to recall some of the many people Jesus took the time to visit, to talk with, to help. Then tell the children the incident recounted in Mk 10:13-14a, 16. Do not let the children think that the disciples were showing dislike of children, but rather that they were trying to free Jesus from what must have been constant demands on his time.

3. Ask the children to stand. Acclaim the gospel in song, help the children with the responses, and then proclaim Mk 10:13-14a, 16.

Make the Good News Our Own

1. To help the children internalize the gospel message of the love of Jesus for them and for all of us, make a poster:

• Have ready a figure of Jesus, perhaps one already made by some of the children. Let a child write "Jesus" on the figure. Glue the figure in the center of a poster board.

• Give each child a smaller figure of a child. Let the children personalize their figures in some simple way, for example, by writing their names, drawing their faces, coloring some clothes.

• Collect the figures from the children and glue them onto the poster board surrounding the figure of Jesus. As the children watch, write "Mark 10:14" in one corner of the poster, explaining that the words and numbers tell us where in the bible we can find the story of Jesus and the children.

• As the children rejoin the assembly, have several of them carry the poster into the church and present it to the presider, who should place the poster where the assembly can see it. If the presider were to comment on the poster, it would make the children happy.

2. Keeping in mind how Jesus welcomed the children even when he was busy and tired, discuss with the children how we can try to be kind to people always, as Jesus was. Dwell especially on how we can be loving and available at home. Help the children to be practical.

3. As a reminder of our liturgy of the word today give each child a picture of a larger figure with his arm around a smaller figure. Ask the children to take their pictures home and to color the figures so that they represent Jesus with his arms around a child.

Other Possibilities:

1. The better part of today's gospel turns our thoughts to the ideal of faithful love in marriage. So many of our children live in families in which there are, or have been, serious marriage problems. Rather than discuss these problems directly with little children, we have chosen, in the above presentation, to encourage the children to strive to be faithful in their love for those in their immediate families, as well as more generally for those in the entire human family.

2. Older children are acutely conscious of how even one selfish action can disrupt harmony in their lives at home. Perhaps they would be willing to formulate some positive suggestions about how whole families can work together to respect each other, to help each other, to enjoy each other's company, to live happily together. If the children become unusually interested in the activity, the leader can record the children's ideas, reproduce them, and give them to the children next Sunday to take home.

3. Elaborating on the theme of faithful love in marriage, perhaps the older children would like to suggest promises which young couples could include as part of their marriage promises to each other.

4. Jesus is the perfect model of unselfish love, and the way in which he displays his love for children in today's gospel is touching. An alternative approach to today's liturgy, whose primary theme is difficult for little children, would be to center the entire celebration on the love of Jesus for children. The leader should make the decision about whether to do this with the needs of his or her particular group in mind.

5. Discuss with older children what Jesus meant when he said that we must accept the kingdom of God like little children or else we cannot enter it. What admirable qualities do we older people see in little children? Certainly not every characteristic of little children is worthy of imitation, as the children in the group who have younger siblings can undoubtedly attest!

6. For an extremely interesting commentary on the "sexist" creation accounts, read the appropriate sections of Phyllis Trible's provocative book *God and the Rhetoric of Sexuality*.

7. Since we will read from the letter to the Hebrews for the next seven weeks, a few words of background information are in order. The style of the letter, if indeed it was a letter, is "the most polished of all the New Testament writings" (McKenzie, DOB, p.349). The author of the letter, the date and place of its composition, and the particular group for whom it was intended are all subject to scholarly debate. Very few modern scholars still maintain that it is the work of Paul. Reginald Fuller suggests that it was written about 85 CE to Greek-speaking Jewish Christians in Italy. He suggests further that the group to whom it was written was an "esoteric group within the church" which "had stagnated instead of growing to Christian maturity." The writer

of Hebrews used the centrality of Christ's high priesthood as the basis for a series of "pep talks" to urge the community to be strong in its faith, despite whatever difficulties it encountered. (See Fuller, PNL.)

In our reading today, the writer affirms the humanity of Jesus, through which he became our brother, and announces that it was fitting that Christ suffer as our leader to bring us to salvation. In light of the message of our other readings today, we might use the reading from Hebrews to urge the children to be patient and faithful in their everyday difficulties.

8. In encouraging parishes to plan special liturgies of the word for children, the church had in mind the words and action of Jesus that we read today. The Directory for Masses with Children states, quoting Mk 10:16: "The Church follows its Master, who 'put his arms around the children . . . and blessed them'" (#3). Let us who lead children in liturgy of the word be encouraged by today's gospel!

Twenty-Eighth Sunday of the Year

Lectionary for Masses with Children	Lectionary for Mass
*Wis 7:7-11	*Wis 7:7-11
Ps 90:12 and 14,16-17	Ps 90:12-13,14-15,16-17
*Heb 4:12-13	*Heb 4:12-13
**Mk 10:17-27	**Mk 10:17-30 or 10:17-27

Focus: Jesus calls us to value treasure in heaven above all our earthly possessions.

Gather the Children

1. Gather the children with joy and remind them why we have our special liturgy of the word.
2. Lead the group in song to celebrate the presence of God among us, and then pray quietly together that we will listen attentively to the word of God today and always.

Proclaim the Gospel

1. Prepare the children for the gospel proclamation:
• Ask the children to imagine that they are rich and can have anything they want. Ask them to name things they would like to have.
• Continue to describe a "rich person" in terms suited to the understanding of the children. The person would have lots of money, fine clothes, lots of food. Sketch the person simply. (Simple sketches are not hard, even for the non-artist.) Give the person a fine coat, hat, shoes. In one hand draw a bag with a dollar sign on it, and in the other hand draw an ice cream cone of many scoops and topped with a cherry. Draw the person's eyes and nose, but do not add the mouth.
• Ask the children to imagine that the person is also a good person. Let the children share briefly their ideas about what it means for a person to be good.
• Tell the children that one day Jesus met a man who was both rich and good. Our gospel is the story of what happened when Jesus and the man met.
2. Tell the children the story of Mk 10:17-22. Tell the story vividly and with feeling. The rich man apparently was quite sincere in his desire to do more than the minimum for salvation, and his decision not to follow Jesus was a difficult one which might well have haunted him for the rest of his life. Jesus loved the rich man (the LMC weakens the touching phrase of the New American Bible "Jesus looked at him with love" to "he liked him"), and must have been disappointed, even hurt, when the man chose his material possessions rather than life with him.
3. Ask the children to stand and listen well to the story of the rich man as we find it written in the bible. Acclaim the gospel in song. During the singing have one child carry the lectionary reverently to the leader. Then proclaim the gospel, shortening the reading to include only through verse 22.
4. To help the children understand the story return to the picture of the rich person:

• Ask the children how the rich man felt when Jesus asked him to give away all that he had. Then draw the figure's mouth, making a sad face.
• Sketch another figure, this time a picture of what the rich man could have become if he had answered the call of Jesus. Dress the person in rags, with bare feet and empty hands, but put a big smile on his face.

Respond to the Good News

1. To help the children remember what Jesus promised the rich man if he would give up all and follow him, have ready "silver" or "gold" letters (use silver or gold poster board or Christmas gift-wrapping paper) spelling "treasure in heaven." Without telling the children the message, pass out the letters. Tell the children that the letters will remind us of the reward the rich man could have had. Ask for the letters, one by one in order. Even if the children cannot read, most will be able to recognize the letters. Let the children holding the letters stand side by side so that the message is finally readable.
2. Discuss briefly the difference between treasure in the worldly sense and treasure in heaven.
3. Pray with the children that we will try to think more about following Jesus and less about our worldly possessions.
4. As a reminder of our liturgy today, give each child a large "silver" or "gold" disc with the sentence "Have treasure in heaven" written on it.

Tell the Children about St. Francis of Assisi

1. Introduce Francis as a man who took to heart Jesus's words to the rich man to sell all that he had and give to the poor. Francis, in fact, probably took to heart and acted more literally upon these words of Jesus that any other person i*Encyclopaedia Britannica* cites this as "the key to the character and spirit" of Francis. "To neglect this point is to show an unbalanced portrait of the saint as a lover of nature, a social worker, an itinerant preacher, and a lover of poverty" (*Britannica*, 1974, v. 7, p.682).
2. In preparation for telling the children about Francis the leader should read an account of his life. There is much good literature about this very popular saint. Most any encyclopedia contains at least a short article about him. The September 1982 issue of *Maryknoll* highlights, in lovely text and lovely pictures, the life of Francis and the relevance of his life and work to our world today.

3. Summarize the life of Francis for the children, including such details as:
- His birth in Assisi in Italy in 1181-82, his wealthy youth, his love of sports and games, his many friends;
- His year-long imprisonment during the war between Assisi and Perugia and his serious illness as soon as he returned home;
- His decision to give everything to God;
- The incident with his father before the bishop;
- His love for the poor and neglected—it is said that Francis never refused to give to a beggar;
- His own poverty;
- His love of nature, which Francis saw as a mirror of God;
- His stigmata and his great suffering before his death. Francis died on October 3, 1226.

4. Deepen the children's acquaintance with Francis by showing them a reproduction of a famous work of art depicting Francis. Giotto, Ciambue and El Greco, to mention but a few masters, have painted the saint. Or tell some of the children the story of Francis before the liturgy, have them illustrate scenes from his life, and use the children's pictures during the liturgy of the word. Later share the children's pictures with the entire parish by displaying them in a place where many will see them.

5. Discuss how we might imitate Francis. God does not call all people, as God called Francis, to a life of total poverty; but God does ask each of us not to let whatever material goods we have stand in the way of a life of dedication to the gospel. Help the children to be practical in their application of the message of today's gospel and in their imitation of Francis. Perhaps with little ones we should focus simply upon sharing.

6. Pray in thanksgiving to God for the beautiful life of Francis and his example to us of how to follow Jesus.

7. Listen to John Foley's "Peace Prayer" (from *Neither Silver Nor Gold*). Use the song as background music during a meditation on the life and love of Francis and on our desire to follow Jesus in our own way, as Francis did in his.

Other Possibilities:

1. For older children, use a different approach to the gospel story:
- On the gathering cloth have a large pile of "possessions," for example, a pile of "money," "furs" (imitation furs from a fabric shop), "diamonds," sports equipment, a bathing suit and a poster of a Hawaiian beach, a hub cap and a picture of a Porsche. Find a willing volunteer and load the "possessions" into his or her arms. There should be enough "possessions" so that the child can hardly hold them all.
- Tell the child that there is one more thing which he or she may have. Produce a very large wrapped gift and present it to the child. Our objective in this activity is to cause the child to choose between keeping all the "possessions" and relinquishing at least some of them in order to take the gift.

- Discuss briefly with the children how hard it is to make choices between things we value. If the concept seems too difficult for the children, do not attempt to explain it thoroughly, but simply rely on the activity.
- After the proclamation of the gospel, ask the children what they think the wrapped gift might symbolize. In this way lead the children to recognize the vast worth of "treasure in heaven," especially in relation to all our material possessions.

2. Ask older children what might have happened to the rich man during the rest of his life. Did he ever change his mind about his possessions and give them all away? Did he spend his life doing other generous and praiseworthy things, but still fall short of the total renunciation to which Jesus called him? Share with the children the words Jesus spoke to his disciples after the rich man left him. Help the children to understand that we cannot "explain away" Jesus's words about poverty and the poor. He confronts us with a challenge which most of us will never take seriously.

3. Our first reading, from the book of Wisdom, is part of a speech placed on the lips of Solomon, glorious king of Israel, known for his great wisdom as well as his great wealth. In his speech Solomon expresses his love of wisdom above wealth and power, and recalls his choice of wisdom above all things. Fortunately for Solomon God was so pleased with his choice of wisdom that God granted him also riches and honor. (See I Kgs 3:3-14.) Proclaim the reading to older children. Let the children discuss the meaning of "wisdom," then comment on Solomon's description of the value of wisdom. Discuss some of the dominant values in our own society and ask them to rephrase Solomon's speech as if he were alive and young and making it today. Help the children to relate the reading from the book of Wisdom to today's gospel.

4. Our reading from the letter to the Hebrews is profound, and also poetic. It describes the choice of the rich man and the choice of Solomon, as well as some of our own choices. Explain the reading to older children and use it to meditate upon the constant challenges of God's word.

5. Pray St. Francis's great prayer of praise, the "Canticle of the Sun." Accompany the prayer with slides. Give the children copies of the prayer to take home and illustrate. Simplify the prayer for children who are not mature enough to appreciate it in its fullness. The well-known, well-loved hymn "All Creatures of Our God and King" is, of course, a musical rendition of Francis's prayer.

Hymn of Saint Francis
"Canticle of the Sun" Simplified for Younger Children

Praise to You, my Lord,
with all the things you have made.

Praise to You, my Lord, for the Sun.
He brings us day and gives us light.

Praise to You, my Lord, for the Moon and the Stars.
They shine in heaven.

Praise to You, my Lord, for the Wind.
He keeps us alive.

Praise to You, my Lord, for the Water.
She is so very useful.

Praise to You, my Lord, for Fire.
He lights up the night.

Praise to You, my Lord, for the Earth.
She gives us food.

Praise to You, my Lord,
for those who forgive each other in love.

Praise to You, my Lord,
for those who are sick and suffering.

Praise to You, my Lord, for our Death.
She is lovely for those who do your will.

O praise and bless my Lord!
Thank Him and serve Him!

Canticle of Brother Sun

Praised be You, my Lord, in all your creatures,
Especially Sir Brother Sun,
Who makes the day and enlightens us through You.
He is lovely and radiant and grand;
And he heralds You, his Most High Lord.

Praised be You, my Lord, for Sister Moon
And for the stars.
You have hung them in heaven shining and precious
and fair.

And praise to You, my Lord, in Brother Wind,
In air and cloud, calm, and every weather
That sustains your creatures.

Praised be You, my Lord, for Sister Water,
So very useful, humble, precious and chaste.

Yes, and praise to You, my Lord, for Brother Fire.
Through him You illumine our night,
And he is handsome and merry, robust and strong.

Praised be You, my Lord, for Sister, Mother Earth
Who nourishes us and teaches us,
Bringing forth all kinds of fruits and colored flowers
and herbs.

Oh, and praise to You, my Lord,
For those who forgive one another in Your love
And who bear sickness and trials.
Blessed are they who live on in peace,
For they will be crowned by You, Most High!

Praise to You, my Lord, for our Sister Bodily Death,
From whom no living person may escape:
How dreadful for those who die in sin,
How lovely for those who are found in Your Most Holy
Will,
For the second death can do them no harm.

O praise and bless my Lord,
Thank Him and serve Him
Humbly but grandly!

Twenty-Ninth Sunday of the Year

Lectionary for Masses with Children	Lectionary for Mass
- - - - -	**Is 53:10-11
Heb 4:14-16	Ps 33:4-5,18-19,20,22
Ps 33:4-5,20 and 22	Heb 4:14-16
**Mk 10:35-45	**Mk 10:35-45 or 10:42-45

Focus: Whoever wants to be first in the eyes of God must serve others.

Gather the Children

1. Welcome the children with joy to their special liturgy of the word. Remind them that our celebration of God's word, though separate from the adult celebration, is the same liturgy of the word. Join the children in prayer that we will listen well to God's word today and always.

2. Sing a song of praise to God who loves us, cares for us and calls us. During the singing have one child hold the lectionary high, then lay it in a place of honor where all the children can see it.

Proclaim the Gospel

1. The leader might arouse the interest of younger children and introduce the message of the gospel by recalling the story of Cinderella:

- The leader might tell the children that he or she has in mind a story they all know. In the story there are two sisters who think they are better than other people, and one sister who always must do what others ask of her. At the end of the story the sister who always serves others finds happiness. Ask the children if they know what the story is. Let the children briefly share their memories of the fairy tale. Show a few pictures from a book.

- Then, to emphasize the point, ask the children what they think would have happened if Cinderella's stepsisters had changed their selfish ways and been more humble and helpful to others. Not all three sisters, of course, could have married the prince; but the three sisters could certainly have lived in a harmonious and happy relationship.

2. Turn the thoughts of the children to the gospel:

- Tell the children that today's gospel story is about two brothers, James and John, who want to be greater than other people. In the story Jesus tells James and John what they must do if they want to be great. It is not at all what the brothers had been thinking of.

- Tell the children of the request of James and John. Tell them further that the other disciples, not surprisingly, became angry when they heard the self-centered request of the brothers.

- Ask the children to listen carefully to the words of Jesus in our gospel, because Jesus tells us what we should do if we want to be great in the most important way.

3. Ask the children to stand. Acclaim the gospel in song, and have one child carry the lectionary reverently to the leader during the acclamation. Then proclaim the gospel. In the interest of being realistic, the leader might consider retaining the word "serve" of the LM, rather than replacing it with the word "slave" of the LMC. Be sure, of course, that the children understand that service means unselfish help.

Respond to the Gospel

1. Talk with the children about the meaning of the gospel. Little children may not be motivated to be the most important, but they do wish to have their own ways.

2. In an effort to be practical in our application of God's word today, ask the children what kinds of things we can do to serve others, for example, parents, siblings, grandparents, friends, teachers. Encourage the children to supply specific, sensible examples.

3. Make a symbol of Jesus's injunction to us to serve others:

- Focus on serving those with whom we live by suggesting that a broom might be a symbol of helping with housework.

- Have ready a pile of paper straws and a broom handle of heavy cardboard. Give each child a straw. Ask the children to think of particular things they will do today for those with whom they live.

- Tell the children that we will let the straws be a sign of our willingness to serve others. Then collect the straws from the children and glue them to the broom handle.

- Conclude the activity by praying that we will try to serve others. The leader might lead the children in prayer as follows:

> Loving God,
> we want to be first in your eyes
> and happy with you.
> We know what you want us to do:
> you want us to serve other people.
> We've thought of special ways to serve others.
> Please help us to do these things.
> We ask this in the name of your child, Jesus,
> who lives in heaven with you and the Holy Spirit.
> Amen.

4. Teach the children a song in which we pray to serve others.

5. Give each child a small paper broom to take home as a reminder to our intention to serve others.

Other Possibilities:

1. There are numerous good children's books whose

theme is unselfish service of other people. One such book is *What's the Matter with Carruthers?* by James Marshall. The humorous story tells of how Emily Pig and Eugene Turtle try to cheer up their old friend Carruthers who has become strangely grouchy. The leader might prefer to use this story instead of the story of Cinderella. In this case let the children make a rake.

2. Discuss the gospel more deeply with older children:

• Before proclaiming the gospel, discuss our natural human tendencies to "lord it over" others. Perhaps some of the children would enjoy planning and presenting scenes in which children or adults act like James and John by asking for special treatment they do not deserve.

• Tell older children of Jesus's words about his own suffering and about the suffering which James and John would one day undergo. James was beheaded, the first of the Twelve to suffer martyrdom (Acts 12:2). John's identity is uncertain. He may have been martyred at an early date, but if this John was the author of the fourth gospel, which fact is by no means certain, tradition has it that he was tortured and then exiled to the island of Patmos, where he lived until he was very old. Help the children to understand the depth of a resolution to follow the way of Jesus.

• Point out that the ten became "indignant" with James and John, while Jesus did not at any point in the episode become angry. Contrast the impatience of the ten with the two brothers with the patience of Jesus as he once again explained to his own that he and they (and we) must suffer.

• After proclaiming and explaining the gospel, the leader might involve older children more actively by letting them read the gospel together in parts.

• Let the children make a poster symbolizing their resolution to serve others. Let them trace and cut out their hands and write on them specific ways in which they intend to serve others. Glue the hands onto a poster surrounding the words, "If you want to be first, serve the rest."

3. Our reading from the book of Isaiah, which the LMC omits, is part of the fourth "Suffering Servant Song." It describes the suffering of the innocent servant, ending in his death "possibly by execution, certainly with an evil reputation" (McKenzie, DOB, p. 791). Through his willing suffering the servant atones for the sins of "many." After his death he is rewarded by the Lord, apparently with resurrection, although the poem is "earlier than any attested belief in the resurrection" (AB, 20, p.135). Christians, of course, apply this prophecy to Jesus. Read parts of the poem to older children and ask them if they think the servant's experiences influenced Jesus's understanding of his work on earth.

Thirtieth Sunday of the Year

Lectionary for Masses with Children	Lectionary for Mass
*Jer 31:7-9	*Jer 31:7-9
Ps 126:1-2,4-5,6	Ps 126:1-2,2-3,4-5,6
Heb 5:1-6	Heb 5:1-6
**Mk 10:46-52	**Mk 10:46-52

Focus: We praise God for the gift of our sight.

Gather the Children

1. Welcome the children joyfully and gather them in a circle. Remind them why we come together for our special liturgy of the word.
2. Turn off the lights in the room. Ask the children to close their eyes and imagine for a few moments what it would be like if we could not see.
3. Light candles near the lectionary and sing a song to praise God for the gift of our sight. Or sing about Jesus as the light of our lives.
4. Pray with the children that God will light our minds and our hearts with the word we will hear.

Praise God for the Gift of Our Sight

1. Introduce today's readings by helping the children to grasp something of what blindness is like:
- Ask several children to tell the group things they like to look at.
- Show the children pictures of people, animals, flowers, famous works of art, other things pleasant to look at.
- Turn all the pictures face down or cover them with a black cloth. Ask the children to close their eyes and think of what they would most miss seeing if they were blind.
2. Drawing upon our reading from the book of Jeremiah, tell the children that one sign of the love of God for the people was God's care of the sick and disabled, including the blind. Read some of Jeremiah's words about the care of God for the blind.
3. In response to the reading and in thanksgiving to God for the gift of our sight, pray today's selection from Ps 126. The leader should take the time to teach the children to repeat the psalm refrain. It is important that children use the adult ritual when they can do so with understanding.

Proclaim the Gospel

1. Tell the children the story of the cure of blind Bartimaeus. The story is fresh and full of action, as we have come to expect of Mark's gospel. Tell the story vividly, but faithfully to the gospel account, involving the children in the action as much as possible:
- Ask the children to imagine that they were children in the city of Jericho at the time the story takes place. Many times they would have seen Bartimaeus sitting by the gate of the city, begging for money so that he could buy food. He would have had no other means to support himself.
- Ask the children to imagine that their parents had heard of Jesus and had spoken to them of the wonderful things Jesus had done. Ask them to imagine that on the day Jesus came to their city, the children with their parents were among the large crowd present when Jesus met Bartimaeus.
- Describe the feelings and actions of Bartimaeus:

He must have been curious as he sat by the roadside and heard the commotion which a large crowd would have made.

How excited Bartimaeus must have been when he heard that Jesus was at the center of the crowd! It seems clear from Bartimaeus's reaction to the information that Jesus was near that he had heard of Jesus and his wonderful compassion for the blind.

What must Bartimaeus have thought when the people tried to keep him quiet? He obviously decided that he would ignore their scolding and risk their displeasure in the hope that Jesus would help him.

How excited he must have been when Jesus called him! He must also have been frightened.

What might have been the first thing he saw? Was it the sky? Was it faces in the crowd? Was it the face of Jesus? What might have been his words to Jesus?

2. Acclaim the gospel in song, and then proclaim it.

Respond to the Gospel

1. Talk with the children about other ways of being blind besides not being able to use our eyes. The concept will be difficult for very young children because they do not think abstractly. Supply a few examples, but do not dwell on explanations. We are blind when we do not notice that other people need our love and our help. We are blind when we ignore people who are sad or lonely. We are blind when we think only of ourselves. Pray with the children that Jesus will heal all our blindness, just as he healed Bartimaeus's eyes. Teach the children verse one of "Amazing Grace" with its lovely voicing of today's message about spiritual blindness "I once was blind, but now I see."
2. Talk about Bartimaeus's faith in Jesus, which Mark tells us was the occasion of his cure. Then say a profession of faith. The leader might use the following profession of faith, asking the children to respond in song "Amen! We believe!" to each of these statements:

We believe in God who made us.
We believe that God fills us with joy.
We believe in Jesus, God's child.
We believe that Jesus helps us to see.
We believe that Jesus calls us to follow him.

We believe in the Holy Spirit.
We believe that we will live with God forever.

3. Give each child a paper magnifying glass to take home as a reminder of our resolution to use our eyes to see all the things, physical and otherwise, that God wants us to see.

Other Possibilities:

1. Invite a blind person to speak with the children about blindness. If one of the children is blind, be sure to invite the special participation of that child in today's presentation.

2. *Jesus Heals a Blind Man*, from the Augsburg Publishing House *What the Bible Tells Us Series*, tells the story of today's gospel. The wording is simple yet faithful to the gospel. The pictures are beautiful. Use the words and the pictures in the book to review the story with the children.

3. With older children the gospel of the LM may be proclaimed unchanged, and, whenever it is possible, it is good to do just that in order to facilitate the eventual presence of the children at the adult liturgy of the word. After the proclamation of the gospel augment the above discussion of the feelings and actions of Bartimaeus:

• How did Bartimaeus explain later to his friends what had happened to him? What might he have said to other blind beggars at the city gates?

• Was Bartimaeus's life different because of his encounter with Jesus? The gospel says that he followed Jesus up the road. Did he stay with Jesus and become one of his disciples? Did he remain in Jericho and dedicate his life to helping the blind and the otherwise disadvantaged? Did he eventually forget the compassion of Jesus?

• Just how well did Bartimaeus "see" Jesus? Did he "see" him only as a miracle-worker? Or did he, in some however imperfect way, "see" Jesus as the love and care of God incarnate?

• Because the gospel is so word- and action-packed it would be good to dramatize it. Let several children pantomime the action while the rest read the passage, perhaps arranged so that one child is Jesus, one is Bartimaeus, several are the crowd, and the rest are the narrator. Or let several children simply act it out. Or, especially for younger children, proclaim the gospel and then let several children pantomime the action while the leader retells or rereads the story.

5. If we recall the gospels of the past several Sundays, we see that the faith of Bartimaeus stands in striking contrast to the repeated failure of the disciples to grasp what Jesus was trying to teach them about himself, specifically, that he was calling them to the way of suffering and death. Considering its position in Mark's gospel, the story of Bartimaeus thus tells us that the cure of real blindness is none other than the way of the cross.

• Let older children discuss what "real" blindness is and what Jesus might do today to cure it. Pray in the general intercessions for the healing of the blind in our world.

• Let older children formulate a profession of faith based on what they believe about Jesus.

6. Introduce Braille to older children. Send them home with a copy of the Braille alphabet and with a Braille message to translate.

7. Remind older children that the care of God for the weak and the disabled was a constant Old Testament promise. Explain and proclaim the reading from the book of Jeremiah. Talk about how in Jesus the promises of God through the ages were fulfilled. Did the people of Jesus's time notice? Do people today notice? What might God promise us today as a sign of God's presence among us?

Thirty-First Sunday of the Year

Lectionary for Masses with Children	Lectionary for Mass
**Dt 6:2-6	**Dt 6:2-6
Ps 18:1-2,46	Ps 18:2-3,3-4,47,51
Heb 7:26	Heb 7:23-28
**Mk 12:28-31	**Mk 12:28-34

Focus: Love sums up all the commandments. We pray to love God above all things and to love our neighbor as we love ourselves.

Gather the Children

1. Welcome the children with joy and remind them why we gather for our special liturgy of the word.
2. Sing in praise of God for God's word which guides our lives. Then pray quietly with the children that we will listen well to God's word today and always.

Proclaim the Gospel

1. Help the children to understand the meaning and the purpose of the commandments:
• Focus on the meaning of the word "rule":

Before the liturgy ask a child to make a fist and extend the index finger as if pointing to something. Trace the child's hand and cut out ten or twelve copies. Even better, use the hands of ten or twelve children.

During the liturgy, ask the children what a rule is. As an example of a rule, show a picture of a traffic light. After discussing the traffic light, write the numeral "one" on one of the hands. Ask the children to think of other rules. Each time a child mentions a rule, take another hand and write on it the next numeral. Then talk with the children about the vast number of rules we have.

Discuss why we have rules:

We have rules for life and growth and maintaining good health, rules, for example, about food and rest and exercise, about brushing our teeth, bathing, having regular medical check-ups and immunizations.

We have rules for safety, rules, for example, about traffic lights and speed limits, about matches, knives and guns.

We have rules for fostering good relations with other people, rules, for example, for good manners.
• Tell the children that there are other words that mean the same thing as the word "rule." Introduce the word "commandment," write it in large letters on a piece of paper and lay on the paper all the hands, pointing to the word. Comment on how many commandments there are.
2. Introduce today's gospel:
• Tell the children that there are many commandments in the bible. Some are very important; some are of less-

er importance. The commandments help us in our relationships with God and with each other. The "ten commandments" are the most famous of the Old Testament commandments, but there are many other Old Testament commandments as well.
• Tell the children that Jesus, as always concerned about our worries, knew that the people of his time had many commandments to obey. He did not want them to become confused and discouraged in trying to do what God wanted.
• A Jewish scribe in New Testament times was a person who studied and knew "the law," that is, a person who knew the Jewish scriptures well and was an expert in how to keep all its commandments. Our gospel describes a conversation between Jesus and a scribe. The conversation centered around the many commandments of the law and resulted in a simple way to remember them all: a one-word summary. Although the LMC, in shortening the LM reading, omits the subsequent exchange between Jesus and the scribe, the leader might want to include it anyway: present the scribe to the children as a person who was honestly seeking the opinion of Jesus, and who recognized Jesus, through Jesus's response to his question, as one who spoke in a special way for God; Jesus, in turn, acknowledged the scribe as one whose understanding of the law was deep and valid and was bringing him to true happiness.
3. Proclaim the gospel:
• Ask the children to stand and listen carefully to the gospel. Ask them to see if they can spot the one word that sums up all the commandments of the law.
• Acclaim the gospel in song. During the acclamation, have one child carry the lectionary, held high and reverently, to the leader. Help the children to say the proper responses. Then proclaim the gospel.

Make the Good News Our Own

1. Help the children extract the word "love" from the gospel as the one-word summary of the law. Remind them briefly that "your neighbor" means "all people." Help the children to see why love really does sum up the law. Be practical rather than abstract, especially for younger children.
2. To help the children visualize and assimilate the message of the gospel, have a large envelope. Write "Love God" on one side of the envelope and "Love your neighbor" on the other side. Then put into the envelope all the pointing hands.

Respond to the Good News

1. Pray in the general intercessions that we will love God and love our neighbor. If the children do not know how to respond properly to the intercessions, the leader should take the time to teach them, though a liturgy of the word is not the time for "drill." The leader might formulate the prayer as follows:

Leader: Sisters and brothers in God's family, let us pray that all people will try to love God and to love each other.

For those who argue and fight, that they will show their love for God and their neighbor by being people of gentleness and peace, we pray to the Lord.

All: Lord, hear our prayer.

Leader: For those who selfishly keep all that they have for themselves, that they will show their love for God and their neighbor by sharing their possessions, we pray to the Lord.

All: Lord, hear our prayer.

Leader: For those who do not notice when other people need their time and their attention, that they will show their love for God and their neighbor by giving of their time and their attention, we pray to the Lord.

All: Lord, hear our prayer.

Leader: For those who are sick or sad, especially for the dying, for those who are trying to be good, that they will know the love of God and their neighbor, we pray to the Lord.

All: Lord, hear our prayer.

Leader: Loving God, hear all our prayers, those which we speak aloud and those which we speak only in our hearts. Help us and all your children to love you as much as we can, and to show our love for you by loving other people. We pray in the name of Jesus through the Holy Spirit.

All: Amen.

2. As a practical reminder of today's gospel, give each child a "love locket" to wear home. Make the locket by cutting a double disc, flat on one edge, leaving the two discs attached on the flat edge. Let older children write on one side of the disc "Love God" and on the other side "Love your neighbor." On the inside of the locket the children should write a practical, simple suggestion for how they can show their love for God and other people. Hang the lockets on yarn strings. Ask the children to wear their love lockets home and to explain them to their parents. The leader of a group of younger children might enlist the help of older children in preparing the lockets before the liturgy.

3. Teach the children to sing a hymn which encourages our love of each other.

___

Other Possibilities:

1. For a humorous story about the necessity of rules, read Joann Stover's *If Everybody Did*. To read the story to the children before the liturgy would be good preparation for a discussion of rules. During the liturgy of the word, the leader will probably have time only to use a few examples from the story. The children might enjoy making up other "what if's."

2. For older children, instead of placing pointing hands in an envelope, write the rules they think of on twelve strips of paper, and then lay out the strips to form the word "love" in box letters. Or have a pile of stones to represent the rules and talk about the burden which the law can become.

3. Share with older children the beautiful and theologically important reading from the book of Deuteronomy:

• The words of our reading (as, indeed, the words of the entire book of Deuteronomy except its closing verses) were supposedly spoken by Moses to the Israelites just before they entered the promised land. The words were a reminder to the people of God that they were to keep their part of the covenant which they and God had made. Proclaim the reading solemnly to the children, as would be fitting for such an occasion.

• The verse Dt 6:4 is the very important Jewish daily prayer, the "shemah." The command to love God with our whole being follows from the revelation of God to us that God is the one God. "Shemah" is the imperative of the Hebrew verb "to hear."

Tell the children that some Jewish families write the words of Dt 6:4 (more precisely, Dt 6:4-9 and Dt 11:13-21) on tiny scrolls and fix them to the doorways into their homes, where they are a frequent reminder of their faith. Such a scroll is called a "mezuzah" from the Hebrew word for doorpost. Suggest to the children that they make mezuzahs to use in their homes.

Or give the children papers with the words of Dt 6:4 written in fat letters. Ask the children to color the letters and decorate the papers, then hang their papers in their homes.

Older children might like to see the shemah written in Hebrew. Enlist the help of a Jewish friend to write Dt 6:4 in Hebrew.

• After a discussion of the first reading, proclaim the gospel in its entirety to older children.

4. It is interesting to ask just what was "excellent" about the reply of Jesus to the question of the scribe. Jesus did not make up the commandment "love God" (see Dt 6:4) and he did not make up the commandment "love your neighbor" (see Lv 19:18); they were very much a part of his Jewish tradition. Further, Jesus was probably not the first to associate the two commandments. What was, however, radical about the teaching of Jesus was the way in which he perceived that the two commandments are, in fact, inseparable. To obey one commandment is to obey the other. (See Vawter, FG, vol. 2, p.152.) Share these thoughts with older children.

5. As a fitting response to the shemah and to the great commandment, pray the selection from Ps 18.

Thirty-Second Sunday of the Year

Lectionary for Masses with Children	Lectionary for Mass
**I Kgs 17:10-16 Ps 146:6-7,8-9,9-10 - - - - - **Mk 12:41-44	**I Kgs 17:10-16 Ps 146:7,8-9,9-10 Heb 9:24-28 **Mk 12:38-44 or 12:41-44

Focus: We pray that we, like the widows, will share generously what we have.

Gather the Children

1. Gather the children joyfully in their separate space. Ask them why we come together for our special liturgy of the word and listen respectfully to their answers. Then lead the children in prayer that we and the adult assembly will listen well to the word of God today and always.

2. Sing to celebrate the presence of God in the word and in the gathered community. Add simple gestures to heighten the interest of younger children.

Proclaim the Old Testament Reading

1. Tell the children the story of Elijah and the widow of Zarephath. The story is gripping and vivid, and the leader should tell the story in just that way. The leader should be faithful to the biblical account, yet encourage the children to become involved in the story. A few props always help hold the attention of the children. For this story use some sticks, a nearly empty jar of flour, a nearly dry jug of oil, a bit of bread.

• As background to the story tell the children that Elijah was a prophet, that is, a man who listened to God and then spoke for God to the people. Elijah lived long ago, many years before Jesus, in the kingdom of Israel. Elijah's mission as a prophet was to keep the people from forgetting Yahweh, their God, and so to keep them from turning instead to the worship of false gods. Elijah came on the scene suddenly to predict three years of drought in the land. God then ordered Elijah to go east and hide, where he was fed by ravens. Then the Lord sent Elijah to Zarephath, a harbor city in ancient Phoenicia, where God had chosen a widow to take care of the prophet. (See I Kgs 17:1-9.) Our reading today takes up the story at this point.

• Make sure the children know what a widow is. Be concerned that they realize that the widow of our story was very poor. Tell the children what the woman was doing at the beginning of our reading, and talk with them about the worries and the fears she must have had.

• Tell the children of Elijah's request of the poor widow, and discuss her likely feelings. The woman must have been frightened at the thought of sharing her meager supplies, but still she decided to share her food.

• Tell the children of the reward God gave the widow.

Stress that God rewarded her because she showed love and concern for Elijah in his great need.

2. Suggest that Elijah and the widow and her son might have prayed together prayers like the psalms, the biblical song-prayers of Israel. Teach the children to sing the psalm refrain, and them pray selections from Ps 146.

Proclaim the Gospel

1. Introduce the gospel by telling the children that today Jesus talks about another poor widow, and he praises her for giving away some of the little money she has.

2. Remind the children that the temple, like our church, was the place where people gathered to worship God. The money collected in the temple was used to take care of the temple and to help the poor, like the money we collect today in our church.

3. Ask the children to stand to listen to God's word as we read it in the gospel. Acclaim the gospel joyfully in song. During the singing have one child carry the lectionary reverently to the leader. If necessary, help the children to say the responses properly. Proclaim the gospel.

Make the Good News Our Own

1. Review the gospel story by asking the children questions such as the following:

• Whom did Jesus see putting money into the collection box?

• What did Jesus say about the gifts of the rich people?

• What did Jesus say about the gift of the poor widow?

• Why do you think the poor widow would give away some of her money when she had so little?

• What do you think Jesus was trying to teach his disciples by telling them about the widow?

• How do you think God might have rewarded the poor widow for her generous gift?

2. Relate the gospel to our lives:

• Ask the children what they think we can learn from today's gospel.

• Help them to see that Jesus calls us also to generous giving of things besides our money. Be imaginative and practical in examples of how children can give generously to others.

3. Give each child two pennies to keep for the remainder of the liturgy today and then to put in the parish poor box as they leave the church with their adult companions. Or give each child "a near-empty jar of flour" as a reminder of the generosity of the widow of Zarephath.

4. Pray in the general intercessions that people will give generously of their money, their time, their talents.
5. Conclude the liturgy with a song whose theme is generous sharing.

Other Possibilities:

1. Let several children pantomime the gospel. Dress the rich appropriately and let them put many noisy coins into the collection box. Dress the poor widow appropriately and let her put two coins quietly into the box. Then ask the whole group which gift pleased God the most.
2. Act out the story of Elijah and the widow of Zarephath.
3. Have a collection pantomime with older children: Pass an imaginary box from person to person and let each one pretend to put an offering into the box. Each person should explain his or her offering in a few words, for example, "I offer time today to read to my little sister" or "I offer to set the table tonight without being asked" or "I offer not to yell at my family the next time I become angry."
4. Suggest to older children that they write up the story of Elijah and the widow of Zarephath or of the rich people and the poor widow like a modern child's book. Illustrate it. Make up a modern story of generous giving.
5. In prayer with older children acknowledge our failures and our successes with regard to generous giving and sharing:

We are like the rich people when . . .
Loving God, forgive us for our selfishness.
We are like the poor widow when . . .
Loving God, help us to give and share more often.

Continue with other examples until the children lose interest.

Thirty-Third Sunday of the Year

Lectionary for Masses with Children	Lectionary for Mass
**Dn 12:1-3 Ps 16:5 and 8,9-10,11 ----- *Mk 13:24-32	**Dn 12:1-3 Ps 16:5 and 8,9-10,11 Heb 10:11-14,18 *Mk 13:24-32

Focus: We prepare for life after death by living every moment fully.

Gather the Children

1. Welcome the children happily and remind them why we come together for our separate liturgy of the word.
2. Light candles as a sign of God's presence among us. Praise God in song because God gives us the word to light our hearts and minds and lives.
3. Lead the children in prayer, asking God to help us listen well to the word. The leader might ask the younger children to repeat the following simple prayer, line by line:

> Loving God,
> You speak to us
> in many ways.
> We praise you for your word
> which lights our minds and our hearts
> and shows us how to live.
> You speak to us right now
> through the words of the bible.
> We want to listen to you.
> Help us to listen well to you
> now and always.
> Amen.

Proclaim the Old Testament Reading

1. In magnificent poetry the author of the book of Daniel describes the resurrection of the dead to everlasting life or to everlasting shame. We use the reading to focus the attention of the children on our belief in, to quote the Apostles' Creed, "the resurrection of the dead and life everlasting." For little children it is not necessary to talk about everlasting punishment, but only about everlasting joy.
2. Ask the children what happens to us after we die. Listen carefully and respectfully to their answers. Then speak to them lovingly of our God who takes care of us always, even after death. Tell the children that after death we will rise to new life with God, a life which we cannot yet understand, but which we know will be a happy one.
3. Proclaim the beautiful words of the book of Daniel:
- Tell the children that a man whom we know as Daniel once wrote about life after death. He didn't tell us exactly what that life would be like, but in a beautiful word-picture he told us that our new life would be wonderful. His words are so important that they are written in our bible.
- Ask the children to be still, to listen carefully, and to remember what Daniel said we would be like after death.
- Proclaim Dn 12:2-3.
4. Strengthen the children's belief in life after death and their love for God who gives us life forever:
- Ask the children if they noticed, when we read Daniel's words, what he said we shall be like after we rise from the dead. Focus their attention on the beautiful promise that we shall "shine like the stars forever." Then lay out gold foil or gold poster board stars on a dark blue or black poster board.
- Pray with the children that we will live every day as God wants so that we will share the wonderful happiness that God has prepared for those who love God. Use the words of Ps 16, simplified appropriately. The leader should take the time to teach the children to say, better, to sing, the psalm refrain, if possible the one which the adult assembly will sing.

Proclaim the Gospel

1. Today's gospel is difficult for little children. Because we never wish to frighten them, especially in talking about things of God, we omit most of the selection and share only the last sentence. Our emphasis is on being good right now in order to be ready for death and new life whenever it comes to us.
2. Speak to the children gently about the fact that we will all die one day and then rise to new life, but we do not know when that will happen. Tell them that in our gospel Jesus explains this to his disciples.
3. Ask the children to stand and be ready to listen attentively to some words of Jesus. Acclaim the gospel joyfully in song, perhaps accompanying the acclamation with simple gestures. During the singing have one child carry the lectionary reverently to the leader. Help the children to say the responses before the gospel, then proclaim Mk 13:32-33.

Respond to the Word

1. Help the children assimilate the message of today's readings, that death and new life will come and that we prepare for them by the way we live now:
- Ask the children what we can do to be ready for our death and for the new life that God will give us after death. Help the children to see that God asks only that we live as well as we can every day.
- Remove the stars from the poster board. As the children suggest ways in which we can live in accord with

God's will for us, replace the stars on the poster board as reminders of what we must do to gain everlasting life. Or, if the size of the group permits, write the names of the children on the stars.

- Spell out across the bottom of the poster "Shine like the stars!" and "Dn 12:3." Or lay out the words in gold foil letters.

2. Teach the children to sing "Grow Strong" (from Jack Miffleton's *Promise Chain*). Teach the children the gestures, perhaps even the dance, described in the songbook. The song suggests our patient waiting for the coming of Jesus who is our source of eternal life. Plan to use the song with the children for the next two Sundays also when the readings continue to look to the end of the world and the coming of Jesus in glory.

Other Possibilities:

1. The story *Stevie*, by John Steptoe, is a touching, realistic story of a little boy who appreciates another child only after the other child is gone forever. The message of the story, to appreciate what we have and to use our lives well right now, is similar to the message of today's readings. Younger children will enjoy the story even if they fail to comprehend its remarkably deep meaning. Older children will also enjoy the story and it will help them to assimilate the message of these "end-time" Sundays.

2. Tell older children about more about the book of Daniel:

- The book of Daniel was written during the bitter persecution of the Jewish people by Antiochus Epiphanes, king of Syria in the second century BCE. Antiochus attempted to impose Hellenistic culture and religion on the Jewish people by suppressing their worship, their sacred books, their religious practices, etc. His most notorious action was the erection in the temple sanctuary of an altar to Zeus, which was so hated that it became known as the "abomination of desolation." Writing under the fictitious name Daniel, a legendary righteous man, the author of the book of Daniel told stories to his suffering fellow-believers to console them and to encourage them during their trials. The resistance of the Jewish people finally erupted into revolt under the leadership of Judas Maccabeus and his family, the story of which is recounted in the books of Maccabees.

- Our reading today from the book of Daniel concludes, in beautiful poetry, the revelation of an unknown angel to Daniel in a vision. The message of the angel was one of great hope: it was a prediction of ultimate salvation, in spite of the "unsurpassed distress" of the present. Our passage is remarkable in that it is one of the earliest Old Testament passages which speak of the resurrection of the dead.

- Tell older children something of the background of the book of Daniel. Help them to appreciate the tremendous hope that the words of Daniel must have inspired in his near-despairing people. Help them to see that the words of Daniel should fill all people today with hope arising from the assurance that God is in control of history.

- The book of Daniel is an example of "apocalyptic" literature. Abounding in visions and symbols, an apocalypse pictures all of history from the vantage point of God, and looks to a final consummation in which God will overthrow the powers of evil and vindicate the righteous. It should interest today's children, taken by the fantasy of modern videos, to know that the bible is unexcelled in gripping, imaginative concepts and stories.

3. Show older children a picture of a medieval rendition of the last judgment: Jesus in judgment, with the souls of the good coming toward him on his right and the souls of the damned departing from him, perhaps into the jaws of hell, on his left. Use the picture to introduce a discussion among the children of the reality of judgment and life after death. The magnificent central portal of the wonderful twelfth-century cathedral of Autun in central France depicts such a scene.

4. The liturgical year will end next Sunday with the feast of Christ the King. From there we immerse ourselves in the season of Advent, whose readings will lead us from our thoughts of the final coming of Christ at the end of time to thoughts of his historical coming, which we celebrate at Christmas. To help older children grasp the rhythm of the liturgical year, give them simple liturgical calendars to take home. Suggest that each Sunday they write on their calendars some thought from the day's liturgy of the word.

Lectionary for Masses with Children	Lectionary for Mass
*Dn 7:13-14	*Dn 7:13-14
Ps 93:1,2 and 5	Ps 93:1,2 and 5
*Rv 1:5-8	*Rv 1:5-8
**Jn 18:33-37	**Jn 18:33-37

Thirty-Fourth or Last Sunday of the Year Christ the King

Focus: Jesus is king of our hearts. Jesus matters most in our lives. We love him! We praise him!

Gather the Children

1. Gather the children in their separate space, welcoming them with joy. The lectionary should be in a place of honor where all the children can see it. Remind the children why we come together for our special liturgy of the word, then join them in a few moments of prayer that God will fill our hearts, our minds, our lives with the word.
2. Light a candle as a sign of the presence of God among us. Light several smaller candles as a reminder of last week's reading from the book of Daniel and our destiny to "shine like the stars forever."
3. Praise God by singing to celebrate the kingship of Christ. The leader might teach the children "To Jesus Christ, Our Sovereign King" or another hymn which the adult assembly knows and will sing today. Or teach them the Afro-American spiritual "He Is King of Kings" (in *Worship III*).

Introduce Jesus Christ as Our King

1. Talk with the children about the meaning of "king":
● Show the children a poster board crown and ask them who wears a crown. Ask them what a king is and does. Listen with interest to their ideas, noting especially the good things they say about kings.
● Summarize and deepen the discussion about kings by sketching a crown on a large piece of newsprint and drawing near the crown symbols of the qualities of a good king, for example, a large heart for the love of the king for his people, several smaller hearts for the love of the people for their king, a scepter for the king's power, a shepherd's staff for his care.
2. Turn the thoughts of the children to Jesus, who reigns in our hearts:
● Tell the children that today we celebrate the kingship of someone we cannot see or hear or touch; someone who is king, but not of any special place; someone who is king of all of us, no matter where we live or who we are. No doubt the children will guess about whom we are talking. Use the words "Jesus Christ" today, so that the children will become familiar with the title "Christ." They are surely more familiar with the name "Jesus."
● Relate to Jesus Christ our King the qualities of a good

monarch which the children suggested a few moments ago. Spell out with glue on the crown the words "Jesus Christ." Sprinkle the glue with glitter (children love glitter), wait a moment, then shake off the excess.

Proclaim the Gospel

1. Tell the children that in our gospel today we hear Jesus himself describe what kind of king he is. He was talking to Pilate, the governor of the land of the Jewish people where Jesus lived. Pilate had heard that Jesus was a king and he wanted to know more about it. Jesus told him that he was not the kind of king Pilate was thinking of, but that he wanted to be king of people's lives.
2. Proclaim the gospel:
● Ask the children to stand to listen to the words of Jesus in our gospel. Acclaim the gospel in song. During the singing have one child carry the lectionary reverently to the leader.
● Today's gospel is abstract and involved, thus difficult for little children to understand. For very young children, the leader might simplify the reading even more than does the LMC, though striving not to distort its meaning or its spirit.
3. Do not attempt to explain the gospel in depth, but focus the attention of the children on the fact that Jesus wants to be king not in any earthly sense, but of our hearts and of our lives.

Accept Christ as Our King and Praise Him

1. Symbolize our acceptance of Christ as our king:
● Give each child a small paper heart. Let the children personalize the hearts in some simple way; for example, they may write their names or sketch their faces.
● Ask the children to let the hearts represent their acceptance of Christ as king of their hearts and lives. Then collect the hearts from the children, one by one, asking each child, "Do you accept Christ as king of your heart and life?" Glue all the hearts on the crown. If the number of children is large, the leader might draw one heart in glitter on the crown and let the children simply take home their small hearts.
● When the children rejoin the assembly, let them carry the crown into the church and place it near the ambo where everyone can see it.
2. Pray the general intercessions, focusing on the com-

ing kingship of Christ. The leader might formulate the prayer as follows:

Leader: My brothers and sisters in God's family, let us ask God to bring to perfection the kingdom of Christ on earth. Please respond, "May the kingdom of Christ come!"

Loving God, gather your people from every land and every age. Bring them together in the kingdom of Christ. For this, we pray:

All: May the kingdom of Christ come!

Leader: Loving God, comfort the sorrowful and heal the sick, forgive the sinner and call back the lost. For this we pray:

All: May the kingdom of Christ come!

Leader: Loving God, welcome all who have died into happiness with you. For this, we pray:

All: May the kingdom of Christ come!

Leader: Loving God, grant all power and glory to your child, Jesus Christ, who will give himself and all creation to you. For this, we pray:

All: May the kingdom of Christ come!

Leader: All powerful God, through your child, Jesus Christ, you make all things new. Christ is king of all creation. May all on earth know his kingship and proclaim his glory. May all in heaven give you praise through him. He reigns with you in heaven with the Holy Spirit forever and ever.

All: Amen.

3. Sing once again a hymn which praises Christ as king of our lives.

4. As a reminder of our acceptance of Christ as king of our hearts and lives, give each child a small paper crown to take home. If the children have their small hearts, they may glue them onto the crowns.

Other Possibilities:

1. In the above outline we concentrate on celebrating the kingship of Christ. For older children discuss the practical consequences of this concept: in terms of our daily living, what does it mean for Christ to be king of our hearts and our lives?

2. Remind the children that Jesus taught us to pray "Your kingdom come, your will be done on earth as it is in heaven." What does it mean for the kingdom of God to come? Help the children to see that Jesus lived his life to show us the meaning of God's kingdom and the way to attain it. Encourage the children to pray the Lord's Prayer slowly and thoughtfully during the liturgy of the eucharist. Suggest that, during the coming week, the children illustrate creatively the meaning of "the kingdom of God on earth."

3. The leader should read Jn 18:28-19:16 for John's full description of Jesus before Pilate. Talk with older children about the occasion and the outcome of Jesus's conversation with Pilate. The enemies of Jesus, the religious leaders of his own people, had captured him and brought him to Pilate, the Roman governor, because Pilate alone had the power to order Jesus to be put to death. As John and the other evangelists make clear, Pilate did not think that Jesus deserved death, but he eventually gave in to the demands of the chief priests and the people. Jesus stood before Pilate physically bound, but by far the more powerful of the two men. The reader feels sorry for Pilate, blind to what was really going on around him and insecure in the face of the people he supposedly ruled. What if Pilate had been wise and strong?

4. The book of Daniel was probably written during the bitter persecution of the Jewish people by Antiochus Epiphanes, king of Syria in the second century BCE. The book of Revelation was probably written during the ruthless persecution of the early Christian church by the Roman authorities. Both books are examples of apocalyptic literature, in which the writers, to encourage their readers to be strong and faithful to their religious beliefs in most difficult times, look with confidence to the final victory of God over the forces of evil. Both our readings today present us with magnificent images which the church applies to the coming of Christ in glory at the end of the world. Share one of these reading with the older children, reading it with great solemnity and great joy. Help the children to see that the readings should be a source of comfort for us, too, assuring us, as they have assured the people of God through the ages, that God is in control of the world, no matter what difficulties humankind may face.

5. Explain to older children the sacred monogram "chi rho." The Greek letters chi and rho are the first two letters in the name "Christ." Find out how to write the monogram in the traditional way, with the letter rho superimposed on the letter chi. Decorate a crown with the sacred monogram. Explain the symbol "the alpha and the omega." Alpha is the first letter of the Greek alphabet and omega is the last. Today's second reading gives both the origin and an explanation of the symbol. Find out how to write the two letters in Greek and decorate a second crown with the symbol. Explain that at the end of the world Christ will hand over the all things to the God who will reign with the him and the Spirit in power and glory forever. (See I Cor 15:20-28.)

6. Today is the last Sunday of the liturgical year. With older children make use of a liturgical calendar to give them a sense of the rhythm of the church year. Next week we begin the great season of Advent, and turn our thoughts gradually from the final coming of Christ in glory to his historical coming.

7. Jack Miffleton's "Grow Strong" (from *Promise Chain*) suggests our patient waiting for the end of the world and the coming of Christ in glory. The song is appropriate for these "end-time" Sundays. Sing the song with the children, leading them in the gestures described in the songbook. If the group is cooperative, teach them the dance steps.

Music
to
Gather the Children

by Fred Moleck

Gramma Grunts said a curious thing,
"Boys must whistle and girls must sing."

This piece of Americana myth is dismissed rapidly when Catholic boys and girls gather to celebrate the liturgy of their church. Girls whistle and boys sing, and, what's more, they do it all within the context of the celebrating community in which they were baptized. Not only is that context of celebration so broad and generous that the style and manner of the children celebrating permit the diversity which Granma Grunts would not allow, but it demands that the diversity be present in all celebration. Girls whistling, boys singing, leaders proclaiming and colors exploding are all quite appropriate in the celebration of Roman Catholic liturgy with children—especially the music.

The music suggested for use in the three year scheme of Gather the Children seeks to encourage that diversity which the liturgy values. The musical items also try to express the children's worship view and fulfill the language needs of the children at worship. All of these elements are placed in relationship to the child, to the liturgical moment or ritual and to the whole community at worship. It is all in scale. "Scale" here is not a series of tones grouped in patterns of tone and semitone, but "scale" here means in proportion. Frequently, the proportion of a musical item in relation to the child is distorted. Demands are placed on children to sing while they pray, move, sit, stand and jump for joy—all of which are out of proportion to what the music could do to excite prayer and to unite prayer. Too many times children are asked to do at liturgy what no adult assembly could ever do nor choir ever perform. The most obvious distortion is too many items in one liturgy.

After one year of weekly celebrations, the children should know about a dozen items they can sing comfortably without the printed page. That can happen only by repetition, and repetition works only if the music is delightful and asks to be sung again and again. That delight comes about when both the musical and the textual language needs of the child are fulfilled as to simpler statements.

(The Athanasian creed set to a Baroque aria fails miserably in fulfilling those needs.) Many of the items cited in the following pages seek to create instant participation by the echo form and/or the antiphonal form. The value in these formulae is that take account of the fact that the time spent with the children is usually only about one-half hour every week and permits little rehearsal time. Echoing is one way to get children singing.

Hymns are included. Chosen for the appropriateness to the season they are an important part of the Christian's prayer life. For reasons of expediency children frequently are reared in the church without any knowledge of the treasury of hymnody, hardly a desirable effect. Some chant and Latin repertory are included.

Major sources of music are listed, but many items may be found also in other sources. It is thought that the items chosen should be available to the parish without complicated copyright releases or searches in composers' warehouses. Original items are included and require no special permission for their reproduction. The music has been chosen with the needs of both particular Sundays and particular seasons in mind. A leader, then, in looking for suggestions for music, should not only look in the list for a specific Sunday, but should also consider the season. For example, the leader should consider all the music listed during Advent as possibilities for use on each of the four Sundays of Advent. The leader is urged to view the list of music only as a list of suggestions, and not to adhere slavishly to its contents.

As the children gather, may they reflect Paul's admonition that there not exist among you "Jew or Greek, slave or freeman, male or female. All are one in Christ Jesus" (Gal 3:28). Might we add, whistlers and singers all are one, too.

Music for Sundays and Seasons
Selected by Fred Moleck

The following abbreviations are used in the list of music:

GIA   GIA Publications
NALR   North American Liturgy Resources
WLP   World Library Publications
OCP   Oregon Catholic Press

First Sunday of Advent
"No Shadow of Turning," Heirborne (cassette), Meadowlark Records/Sparrow Corp.
"Prepare the Way of the Lord," Taizé, GIA
"The King of Glory Comes," Willard Jabusch, GIA
"A Voice Cries Out," Michael Joncas, *Every Stone Shall Cry*, NALR
"My Soul In Stillness Waits," Marty Haugen, GIA
"O, That You Would Come," Verse, Fred Moleck, in *Gather the Children*, Pastoral Press

"O Come, O Come, Emmanuel," Chant, in *Worship II* and *Worship III*, GIA

Second Sunday of Advent
"Of the Father's Love Begotten," Chant, in *Worship III*, GIA
"Like a Shepherd," Bob Dufford, *A Dwelling Place*, NALR
"Soon and Very Soon," Andrea Crouch, in *Songs of Zion*, Abingdon Press
"Sing Out, Earth and Sky," Marty Haugen, GIA

Third Sunday of Advent
"Rejoice in the Lord Always," Round, Copyright unknown, Music may be found in *Hi God!*, NALR

Fourth Sunday of Advent
"Jesu, Joy of Man's Desiring," J.S. Bach, Cassette (Any number of settings is available)

136

"The Angel Gabriel," Basque carol, in *Worship III*, GIA

"I Sing of a Maiden," Dell Ridge, GIA

"My Soul Proclaims the Lord, My God," Tune of "Amazing Grace," in *People's Mass Book*, WLP

"My Soul Gives Glory to the Lord," Michael Joncas, in *Praise God in Song*, GIA, also in *Worship III*, GIA

Christmas
"Children, Run Joyfully," Bob Dufford, *Gentle Night*, NALR

"Joy to the World," Traditional

Holy Family
"Once in Royal David's City," in *Worship III*, GIA

"Canticle of Simeon," Tune of "Consolation," in *People's Mass Book*, WLP

Epiphany
"All the Ends of the Earth," Marty Haugen and David Haas, in *Psalms for the Church Year*, GIA

Baptism of the Lord
"Come to the Water," John Foley, *Wood Hath Hope*, NALR

"Glory and Praise to Our God," Dan Schutte, in *Glory and Praise*, NALR

"You Have Put on Christ," Howard Hughes, *ICEL Collection*, GIA

"I Want to Walk as a Child of the Light," Kathleen Thomerson, in *Worship III*, GIA

Second Sunday of the Year
"Here I Am, Lord," Dan Schutte, *Lord of Light*, NALR

"Two Fishermen," Suzanne Toolan, in *Worship III*, GIA

Third Sunday of the Year
"I Lift Up My Soul," Tim Manion, *A Dwelling Place*, NALR

"Two Fishermen," Suzanne Toolan, in *Worship III*, GIA

Fourth Sunday of the Year
"Great Is the Lord," Suzanne Toolan, GIA

"Great Are the Wonders," Jack Miffleton, *Promise Chain*, WLP

"Silence, Frenzied Unclean Spirit," Carol Doran and Thomas Troeger, Oxford University Press, in *Worship III*

Fifth Sunday of the Year
"Lord, You Have the Words of Everlasting Life," Marty Haugen and David Haas, in *Psalms for the Church Year*, GIA

"Thy Strong Word," in *Worship III*, GIA

"There Is a Balm in Gilead," in *Worship III*, GIA

"In Days of Old," in *Worship III*, GIA

Sixth Sunday of the Year
"Do You Believe," Profession of Faith, Fred Moleck, in *Gather the Children*, Pastoral Press

"Be with Me, Lord," Michael Joncas, in *Today's Missal*, OCP

Seventh Sunday of the Year
"The Heavens Are Telling," Marty Haugen, *Canticle of the Sun*, GIA

"Father, Mercy," Bob Dufford, *Neither Silver nor Gold*, NALR

"He Is King of Kings," Afro-American Spiritual, in *Worship III*, GIA

"In the Breaking of the Bread," David Hurd, OCP

First Sunday of Lent
"Pange Lingua," Chant, in *Worship III*, GIA

"Attende Domine" or "Hear Us, Almighty Lord," Chant, in *Worship III*, GIA

"He's Got the Whole World in His Hand," Negro Spiritual

"Yahweh, I Know You Are Near," Dan Schutte, in *Glory and Praise*, NALR.

"Yahweh, the Faithful One," Dan Schutte, in *Glory and Praise*, NALR

Second Sunday of Lent
"Rejoice, Be Glad," Dick Hilliard, *My Heart Is Happy*, Resource Publications

Third Sunday of Lent
"Praise Go

"Lord, Have Mercy," Penitential Rite, Fred Moleck, in *Gather the Children*, Pastoral Press

"By the Babylonian Rivers," in *Worship III*, GIA

Fifth Sunday of Lent
"All Glory and All Praise to You," Gospel Acclamation, Fred Moleck, in *Gather the Children*, Pastoral Press

"Song of the Mustard Seed," Hal Hopson, GIA

"Tree Song," Ken Medema, in *Tree Song Medley*, Word, Inc.

"Behold the Wood," Dan Schutte, *A Dwelling Place*, NALR

Passion Sunday
"Hosanna," Howard Hughes, *Divine Word Mass*, GIA

"Hosanna," Lucien Deiss, in *People's Mass Book*, Vol. 1, WLP

"Christ Has Died," Marty Haugen, *Mass of Creation*, GIA

"In the Breaking of the Bread," Bob Hurd, OCP

"Jesus, Remember Me," Taiz_, GIA

"I Will Praise Your Name," Marty Haugen, in *Psalms for the Church Year*, GIA

"Jesus the Lord," Roc O'Connor, *Lord of Light*, NALR.

Easter Sunday
"This Is the Day," Echo Song, Copyright unknown, Music may be found in *Hi God 2*, NALR

Alleluia of "Ye Sons and Daughters," Chant, in *Worship II*, GIA

"I Do, Alleluia," Response, Fred Moleck, in *Gather the Children*, Pastoral Press

"Keep in Mind that Jesus Christ," Lucien Deiss, in *Biblical Hymns and Psalms*, WLP

"Springs of Water," Acclamation, Fred Moleck, in *Gather the Children*, Pastoral Press

"You Have Put on Christ," Howard Hughes, *ICEL Collection*, GIA

Second Sunday of Easter
"We Walk by Faith," Marty Haugen, in *Worship III*, GIA

"Shalom, My Friends," Israeli Folk Song, in various collections

"I Want to Walk as a Child of the Light," Kathleen Thomerson, in *Worship III*, GIA

Third Sunday of Easter
"Father, Lift Me Up," Honeytree, Word, Inc., through OCP

Fourth Sunday of Easter
"We Are His People," David Haas, in *Psalms for the Church Year*, GIA

"We Are His People," Alexander Peloquin, in *Songs of Israel*, GIA

"The Lord Is My Shepherd," Negro Spiritual, in *Worship III*, GIA

"Loving Shepherd of Your Sheep," in *Morning Star Choir Book*, Vol. 2, Concordia Press

"Jesus, Shepherd of Our Souls," Alexander Peloquin, in *Worship II* and *Worship III*, GIA

Fifth Sunday of Easter
"We Are the Branches" Jack Miffleton, *Make a Wonderful Noise*, WLP

"God Is Love," Clarence Rivers, in *People's Mass Book*, Vol. 2, WLP

Sixth Sunday of Easter
"God Is Love," Clarence Rivers, in *People's Mass Book*, Vol. 2, WLP

"Amen. Alleluia," Michael Joncas, in *Gather To Remember*, GIA

"Father, May They All Be One," John Foley, *Neither Silver nor Gold*, NALR

Seventh Sunday of Easter
"Father, Lift Me Up," Honeytree, Word, Inc., through OCP

"God Sends Us His Spirit," Gonja Folk Song, in *Worship III*, GIA

"Years and Seasons," Jack Miffleton, *Promise Chain*, WLP

"Spirit of God," Jack Miffleton, *Promise Chain*, WLP

Pentecost
"Lord, Send Out Your Spirit," Dean Olawski, in *Pilgrim Praise*, OCP

"God Sends Us His Spirit," Gonja Folk Song, in *Worship III*, GIA

"Come, Holy Spirit," Response, Fred Moleck, in *Gather the Children*, Pastoral Press

"Father, Lift Me Up," Honeytree, Word, Inc., through OCP

"Father, I Adore You," Round, Terrye Coelho, *Gathering to Praise*, Word, Inc., through OCP

Trinity Sunday
"Father, Lift Me Up," Honeytree, Word, Inc., through OCP

"Father, I Adore You," Round, Terrye Coelho, *Gathering to Praise*, Word, Inc., through OCP

Corpus Christi
"Taste and See," James Moore, GIA

"Taste and See," Marty Haugen, GIA

"The Blessing Cup," Michael Joncas, NALR

Tenth Sunday of the Year
"Give Thanks to the Lord," *Creation Song*, by Dean Olawski, Word, Inc., through OCP

"Lord, Have Mercy," Fred Moleck, in *Gather the Children*, Pastoral Press

"Kyrie," Fred Moleck, in *Gather the Children*, Pastoral Press

Eleventh Sunday of the Year
"Song of the Mustard Seed," Hal Hopson, GIA

"I'm Growing Tall," Ken Medema, in *Tree Song Medley*, Word, Inc.

Twelfth Sunday of the Year
"All Creatures of Our God and King," in *Worship II* and *Worship III*, GIA

"Yahweh, I Know You Are Near," Dan Schutte, *Neither Silver nor Gold*, NALR

"Precious Lord, Take My Hand," Thomas Dorsey, in *Songs of Zion*, Abingdon Press

Thirteenth Sunday of the Year
"Canticle of the Sun," Marty Haugen, GIA

"When Love Is Found," in *Worship III*, GIA

Fourteenth Sunday of the Year
"Canticle of the Sun," Marty Haugen, GIA

"Father, I Adore You," Round, Terrye Coelho, *Gathering to Praise*, Word, Inc., through OCP

Fifteenth Sunday of the Year
"Two Fishermen," Suzanne Toolan, in *Worship III*, GIA

Sixteenth Sunday of the Year
"My Shepherd Is the Lord," Joseph Gelineau, in *Worship III*, GIA

"The Lord, the Lord, the Lord Is My Shepherd," Afro-American Spiritual, in *Worship III*, GIA

Seventeenth Sunday of the Year
"In the Breaking of the Bread," David Hurd, OCP

"We Praise You," Memorial Acclamation, Fred Moleck, in *Gather the Children*, Pastoral Press

"I Come with Joy to Meet My Lord," in *Worship III*, GIA

"One Bread, One Body," John Foley, *Wood Hath Hope*, NALR

Eighteenth Sunday of the Year
"The Lord, the Lord, the Lord Is My Shepherd," Afro-American Spiritual, in *Worship III*, GIA

Nineteenth Sunday of the Year
"Canticle of the Sun," Marty Haugen, GIA

Twentieth Sunday of the Year
"Glory and Praise to Our God," Dan Schutte, *A Dwelling Place*, NALR

"Great Is the Lord," Suzanne Toolan, in *Today's Missal*, OCP

"Eat This Bread," Taiz_, GIA

Twenty-First Sunday of the Year
"Jesu, Jesu, Fill Us with Your Love," Ghana Folk Song, in *Worship III*, GIA

Twenty-Second Sunday of the Year
"Wonderful and Great," Lucien Deiss, *Biblical Hymns and Psalms*, Vol. 1, WLP

Twenty-Third Sunday of the Year
"Praise the Lord, My Soul," John Foley, *Earthen Vessels*, in *Glory and Praise*, NALR
"You Are My Own," Dan Schutte, *Neither Silver nor Gold*, NALR

Twenty-Fourth Sunday of the Year
"I Want to Walk as a Child of the Light," Kathleen Thomerson, in *Worship III*, GIA
"Jesus Walked this Lonesome Valley," American Folk Hymn, in *Worship II* and *Worship III*, GIA

Twenty-Fifth Sunday of the Year
"We Walk by Faith," Marty Haugen, in *Worship III*, GIA
"Father, Lift Me Up," Honeytree, Word, Inc., through OCP

Twenty-Sixth Sunday of the Year
"Whatsoever You Do," Willard Jabusch, in *Worship II*, GIA

Twenty-Seventh Sunday of the Year
"In Perfect Charity," Randall DeBryn, OCP

Twenty-Eighth Sunday of the Year
"O the Beautiful Treasures," American Shaker Melody, in *Worship III*, GIA
"Canticle of the Sun," Marty Haugen, GIA

Twenty-Ninth Sunday of the Year
"We Walk by Faith," Marty Haugen, in *Worship III*, GIA

Thirtieth Sunday of the Year
"The Lord Is My Light and My Salvation," David Haas, GIA
"Amazing Grace," Verse 1, in *Worship III*, GIA
"Son of David," John Foley, *Wood Hath Hope*, NALR

Thirty-First Sunday of the Year
"God Is Love," Clarence Rivers, in *People's Mass Book*, Vol. 2, WLP

"Whatsoever You Do," Willard Jabusch, in *Worship II*, GIA

Thirty-Second Sunday of the Year
"I Will Praise Your Name, My God and My King," David Haas, GIA

Thirty-Third Sunday of the Year
"Grow Strong," Jack Miffleton, *Promise Chain*, WLP
"Didn't the Lord Deliver Daniel," Negro Spiritual, in *Songs of Zion*, Abingdon Press

Christ the King
"He Is King of Kings," Afro-American Spiritual, in *Songs of Zion*, Abingdon Press, also in *Worship III*, GIA
"Soon and Very Soon," Andrea Crouch, in *Songs of Zion*, Abingdon Press
"Jesus, Remember Me," Taizé, in *Worship III*, GIA

Alleluia Acclamations
"Praise the Lord of All Creation," Marty Haugen, *Mass of Creation*, GIA
"Alleluia in C," Howard Hughes, in *Worship III*, GIA
"Celtic Alleluia," Christopher Walker, OCP
"Alleluia, Praise His Name," Michael Joncas, NALR
Alleluia of "Wonderful and Great," Lucien Deiss, in *Biblical Hymns and Psalms*, Vol. 1, WLP
Alleluia of "Ye Sons and Daughters," Chant, in *Worship II*, GIA
"Happy Those Who Hear God's Word," Jack Miffleton, *Wake Up the Earth*, NALR

Lenten Acclamations
"Lord, You Have the Words," Marty Haugen and David Haas, in *Psalms for the Church Year*, GIA
"Praise to You, Lord Jesus Christ," Frank Schoen, in *Worship II*, GIA
"All Glory and Praise to You," Fred Moleck, in *Gather the Children*, Pastoral Press
"Lenten Acclamation," David Young, in *Worship III*, GIA
"Lenten Acclamation," Richard Proulx, in *Worship III*, GIA
"Lenten Acclamation," Howard Hughes, in *Worship III*, GIA

Selected Children's Literature

The following children's books have been recommended in the liturgy outlines. They are listed here for the liturgy planner's convenience. With the exception of Augsburg's *What the Bible Tells Us Series*, the books can be found in many public libraries. The leader of children's liturgy is urged to read and enjoy children's literature constantly and to share the best of his or her discoveries with the children. A good story, carefully chosen, is worth hours of preaching.

R.C. Bulla	*The Poppy Seeds* Thomas Y. Crowell	
B. Cohen	*The Binding of Isaac* Lothrop, Lee & Shepard	
K. DeKort, Illustrator	*What the Bible Tells Us Series* Augsburg	
T. DePaola	*Nanna Upstairs and Nanna Downstairs* Puffin	
E. Fern	*Pepito's Story* Ariel	
M. Fox	*Wilfred Gordon Mcdonald Partridge* Kane/Miller	
M. Greaves	*A Net to Catch the Wind* Harper & Row	
I. Haas	*The Maggie B.* Atheneum	
F.P. Heide	*That's What Friends Are For* Four Winds	
W. Hutton	*Noah and the Great Flood* Atheneum	
E. J. Keats	*Apt #3* Macmillan	
L. Lionni	*Tico and the Golden Wings* Pantheon	

J. Marshall	*What's the Matter with Carruthers?* Houghton-Mifflin
G. MacDonald	*Little Lost Lamb* Doubleday
E. Ness	*Josefina February* Scribner
Y. Otsuka	*Suho and the White Horse* Bobbs-Merrill
M. Perrine	*Salt Boy* Houghton-Mifflin
S. Silverstein	*The Giving Tree* Harper & Row
J. Steptoe	*Stevie* Harper & Row
J. Stover	*If Everybody Did* David McKay
A. Surany	*Ride the Cold Wind* Putnam
T. Yamaguchi	*Two Crabs and the Moonlight* Holt, Rinehart and Winston
T. Yashima	*Crow Boy* Viking
J. Yolen	*The Emperor and the Kite* Collins, Williams and World
J. Yolen	*The Seventh Mandarin* Seabury
C. Zolotow	*Do You Know What I'll Do?* Harper & Row
C. Zolotow	*The Storm Book* Harper & Row
C. Zolotow	*When the Wind Stops* Abelard-Schuman

Selected Bibliography

An asterisk preceding an entry indicates that a book is recommended for the beginner. An abbreviation following an entry identifies an abbreviation used in the text.

*Achtemeier, Paul J., gen. ed., *Harper's Bible Dictionary* (San Francisco: Harper & Row, Publishers, 1985). Excellent tool for both the biblical novice and the biblical scholar. Contributions by Protestant, Catholic and Jewish authorities, all affiliates of the Society of Biblical Literature. Readable, reliable, with many illustrations.

Achtemeier, Paul J., *Mark* (Philadelphia: Fortress Press, 1975). A volume of the *Proclamation Commentaries,* a series of commentaries which seeks to make the results of modern biblical scholarship available to the interested non-scholar. *Mark* is not a verse by verse commentary, but offers reflections on Mark's intentions, his methods, the main persons and themes of his gospel. Clearly written.

Anderson, Bernhard W., *Understanding the Old Testament* (Englewood Cliffs, N.J.: Prentice-Hall, Inc., 1966). Scholarly yet eminently readable exposition of the Old Testament. Excellent book. (UOT)

*Brett, Laurence F.X., "Share the Word." A good, non-technical commentary on the Sunday lectionary readings, including study helps, published bimonthly by The Paulist Fathers. Write to Subscription Fulfillment Manager, Share the Word, 3031 Fourth Street, N.E., Washington, D.C., 20017.

Brown, Raymond E., *The Gospel according to John I-XII and The Gospel according to John XIII-XXI* (Garden City, New York: Doubleday & Company, Inc., 1966 and 1970). Two volumes of The Anchor Bible, a highly respected series of biblical commentaries prepared by eminent Protestant, Catholic and Jewish scholars. Author's translation, notes and commentary. Complete and scholarly. (AB 29 and AB 29A)

Brown, Raymond E., Joseph A. Fitzmyer and Roland E. Murphy, eds., *The Jerome Biblical Commentary* (Englewood Cliffs, New Jersey: Prentice-Hall, Inc., 1968). Comprehensive modern commentary on the whole bible, proceeding by verse or group of verses with explanation and interpretation. Also includes pertinent topical articles. Designed for educated readers. Scholarly, well-written, very valuable tool in study of the Scriptures. (JBC)

Buttrick, George Arthur, ed., *The Interpreter's Dictionary of the Bible* (Nashville: Abingdon Press, 1962). Comprehensive four volume, plus supplementary volume, dictionary of biblical names, terms, subjects. Many illustrations. Very good reference book for biblical study. (IDB)

Danker, Frederick W., *Jesus and the New Age: A Commentary on the Third Gospel* (St. Louis, Missouri: Clayton Publishing House, 1972). Fresh and interesting commentary, easy to read. Many incisive comments on the relevance of Luke's gospel to modern life.

Deiss, Lucien, trans. by Matthew J. O'Connell, *Springtime of the Liturgy* (Collegeville, Minnesota: The Liturgical Press, 1979). Collection of important liturgical texts from the first four centuries. Beautiful readings which instruct, inspire and enrich the reader. Good comments.

Directory for Masses with Children, prepared by the Sacred Congregation for Divine Worship, trans. by the International Committee on English in the Liturgy (Washington, D.C.: United States Catholic Conference, 1974). This short document addresses the needs of children at worship and offers creative and practical suggestions for adapting liturgical celebrations for children. Every adult who works with children and liturgy should be familiar with this work.

Fitzmyer, Joseph A., *The Gospel according to Luke I-IX and The Gospel according to Luke X-XXIV* (Garden City, New York: Doubleday & Company, Inc., 1981 and 1985). Two volumes of *The Anchor Bible.* Author's translation, notes and commentary. Careful, extensive work. Responsible scholarship. (AB 28 and AB 28A)

Fuller, Reginald, *Preaching the New Lectionary: The Word of God for the Church Today* (Collegeville, Minnesota: The Liturgical Press, 1974). A commentary on the Sunday lectionary readings. Good biblical interpretation and helpful background information. Penetrating, provocative comments on applying the readings to daily life. This very useful book is the work of a competent scholar with a pleasant style. (PNL)

*Jeep, Elizabeth McMahon, et al., ed. by Mary Ann Simco, *The Welcome Table: Planning Masses with Children* (Chicago: Liturgy Training Publications, 1982). Series of short articles to help adults plan liturgies with children. Good insights into liturgy and children. Practical suggestions.

Kingsbury, Jack Dean, *Jesus Christ in Matthew, Mark, And Luke* (Philadelphia: Fortress Press, 1981). This brief work looks at various similarities and dissimilarities of the three synoptic evangelists so that the reader can better understand and appreciate their separate contributions to our understanding of Jesus and his mission. Good information and easy to read. One of the *Proclamation Commentaries*.

LaVerdiere, Eugene, *Luke* (Wilmington, Delaware: Michael Glazier, 1982). Capable commentary on the third gospel, proceeding passage by passage. Very good thoughts about how individual passages fit into their immediate contexts and into their broader contexts. One of the *New Testament Message Series* commentaries. The *New Testament Message Series* is designed for the competent reader who is interested in the results of modern biblical study.

Maly, Eugene H., *Romans* (Wilmington, Delaware: Michael Glazier, Inc., 1983). Clear, insightful, relatively brief, passage by passage commentary on a difficult letter of Paul. One of the New Testament Message Series commentaries.

*McKenzie, John L., *Dictionary of the Bible* (New York: Macmillan Publishing Co., Inc., 1974). Very well done dictionary of Old and New Testament terms, themes and concepts. Broad in scope, accurate and interesting, yet the book is compact and easy to use. (DOB)

McKenzie, John L., *Second Isaiah* (Garden City, New York: Doubleday & Company, Inc., 1968). Author's translation, notes and commentary. Carefully done, but brief enough to appeal to the non-scholar. One of The Anchor Bible commentaries. (AB 20)

Meier, John P., *Matthew* (Wilmington, Delaware: Michael Glazier, Inc., 1980). Good analysis of the first gospel, proceeding passage by passage. Special attention paid to Matthew's use of his sources. Clearly written by competent biblical scholar. One of the New Testament Message Series commentaries.

Reicke, Bo., *The New Testament Era*, trans. by David E. Green, (Philadelphia: Fortress Press, 1968). Describes the world of the Bible from 500 B.C. to 100 A.D. Much information, though somewhat tedious reading.

*Vawter, Bruce. *The Four Gospels: An Introduction* (Garden City, New York: Image Books, 1969). Helpful explanation of the meaning of the four gospels, taken in a continuous narrative. Also contains useful background information. Interesting and easy to read. There are two volumes in the set.

*Von Trapp, Maria. *When the King Was Carpenter* (Harrison, Arkansas: New Leaf Press, 1976). Gentle and interesting book about the daily life of Jesus before his public ministry. Perhaps not accurate in every detail, but imparts well a picture of the holiness and piety of the little Jewish family whose child responded perfectly to God's will.

Index of Readings

Lectionary for Masses with Children

Cycle B

Joel

Amos
7:10-15   Fifteenth Sunday of the Year

Obadiah

Jonah
3:1-5,10   Third Sunday of the Year

Micah

Nahum

Habakkuk

Zephaniah

Haggai

Zechariah

Malachi

Matthew
2:1-12   Epiphany
2:13-15,19-21   Holy Family
28:16-20   Trinity Sunday

Mark
1:1-8   Second Sunday of Advent
1:12-15   First Sunday of Lent
1:14-20   Third Sunday of the Year
1:21-28   Fourth Sunday of the Year
1:29-39   Fifth Sunday of the Year
1:40-45   Sixth Sunday of the Year
2:1-12   Seventh Sunday of the Year
3:20-21,31-35   Tenth Sunday of the Year
3:20-26,31-35   Tenth Sunday of the Year
4:30-34   Eleventh Sunday of the Year
4:35-41   Twelfth Sunday of the Year
5:21-24,35-43   Thirteenth Sunday of the Year
6:1-6   Fourteenth Sunday of the Year
6:7-13   Fifteenth Sunday of the Year
6:30-34   Sixteenth Sunday of the Year
7:1-5,14-15,21-23   Twenty-Second Sunday of the Year
7:31-37   Twenty-Third Sunday of the Year
8:31-35   Twenty-Fourth Sunday of the Year
9:2-10   Second Sunday of Lent
9:33-37   Twenty-Fifth Sunday of the Year
9:38-41   Twenty-Sixth Sunday of the Year
10:13-16   Twenty-Seventh Sunday of the Year
10:17-27   Twenty-Eighth Sunday of the Year
10:35-45   Twenty-Ninth Sunday of the Year
10:46-52   Thirtieth Sunday of the Year
11:1-10   Passion Sunday
12:28-31   Thirty-First Sunday of the Year
12:41-44   Thirty-Second Sunday of the Year
13:24-32   Thirty-Third Sunday of the Year
13:33-37   First Sunday of Advent
14:12-16,22-26   Corpus Christi
15:1-39   Passion Sunday
16:15-20   Feast of the Ascension

Luke
1:26-38   Fourth Sunday of Advent
2:1-14   Christmas
3:15-16,21-22   Baptism of the Lord
24:35-48   Third Sunday of Easter

John
1:19-28   Third Sunday of Advent
1:35-42   Second Sunday of the Year
2:13-22   Third Sunday of Lent
3:16-17   Fourth Sunday of Lent
6:1-15   Seventeenth Sunday of the Year
6:24-29   Eighteenth Sunday of the Year
6:48-51   Nineteenth Sunday of the Year
6:51-58   Twentieth Sunday of the Year
6:60-69   Twenty-First Sunday of the Year
10:11-16   Fourth Sunday of Easter
12:24-26   Fifth Sunday of Lent
15:1-5,7-8   Fifth Sunday of Easter
15:9-14   Sixth Sunday of Easter
17:11   Seventh Sunday of Easter
18:33-37   Thirty-Fourth Sunday of the Year
20:1-9   Easter Sunday
20:19-23   Pentecost Sunday
20:19-29   Second Sunday of Easter

Acts of the Apostles
1:8-11   Feast of the Ascension
1:15-17,20-26   Seventh Sunday of Easter
2:1-11   Pentecost Sunday
3:13-15,17-19   Third Sunday of Easter
4:8-12   Fourth Sunday of Easter
4:32-35   Second Sunday of Easter
9:26-28   Fifth Sunday of Easter
10:25-26,34-35,44-48   Sixth Sunday of Easter
10:34-38   Baptism of the Lord
10:34,37-43   Easter Sunday

Romans
8:14-17   Trinity Sunday
8:31,38-39   Second Sunday of Lent
16:25-27   Fourth Sunday of Advent

1 Corinthians
1:3-9   First Sunday of Advent
5:6-8   Easter Sunday
9:16-18   Fifth Sunday of the Year
10:31-11:1   Sixth Sunday of the Year
12:4-7,12-13   Pentecost Sunday

2 Corinthians
4:16-5:1   Tenth Sunday of the Year
5:6-10   Eleventh Sunday of the Year
5:14-17   Twelfth Sunday of the Year
8:7,9,13-14   Thirteenth Sunday of the Year
12:7-10   Fourteenth Sunday of the Year

Galatians

Ephesians
1:17-21   Feast of the Ascension
2:4-10   Fourth Sunday of Lent
3:1-10   Fifteenth Sunday of the Year
4:1-6   Seventeenth Sunday of the Year
4:31-5:2   Nineteenth Sunday of the Year
5:15-20   Twentieth Sunday of the Year
6:1-4   Twenty-First Sunday of the Year

Philippians

Colossians
3:1-4   Easter Sunday
3:12-17   Holy Family

1 Thessalonians
5:16-24   Third Sunday of Advent

2 Thessalonians

1 Timothy

2 Timothy

Titus
3:4-6   Christmas

Philemon

Hebrews
4:12-13   Twenty-Eighth Sunday of the Year
4:14-16   Twenty-Ninth Sunday of the Year
5:1-6   Thirtieth Sunday of the Year
7:26   Thirty-First Sunday of the Year

James
1:17-18,21-22   Twenty-Second Sunday of the Year
2:1-5   Twenty-Third Sunday of the Year
2:14-18   Twenty-Fourth Sunday of the Year
3:17-18   Twenty-Fifth Sunday of the Year
5:1-6   Twenty-Sixth Sunday of the Year

1 Peter

2 Peter

1 John
3:1-2   Fourth Sunday of Easter
3:18   Fifth Sunday of Easter
4:7-10   Sixth Sunday of Easter
4:11-13   Seventh Sunday of Easter
5:1-6   Second Sunday of Easter

2 John

3 John

Jude

Revelation
1:5-8   Thirty-Fourth Sunday of the Year

Calendar

Cycle B

Sunday/Feast	1993	1996	1999
1st Sun. of Advent	Nov. 28	Dec. 1	Nov. 28
2nd Sun. of Advent	Dec. 5	Dec. 8	Dec. 5
3rd Sun. of Advent	Dec. 12	Dec. 15	Dec. 12
4th Sun. of Advent	Dec. 19	Dec. 22	Dec. 19
Christmas	Wed.	Sat.	Sat.
Holy Family	Dec. 26	Dec. 29	Dec. 26

	1994	1997	2000
Mary, Mother of God	Sat.	Wed.	Sat.
Epiphany	Jan. 2	Jan. 5	Jan. 2
Baptism of the Lord	Jan. 9	Jan. 12	Jan. 9
2nd Sun. in Ord. Time	Jan. 16	Jan. 19	Jan. 16
3rd Sun. in Ord. Time	Jan. 23	Jan. 26	Jan. 23
4th Sun. in Ord. Time	Jan. 30	****	Jan. 30
5th Sun. in Ord. Time	Feb. 6	Feb. 9	Feb. 6
6th Sun. in Ord. Time	Feb. 13	----	Feb. 13
7th Sun. in Ord. Time	----	----	Feb. 20
8th Sun. in Ord. Time	----	----	Feb. 27
9th Sun. in Ord. Time	----	----	Mar. 5
1st Sun. of Lent	Feb. 20	Feb. 16	Mar. 12
2nd Sun. of Lent	Feb. 27	Feb. 23	Mar. 19
3rd Sun. of Lent	Mar. 6	Mar. 2	Mar. 26
4th Sun. of Lent	Mar. 13	Mar. 9	Apr. 2
5th Sun. of Lent	Mar. 20	Mar. 16	Apr. 9
Passion (Palm) Sunday	Mar. 27	Mar. 23	Apr. 16
Easter Sunday	Apr. 3	Mar. 30	Apr. 23
2nd Sun. of Easter	Apr. 10	Apr. 6	Apr. 30
3rd Sun. of Easter	Apr. 17	Apr. 13	May 7
4th Sun. of Easter	Apr. 24	Apr. 20	May 14
5th Sun. of Easter	May 1	Apr. 27	May 21
6th Sun. of Easter	May 8	May 4	May 28
Ascension	May 12	May 8	June 1
7th Sun. of Easter	May 15	May 11	June 4
Pentecost	May 22	May 18	June 11
Trinity Sunday	May 29	May 25	June 18
Corpus Christi	June 5	June 1	June 25
10th Sun. in Ord. Time	----	June 8	----
11th Sun. in Ord. Time	June 12	June 15	----
12th Sun. in Ord. Time	June 19	June 22	----
13th Sun. in Ord. Time	June 26	****	July 2
14th Sun. in Ord. Time	July 3	July 6	July 9
15th Sun. in Ord. Time	July 10	July 13	July 16

16th Sun. in Ord. Time	July 17	July 20	July 23
17th Sun. in Ord. Time	July 24	July 27	July 30
18th Sun. in Ord. Time	July 31	Aug. 3	****
19th Sun. in Ord. Time	Aug. 7	Aug. 10	Aug. 13
20th Sun. in Ord. Time	Aug. 14	Aug. 17	Aug. 20
21st Sun. in Ord. Time	Aug. 21	Aug. 24	Aug 27
22nd Sun. in Ord. Time	Aug. 28	Aug. 31	Sept. 3
23rd Sun. in Ord. Time	Sept. 4	Sept. 7	Sept. 10
24th Sun. in Ord. Time	Sept. 11	****	Sept. 17
25th Sun. in Ord. Time	Sept. 18	Sept. 21	Sept. 24
26th Sun. in Ord. Time	Sept. 25	Sept. 28	Oct. 1
27th Sun. in Ord. Time	Oct. 2	Oct. 5	Oct. 8
28th Sun. in Ord. Time	Oct. 9	Oct. 12	Oct. 15
29th Sun. in Ord. Time	Oct. 16	Oct. 19	Oct 22
30th Sun. in Ord. Time	Oct. 23	Oct. 26	Oct 29
31st Sun. in Ord. Time	Oct. 30	****	Nov. 5
32nd Sun. in Ord. Time	Nov. 6	****	Nov. 12
33rd Sun. in Ord. Time	Nov. 13	Nov. 16	Nov. 19
Christ the King	Nov. 20	Nov. 23	Nov. 26

**** = Sunday Mass replaced by that of a major feast.
---- = Particular Sunday does not occur.